Peril

From Jackboots to Jack Benny

PERIL

From Jackboots to Jack Benny

PEARL GOODMAN

Bridgeross Communications
Dundas, Ontario, Canada

Library and Archives Canada Cataloguing in Publication

Goodman, Pearl, 1954-
        Peril : from jackboots to Jack Benny / by Pearl Goodman.

ISBN 978-0-9878244-6-2

        1. Goodman, Pearl, 1954-. 2. Children of Holocaust survivors--Ontario--Toronto--Biography. 3. Jews--Ontario--Toronto--Biography. 4. Toronto (Ont.)--Biography.
5. Psychotherapists--Canada--Biography. 6. Toronto (Ont.)--History--20th century. I. Title.

FC3097.9.J5G65 2012 971.3'5410049240092 C2012-905085-7

First published in 2012 by Bridgeross Communications, Dundas, Ontario, Canada

ISBN 978-0-9878244-6-2

to
Deanna

for
Fryma and *Zyskind*

because of
Jordan

Introduction

I...FEEL...EVERY...LITTLE...THING...

I am trying to reconcile within me the bizarre extremes in a phrase I've coined: "from jackboots to Jack Benny." The unison beat of thousands of pairs of jackboots clicking and echoing on pavement so many years before my time, and the little girl that I was, listening to the insipid whining of Jack Benny on TV.

I am grappling with what it means to have lived in Toronto in the sixties—"Toronto the Good," or "Hogtown," as it was called—complete with its white Anglo stronghold, which for me was a stranglehold as I faltered and fell unmistakably short of what seemed like the right kind of Canadian.

I learned from the great trendsetter, image maker, and reflector—Television—and those who made decisions that shaped my awareness. Bookended by my parents' trauma, and depictions of the lifestyle I should aspire to, I developed in the middle; between barbed wire and Brylcreem, you might say. I call my conundrum "ad men meet Anne Frank."

Finally, there are the insinuations, like the myriad gray tones in a cloud-filled sky and the constant implications of weather upon me. These shades are about my parents, their presence in my present, their horror story past.

Growing up, I couldn't sleep at night, because I was racked with an inexplicable, primordial fear. I was often alarmed, or at the very least confused, by what my parents said and how they reacted.

1

So I am a stickler for detail, gathering and ferreting to make sense, remembering and remembering, following tangents like a squirrel that traverses every limb of the tree.

Peril...is what I embodied: the ever-threatening feeling of something terrible about to take place, the unwitting imprint of what my parents endured.

Peril...is also the phonetic spelling of the sound of my name in Yiddish, the way my parents pronounced it.

Chapter 1

The Other Side of the Mirror

Out back, three staircases from the second floor apartments descended to the lane. One staircase was used by my family. Those using the other two staircases varied, though the interval between occupants, and hence playmates for me, was interminable. It felt like I had lived here forever.

Rumor had it that a family was moving in next door. I couldn't be privy to the causality, the discussions among their family members about starting a business, the borrowing and lending that would result in some sort of a down payment, the real estate agents, the lawyers, the packing, the moving, the unpacking. Parents making decisions and children having to go along. I would be the last to know, having very little clout as the unknown neighbors' unknown kid.

You couldn't tell from the front. There was a door like mine, into which people slipped and then disappeared. But at the back, you could see and watch and wait. Rumor also had it that there were children, maybe one my age. Hope welled.

There he was...a boy. That was okay. He had an older sister. I had an older brother. We were the same in reverse. That was good. We were going into the same grade. It was summer, lots of time to become friends.

He had blonde hair in a brush cut, and a cowlick that would get lighter and lighter with the sun as his skin turned a protective, ruddy color. His cheeks were always flushed and rosy, and so were his lips. His eyes were a simple, genetic blue, as if he were run on an ordinary setting, "We'll be doing the blonde/blue-eyed batch today. No changes in the format."

He had little arm muscles and a few, new, large, white teeth in front with whiter spots. His voice rang out like an alto in a boys'

3

choir. His fingers were nimble and strong. We began the process of becoming friends in a negotiated rhythm, which took us from pre-liminary exchanges of information such as, age, family con- figura-tion, birth dates, to the informal tests of hanging out, going to the park, improvising a game. So far so good.

He took me on a tour of his father's shop. We came in the back entrance, through a small, adjunct room, then into the main space. It was filled with sheets and panes of glass leaning against tables and waiting to be sized, installed into empty window frames, or silvered. Our footsteps echoed woodenly on the plank floor, in counterpoint to the searing sounds of machinery and breath-stopping wafts of ammonia.

There was something so exquisite about glass. I watched the unassuming glass cutter gliding across the sheet like a skate, yet having the power to cut through the depth, leaving a perfectly clean edge. The silvering solution was like mirror in a bottle, pouring onto a glass surface, gravity determining the flow and the even coverage, which spilled over the edges.

His father said hello to us and tousled his son's hair. His father was nice. Henry loved his father and looked proud. "He's a glazier," Henry proclaimed. The sound of the word *was* glass as far as I was concerned, so close to the Yiddish and German that con-verged and pooled deep within me.

I finally disclosed Henry's pedigree to my parents, fully expecting to be forbidden from playing with him, but the fact that Henry was German seemed to have had no effect whatsoever on them. This shocked me, but was filed under the many inconsisten-cies my parents would offer up for complicated, at best, and im-possible, at worst, comprehension. In a most surprising reprieve, both my mother and father did not blame every German for the atrocities of the Holocaust. "There is good and bad in every group." I knew this meant Jews were no exception.

"Wanna come over?" Henry's next offer after we'd seen the shop.

"Sure." I liked going to everyone else's house.

Once again, we came in from the back. An unexpected perk for me was realizing that Henry's apartment was mine in mirror image, satisfying the constant wondering about what the neighbors could see. The store façades were joined in a row. But behind the front rooms on the second floor there were openings to allow for window wells on inward-facing sides of the respective flats. I had looked out my window at the window directly across about three feet away, and sometimes I could catch someone in a room if the light was on, or see hands and arms lowering or lifting a window blind. Now I knew what they saw too.

There was not much to do, it seemed, once we'd woven in and out of one room after the other until we were done, which took about two minutes. Neither of us was hungry. We took to placing our hands together, first lining up the bases, the palms, and then the fingers.

"Mine's bigger." Henry declared.

Then we stood back to back and reached our hands over our heads to read like Braille the difference between our heights.

"I'm taller." It was true he was.

"Yeah, but you're older," a mitigation I pointed out.

"So," he sniped, with a dismissive affectation that was the trend among young debaters, rendering moot any further statement on my part.

Now Henry was pretending to be an airplane. I still tried to engage him.

"NNNNNYYYYEEEEERRRRRRUMMMM."

"You have blue eyes," I remarked.

"Yeah, I know."

"Do you know what color mine are?"

"Hmmm, brown?"

"No, they're hazel." The fact that Henry had failed to distinguish the finer details of my appearance didn't faze him.

"What's hazel?"

"Well, it's kinda greeny-brown."

"Looks brown to me."

That night I was very busy. I was in my room hoping to escape the notice of parents treading up and down the hall, which was the only thoroughfare that linked one room to the next, the shortest main route there was, with stops too close to one another.

5

At any point I would hear my mother, "Perila, voos tist du?" ("Perila"—my name in the diminutive—"what are you doing?")

"Nothing."

That wasn't true. I was holding a hand mirror as I sat on the edge of the fold-out couch I slept on. I removed the shade from the bedside lamp my brother fashioned in his Grade Eight industrial arts class. The bare bulb was burning hot, but I was careful. I held the lamp up to my left eye and brought the hand mirror closer. I could clearly see the color. My eye was a luminous marble. The outer rim was jade, then avocado green, and, finally, a thin ring around the pupil was golden brown.

I was told that my maternal grandmother had blue eyes and blonde hair, "a blondina" ("a blondie"), my mother would say. Both my aunts had blue eyes; my uncle's and grandfather's eyes were brown. My mother had blue eyes, my father, brown, my brother's eyes were brown. How close is hazel to blue? Close but no cigar. A disheartening reality for me. I yearned for blue eyes.

I was going over to Henry's again.

It was raining today, so we were relegated to the indoors. If we wanted to run we could use the hall as a beeline, all the way from the back, where the kitchen was, to the front room about thirty feet away, and use the front room as a turnabout. I assumed we couldn't make any noise because of the shop downstairs. I knew this all too well. My mind wandered to what my mother always said to me: "Za, shtill!" ("Be quiet!"). My mother shook her finger at me and warned me that the storekeeper and customers could hear everything we did upstairs. She threatened further that the business owner would move away if we were too loud. She was terribly serious. I was angry and defeated at the same time. My days and nights were out of sync with the rest of the world.

It felt good to run, and stifling our laughter was strangely thrilling. We were having fun doing nothing that could be named with a proper noun. While we caught our breath we talked. Since we had already established that my parents were from Poland and his were from Germany, the likelihood of our having our nationality in common had been dispelled. We went back farther hoping for similarities.

"My grandfather fought in the war," Henry said. "He was a soldier in the German army."

"My grandmother died in the war. She was killed because she was too sick to leave her house." Oh well, yet another difference between us.

"Hey!" Henry's face was alive with excitement. It was infectious, and I reflected his delight.

"What?" I asked eagerly.

"Maybe my grandfather killed your grandmother!"

Henry was off and running down the hall. He was his grandfather now. He positioned his hands one behind the other, his two thumbs sticking up assuredly, his forefingers aiming purposefully, his other fingers curled around an imaginary shaft that held a machine gun.

"ACKKACKKKACKKK, ACKKACKKACKK, ACCKKKK-ACCCCKKK." He stood at the first room, leaning back against the post, and then swung around looking for Jews in the room.

In my mind, the Jews were weighed down by their faith. The tall hats housing their skull caps betrayed them above the fences, which they thought shielded them from view. Their caricatural hook noses jutted out beyond the tree they were behind. Their ceremonial garb and accessories, their ringleted sideburns slowed them down as they ran.

"ACKKAKKKACKKK, ACKKKACKKKACKK, ACCKKKK-ACCCKKKK." Down the hall to the next room. The small flat seemed capacious to me now.

In a room, in a town, in Poland, my maternal grandmother lies bedridden. She is "in violation of the order to evacuate," even though she has a good excuse. Teams of Nazi officers are dispatched to scour the neighborhood and make sure everyone has assembled at the train station. The officers yell to each other in German, checking in and confirming the "all clears." They are prepared for the many sneaky ideas a person can have as to where to hide, and they don't take anything for granted in their search. They are both quick and thorough, pounding up and down stairs, stomping to check for loose floorboards, using the barrels of their guns to set aside anything suspicious and to trace areas inside closets.

The suddenness of discovering my grandmother out in the open like that, with no guile, momentarily disrupts their gait as each member of the team joins the other. My grandmother looks at them, assured in the belief that they will appreciate the specific circumstances of why she is there. The soldiers have been given orders and are clear about performing their duty. My grandmother is mistaken about what the soldiers are thinking, and vice versa, so it seems there's no need for either side to explain. In my grandmother's mind, the soldiers have the connections to get her the medical attention she needs. She looks at each one of them in expectation of being helped from her bed. In uniform, all the soldiers look alike. Whichever one ends up raising his gun to aim doesn't matter. In an instant, my grandmother has to make the devastating adjustment to her fate. No one speaks; one shot does the trick. "Arrous!" ("Let's go!"), a soldier says, and the pounding of jackboots on stairs resumes.

I was far from mollified by Henry's enthusiastic suggestion that his grandfather could lay claim to being my grandmother's assailant. The longing for Henry and me to share something was eclipsed by a sneaking revulsion I couldn't shake, but it never went past the pit of my stomach into my throat where words could come out. I didn't know where to begin anyway.

When he was finished, his face was a deep red, his breathing fast, and he was smiling. He had just had a ball, I thought to myself. It was fun to play; I conceded that much.

Henry and I had been like two little fishes sharing a small fish bowl for the summer. When school started, we were released into the greater water, where we gravitated towards familiar species. The first definitive act of distance came in the form of being placed in different classes. Then that extended farther as we found ourselves at different ends of the schoolyard at recess.

The girls played together busying themselves with attaching colored elastic bands in sequences so that patterns of color repeated. There were two positions, which rotated: holding the band taut, and jumping over the increasing heights. Elastic breakage, due to wear, interrupted the game, and meticulous knots forestalled the inevitable replacement. Henry played adversarial games with the boys, using an endless roster of "us against them" versions. I caught a glimpse of him from time to time, and he always seemed active. I was happy for him somehow, new boy at a new school and all.

When I sat at the top of our back staircase, I could see everything I needed to. All the people in the stores came out to the back lane if their cars were parked there. Anyone who lived in the apartments above used the back because it was behind the scenes, like being backstage.

"Perila, voos tist du?" My mother.

"Nothing."

That wasn't true. If I could have seen into the future, I might have been able to determine that the average length of occupants' stays was about two years. But I had an inner sense and knew it was time to begin the vigil. I watched and waited for new people to move in. The first sign of something different would be apparent in the back lane.

Chapter 2

The Forum

The back lane was a forum. I didn't think of it in this way at the time, but upon reflection, the back lane could be thus labeled. Like eras... No one took anyone aside in fourteenth-century Europe to tell the news, "Psst, you know we've been in the Dark Ages, right? Well, the Dark Ages are now over and the Renaissance has begun. Time to shed those depressing grays and browns and try a little color, pass it on."

A forum for business, agriculture, transportation, trade, recreation, meeting, discussion, religion, births and burials...it all took place in the back lane.

The south boundary of the back lane ran the length of the block from east to west—Atlas to Winona—and included various stores and a synagogue. The north boundary of the back lane delineated the shift from commercial to residential. From the lane you could see in plain view the yard and south side of Lydia's house, the first one on the east side of Atlas, the street perpendicular to St. Clair. Less so, the yards of the successive houses going north.

The back of the synagogue, which closed off the lane to the west, shared a fence with the ends of the lots on Barrie, the street one block north and parallel to St. Clair. Using the east egress of the lane, the one way in or out, you could walk around the block without crossing the street and take in a world.

The back lane was the only earth around. The entire block was concrete, from the sidewalk on St. Clair where the storefronts were, to the "yards" behind the stores. Even to the rear of the synagogue, where there was a schoolyard of sorts, the floor was made of wooden slats to allow the weather enough space to disperse, but the earth underneath was completely covered.

The ground of the laneway imparted climatic information, whispering its secrets through its varying textures. The wand of

11

winter immobilized the last expressive nuance of movement in the soil. My feet would negotiate the bumpy terrain as I crossed like a giant over the snow-capped mountains of mud and the frozen lakes in the valleys—the simultaneous result of tires rolling in and out of parking spaces throughout the cold and damp fall.

Then the squishy thaw of spring. A tricky time, having to sidestep the darker sections. In a previous lesson, under the heading of "once bitten...," they had proven to be full of moisture, running shoes sinking, like into quicksand in *Tarzan* episodes. Though only my shoes got swallowed up, and the result was not literally fatal as in the TV show, coming face to face with my mother, whose threshold for dirt was very low, felt hazardous enough. After the spring rains, hot summer air first baked the mud to cake, then continued to dry the earth, separating the particles until powder became airborne as dust.

On one of those days when the earth was drying, I flew out the back door ready to play, ran down the stairs, stopped suddenly on the last tread, and teetered there. It was still, too still for sleep. On the landing, in the path that I would take to get to the back gate, it lay. As the storybooks had indicated, robin's egg blue was a particular shade. There, in the daylight, the rich color was out of place with the deep, dull, utility green of banisters and spindles, gunmetal gray of steps and porch floors, browns of exposed wood in need of paint, and ochre earth. I'd never seen a blue like that that wasn't man-made. Not turquoise and not azure, but a color we tried to mimic in pretty blouses, classy cars, and kitchen appliances of the era. I came closer.

The egg had cracked open upon impact, but had not fallen apart. Inside, pale and wan, was a creature, birdlike and bare, not ready to be born. While I waited for movement, I projected loftily about how I would care for it until it was able to fend for itself. Too many minutes passed with no sign of life. Just as well. My parents would have been furious.

My fantasy had been this:

"Mommy, Mommy can I keep her?" Expectant children close to their mothers' skirts, heads flung back, eyes wide to catch their mothers' reactions, as a glimpse one way or another would deliver the verdict. Mothers, clones of June Cleaver, on TV shows or magnified on the screen in Disney productions, wearing dresses with cinched waists, strings of pearls around their necks, hair always coiffed, lipstick ever applied, shoes with heels.

"Well, now let's see, dear." Mothers would bend down to be at eye level with their child, their skirts flounced and billowing on the floor, like Deborah Kerr in *The King and I*.

"See, Mommy, isn't she cute?"

"Yes, she's very cute, how did you find her?"

"Bobby's cat had babies, and when I went to his house to see them she came right over to me."

"Now *did* she."

"Uh, huh." The child nodded up and down. "I think she likes me."

"I see. Well, she certainly looks comfortable. And you're holding her properly, with one arm underneath for support, and the other in front. You have to be careful with such a small thing."

"I know, and I will be careful, I promise."

"Do you know what it means to take care of a cat?"

"Yes…well, kind of."

"How about we spend some time and think it over, see how the cat feels being here. Your father gets home soon, and we can all discuss it."

"Gee, thanks Mommy, you're the best."

"Dear, don't thank me yet, but we'll figure something out. Now run along."

But that wasn't how it went with my mother.

"Get that out of here!" There's rage. "Sis shmootsic!" ("It's dirty!") I'm trying to listen, but I'm afraid and hurt and insulted.

"Cats aren't dirty, they clean themselves."

"Not dirty! Bist farikt! ('Are you out of your mind!') Do you know where that cat has been? What germs it's picked up? And the hair! Uch!" Her entire body shudders. "Who's going to clean that? Caring about a cat? What's the matter with you? A cat, that's important?" She's disgusted. "Your family, that's what's important. A cat! The Nazis killed six million Jews, and you're worried about a cat."

Did that make me too sensitive, or not sensitive enough?

I looked for a long time at the two halves of the robin's egg, one which cupped the creature's bottom and the other which crowned the tiny head, and then at the strained parchment neck, at the tissue eyelids, and I felt so sorry that it had fallen and that it had to die. The temperature at midday was unforgivingly hot. I knew enough to realize that I had to move the bird and egg from where they lay. I also knew I couldn't tell anybody, because my words would be twisted into some other meaning, and I would be blindsided.

I went inside the apartment and grabbed a handful of Kleenex. I placed one, square, papery sheet on my palm and, careful not to touch the egg, gingerly eased my hand under the whole shell. I covered the poor bird with another Kleenex and wrapped it up as best I could. I looked for a spot in the back lane. I wanted to bury it where there was the least chance that it would be disturbed, deep enough, and away from cars. I could tell by the tire tracks, putting my trust in the habitual parking techniques of the shopkeepers, where the best patch of earth was. I found it somewhere in the middle of the lane and I started to dig. I placed the bundle in the space and then covered it with the unearthed soil.

Some notion about rites had already been impressed upon me. From Hebrew school, I took a prayer I was proud to know by heart, though I didn't know what it meant. There was a "rehearsal" word for God, so as not to use God's name in vain, the first commandment. In Hebrew school, we always used the substitute. I knew that, on this occasion, "everyone" would have insisted on the substitute, but I used God's real name. I said the prayer. From public school, I took the tradition of a moment's silence, that grave, solemn minute at the eleventh hour of the eleventh day of the eleventh month. I was in a trance of feeling, as was the creature's due.

Every single time now, after I began my descent down the back staircase, I would look at the landing first.

On another day in the back lane, an important multicultural conference was underway. There were three delegates. One representing those families who came to Canada from Ireland genera-

14

tions ago, another representing recent immigrants like the Italians, and the third, the Jews from Poland. All of them had convened to compare customs and mores. The participants reflected the changing demographic in Toronto and were here to discuss the challenges they faced.

Roy, Peter, and I stood in the lane, talking about what we were going to do. There was the parkette right across the street, and the synagogue schoolyard at the end of the lane— two excellent choices for activities—yet standing in the lane talking was what we continued to do. The earth beneath our feet was soft enough to flip over clumps, but not so dry as to kick up dirt in someone's face. Our eyes were looking down at three pairs of running shoes, feet that shuffled, and toes that used just enough force to break the earth and coax a pebble loose before flicking it.

We were ensconced in a situation that kept our triad tightly configured. Finally, we decided on a course of action that would determine how we stacked up in relation to one another. The matter was serious, and we were all committed to working it through.

Peter was the first to go. His gesture had an effect on me. I found him to be brave and trusting, yet so easygoing, as if he were about to show us a lucky coin. He unzipped his pants, reached in, and brought out his penis for us to peruse. I was looking at his penis very intently. He held it steady between his thumb on top and his forefinger underneath. I was struck first by the color, a deep, purplish pink with brown undertones. The object was a few inches long, and there was a succession of little folds lined up one behind the other, which accounted for the color gradation. Looking at the end of his penis, I could only compare it to the shape of an acorn, though clearly an acorn's smooth, hard, wooden texture was completely different from what appeared to be pliable skin. Peter kindly twisted his fingers one way, and then the other, so that we could see his penis from every vantage point. When both Roy and I were through with our examination, Peter good-naturedly folded his penis back into his pants and zipped himself up.

Roy said, "I'll go next." Once again, I was impressed with his volunteerism. Perhaps he needed someone to go before him to apprise himself of what to expect. Or, perhaps, putting himself forward even after someone else had taken the plunge still gave him a sense of making up his own mind. In any case, it was another vote of confidence for the process.

Unzipped and now proffered, Roy's penis was ours to behold. The obvious similarity between Roy's and Peter's, as a human organ that is, escaped me. Instead, I was completely surprised by the color. On an artist's palette, the colors would be separate because of their base tones—browns and purples of Peter's, and the hint of yellow, orange, light pink of Roy's. I was fixated on the pallor of Roy's penis; his was barely a color at all. It was even lighter than the flesh-colored, Laurentian pencil crayon I hardly ever used because it didn't really show up on "newsprint," the scratchy grade of paper we used when we had "art" at school.

I spent a long time looking and comparing Roy's to what I recollected Peter's looked like. Since Roy's penis was so faint, it seemed smaller, because it didn't command the eye the way the darker tones did. Actually, Roy's looked kind of scrawny. It shrank back and drooped a little more than Peter's. Not that I thought Peter's was better. Maybe the exercise of penile scrutiny had just run its course. Roy picked up a cue that he could put his penis away.

My two esteemed colleagues now turned their attention to me. It was pretty obvious who was left to go. But something happened. There was a logistical dilemma. They were able to reach inside their fly for their presentation object, which they could hold out, while I would have to pull down my pants and find a position that adequately displayed me. Not so easy.

I had already anticipated how the air would feel on my backside, even before I pulled down my pants. It would feel like a chill, belying the comfortable, outdoor temperature. It would be like many eyes looking at me when I couldn't see behind me. It would be as if I couldn't run away even if I tried, waddling about with my pants around my ankles. They could run away if they chose, unzipped and flapping. Our differences weren't only cultural. On this point, I was the odd man out. I felt the weight of the world upon me now, the stalwart promise we all gave willingly to participate in the exercise, the follow-through actions of two of the three affiliates, which would leave me as the dissembler. The back lane now gaped as an open amphitheatre, the exposing daylight casting no shadows.

"I don't think I want to anymore." There, I said it.

"Okay," they both returned, in their good-natured way, as if we had been talking about something as inconsequential as "Can you come out to play?" Since it was over with, one started, "Guess I'll see you later," and then the other one added, "Yeah, me too." And they were gone.

That was easy, I thought to myself. I was left feeling kind of clever that I had gotten out of something the others hadn't. I saw theirs, and they didn't see mine. My first instinct was to think my mother would have been proud that I had outmaneuvered the other two, but then I began to doubt myself.

My mother would have been irritated by my willing participation in the first place. Why would I have put myself into such a predicament? Her annoyance would have grown. That I had gotten out of it at the last minute would have seemed to her like pulling a rabbit out of a hat. A lucky break, but way too risky. Better to have kept a low profile from the start. This was a strategy that had ensured her survival, as she escaped the notice of the cruel foreman in the slave labor camp where she worked as a welder for three long years, making ammunition for the Nazis by day and dreaming of freedom by night. But I could not make the connection, and it wasn't my experience anyway. I was also left feeling like I had committed an injustice by misleading my friends, and that sat uneasily, like a rickety leg on a wooden chair. My mother would have thought me foolish for thinking about the welfare of others who likely wanted to take advantage of me.

The back lane was a stone's throw from the synagogue schoolyard. Going there calmed my mother because it was so close to home. Though the original vision for the synagogue included both schooling and a place of worship, the reality was that the public educational system was more popular than private, religious-based schools, until the tides turned many years later. And so the schoolyard was never used.

The synagogue walls were long and high; windows were far from the ground, beyond a ball's trajectory. That was good news.

The most common casualty of kids and their balls was broken windows, which kept Henry's father's glass shop in business, but depleted children's coffers painstakingly amassed by weekly allowances. Safely, I could perfect my solitary game of "one, two, three, a-larry" with my tri-colored rubber ball, a seasonal item that appeared in the variety store around spring. Its red, white, and blue paint was pristine when new, but you had to look carefully at the edges of the white band of paint, which separated the two colors, because sometimes the red or blue coverage wasn't always even. So buyer, beware. The ball had to be replaced when the paint started to peel and the outer layer of rubber came away, which affected whether the ball bounced true or not. Important for the game.

If I was lucky, I'd be the only one in the schoolyard. If not, I would be sharing the wall with boys playing handball. When boys played handball, the ball controlled them. Their willingness to suffer any injury, as a consequence of propelling their bodies to get behind the ball and return the throw, was limitless. Their inability to fly seemed not to be a deterrent. That was their affair, until they bumped into you and knocked you off your feet. Though they may have apologized, they were really just telling you that you could expect the same thing to happen again and again, the concept of staying at their end and respecting your side, incomprehensible.

The boys preferred an India rubber ball, a smaller and far denser version of my tri-colored one. One of the sideshows they discovered while playing handball was how funny it was to whip the India rubber ball at someone and watch them howl in pain. Usually they did this to each other to add variety to the rules of their game. You would have *known* if it had ever happened to you, because it was a rare sensation indeed. The impact first took your breath away, and then registered as a deep, dull suffering. Your surface skin smarted wildly, burning hot and icy cold, the outline of the ball clearly demarcated on your skin, just in case you had a lapse of consciousness. All in an evening's fun. If not for the waning light and pangs of hunger...the worry of parents...there would have been no reason to go home.

The back lane provided the quickest route to the ice cream truck. All white, with cartoon images of sundaes, and cones either filled with vanilla ice cream dipped in chocolate, which hardened upon contact, or with vanilla and chocolate ice cream twisting in an upward spiral, a curl at the top. The telltale melody announcing the truck's whereabouts was lighthearted, like skipping. And when the music started, children within earshot were visibly affected. They immediately stopped whatever they were doing, responding with an obedience that no disciplinary system could have elicited. As if programmed, they would go to the nearest authority figure to get permission and ask for money. Then, like robots with homing devices, they sought out the "hub," which could be found idling on Atlas at the mouth of the parkette.

The other truck that delivered something special was the Eaton's truck—dark, royal navy—displaying a subtle white and red logo synonymous with quality and class. It always pulled up and parked on St. Clair to fulfill someone's dream, sometimes one of mine, inspired by the glossy pages of the comprehensive Eaton's catalogue, or a visit to its flagship downtown store.

But two other truck drivers knew to find us by using the back lane. They delivered regularly, not relying on the clumsy, St. Clair address that left everyone baffled, like the Eaton's driver wandering about, or the ice cream man who didn't deliver at all, just waited for everyone to come to him. The trucks that came to us had no fancy pictures or scripts. Not only did the drivers know the back lane, but they would come up the back stairs and rap sharply on *our* door to announce their presence.

One of them was the milkman, the brunt of many romantic speculations on the domestic front, and no wonder. His produce was luscious. Silky sour cream in thick, glass, pint-sized jars with paper lids and tabs. Spooning sour cream dollops over sliced bananas, the tangy, sweet, slippery mixture. Buttermilk in quarts, rich, cold, frothy, refreshing.

The other was the "seltzer vasser mann" (the soda water man), wielding wooden crates with partitions for six thick, glass, soda water bottles and their powerful nozzles. My mother would hand him an empty crate, and he in turn replenished her supply. My parents were *never* without a soda water bottle in the fridge.

The back lane confirmed that I existed, and opened my eyes to the way things worked.

Chapter 3

Lydia

Lydia was a prime example of a "goyeta," a generic term in Yiddish referring to a non- Jewish female, but the connotation was more explicit than that and could be pejorative. "Goyim," the plural form, referred to all non-Jews, but also specifically to a group of "Canadians" who had immigrated generations before from Britain, Scotland, or Ireland. I didn't know how I picked up the notion, but the feeling was strong that the date of arrival on Canadian soil translated into who was more "Canadian" than who, leaving the latest group to land feeling less entitled to the label.

Jews used the term "goyim" preemptively as a kind of signal, an "anti-Semitic red alert," never imagining anything approaching acceptance. The goyim wouldn't necessarily dislike Jews, and Jews were on their guard with respect to non-Jews after the war, no wonder. Distance could very well have been best for all involved.

Living under the radar was something it seemed both Jews and non-Jews agreed Jews needed to do for everyone's sake. One way to accomplish this was to anglicize Jewish surnames, a common practice I imagined some Canadian customs official had a certain flair for. The goal was to clean up these unwieldy and multisyllabic surnames so that they could be easily spelled and pronounced, like the surnames of the goyim, be they Carver or Rogers. Thus, a wand would instantly transform an awkward Mr. Davidovich into Mr. David, or Mr. Davis, or Mr. Davies. And a problematic surname like Utkewitz would be reincarnated as quintessentially Canadian: York.

Obscuring Jewishness may have seemed protective because it had been the salient factor that had proven fatal for Jews in Nazi Germany. But it also played into a more insidious sentiment reinforcing, for both Jews and non-Jews, that being Jewish wasn't desirable or something to be proud of. And so the Jews escaped notice, at least on paper. But in person it was a different story. For the most part the women, like Lydia, were tall, lithe, spindly, compared to the short, portly Jewish matrons. Their features smaller, their skin fairer, compared to Jews. Other than a surname which sounded "Canadian" enough, everything else still gave Jews away. No one confirmed for me that this was what was going on in the recesses of the ethos of the times. It was just how I felt in my bones, and I lived with shame under the yoke of the disparity.

With Lydia, the red alert was downgraded to safe levels, because by all accounts our family could tell that she really didn't mind us.

I would often see Lydia slipping out the side door, which was opposite to our back staircase with the back lane between us, taking the narrow walk to her garden, lifting the latch, and opening the whining gate. I rarely saw her in anything but a housecoat over a night gown, and men's plaid slippers. Her skinny shins and tiny, blue veins looked like they'd never seen the sun. Hard to guess her age, as everyone was old from a kid's perspective, but I would say that she seemed middle-aged, if not chronologically, then energetically.

Usually with a cigarette dangling, her hair divided into little, square sections, hair wound around a finger to make the tightest kiss curls held in place by crisscrossed bobby pins, which would create a cascade of waves, waves I'd never get to see, Lydia would always say hello in her gentle voice. But it was her garden that captured my attention. I longed for it, a large patch of green grass facing west, heady when mowed, a mass of aromatic lilacs in spring and of peonies in early summer, which filled in the end of her yard.

The closest I came to her garden was at her fence. Technically, I was standing on back lane soil, but the weight of the lilac blooms brought the boughs within reach. I could touch their tapering shape, like clusters of grapes on the vine, and, without trespassing, breathe in their purple fragrance (even the white ones had it). But the whiff of the bountiful peonies deep in her yard was too remote and remained unknown to me.

My backyard…wasn't one at all. There was a walkout from the store on the main floor, a concrete patch with a short flight of stairs to street level, and then another flight of stairs to our porch.

I made do.

In the spring, my father and I would go down the stairs after the store was closed, and I would practice my skipping. My father was a "never-ender," not that he knew what it meant. For us who skipped rope, it was the dreaded position of being doomed to repeat an action forever, like a Greek mythological character. But my father thoroughly enjoyed being gainfully employed turning the rope over and over. The post that held up our porch was the other never-ender.

During the summers, when I was a little older, I would haul one of the kitchen chairs down the stairs and set it up for the brief spell when the sun appeared beyond the corner of one building before being eclipsed by the corner of the next one. Not having a lounge chair made it difficult to get an even tan. But I improvised. I slid my body down so that my neck rested on the top of the chair, which probably constricted the blood going to my brain. Then I extended my legs. My arms posed a problem. I had nowhere to put them. If I crossed my arms, I would prevent the sun from getting to my chest and stomach, but I couldn't suspend them in midair for any length of time either. I ended up resting my fingertips on each side of my bathing suit bottoms and froze the posture.

When I turned over to do my back, I was stymied. Straddling the chair was the only option. This meant that, though my back and arms were exposed, the back of my legs would always elude the rays. So much trouble for an activity that turned out to be a huge health risk. The other indignity to be endured was suffering the looks of store personnel coming out the back exit to get into one of their cars parked in the lane. It was hard to be invisible—a girl in a two-piece bathing suit—but I suppose we both tried to pretend the other was not there. For my part, I always felt they were afforded the better view.

During the winters, the snow masked the difference between Lydia's yard and mine. For once, every vista was coated and uniform. If I had anything to boast about, it would be that my cantilevered porch produced the longest icicles, probably lethal when deployed in the spring thaw, but glorious in their frozen extensions, droplets running down the lengths and then freezing before falling, each time getting longer and longer. Enveloped in gear like an astronaut, I would forge a path in the snow, the back stairs now looking like a bobsled run. And at the very bottom where the snow hid the concrete, I would make snowballs and angels and try very hard to create snowmen that vaguely resembled the ones in cartoons, a feat much harder than it looked on TV.

Come summer, Lydia's yard would re-enter my mind like a covetous thought, or the proverbial "grass is greener." No one ever used it. No one took advantage of the west-facing exposure that would guarantee many uninterrupted hours of UV zaps, barring cloud cover. Years of summers came and went. Me with my chair on concrete, Lydia with her intermittent visits to check on her perennials. And a year, let alone many, was a long time for anyone young.

But one day, the events conspired. Summer found me on the back stairs, with Lydia opening her side door. Somehow I felt courageous enough to ask if it would be okay for me to tan in her yard. And she said yes.

Fairly soon after that I also acquired a lounge chair, something that was clearly a luxury for my family, very out of place in our apartment, folded, covered in plastic, and stowed in the deepest part of the largest closet for most of the year, and then brought out to be used in Lydia's yard or carted along for picnic outings.

"In" the yard, as opposed to looking "at" the yard from afar, felt dizzyingly unreal, like it wouldn't last, which in truth it couldn't. But while I was there, I took the opportunity to approach the giant peonies, noticing first the variegated coloration, and next their undulating contours, their maze-like folds. I reached for one large blossom with both my hands, as if to bend down to hold a baby's face. I brought my own face closer so that my lips felt the silky petals, and then did what I had wanted to do for so long. I took in their perfumy bouquet for the very first time in all my life, and now I knew their scent, innocently sweet. Luckily, I also noticed the many tiny ants traversing the hills and valleys of supple terrain, having almost inhaled some of them in my enthusiasm to experience the wonder of peonies.

It seemed grossly unfair in some ways. Lydia should have had my apartment, where the sun couldn't find a footing, since she seemed to eschew daylight anyway, and I her house, so that I could revel endlessly in the backyard.

I didn't know she was a nocturnal creature who preferred the blankety nights, the strobe-like flutter of television images, which broke up the darkness of her living room or the dimness of the bedroom, courtesy of a single, frosted bulb and a shade with caked-on dust, impossible to clean. There in her bedroom, the deep, brown, wood veneer of the furniture soaked up any excess light; two twin beds stood separately, touted as some sort of domestic standard popularized on *The Dick Van Dyke Show*. A protective doily, a wind-up clock vibrating with the impertinent chatter of seconds, the ashtray, a pack of cigarettes, and a book of matches topped the shared night table. Flannel sheet with its signature blue horizontal lines peering over a woolen cover, and another cover folded at the end of each bed…why change out of a housecoat?

I wouldn't have known or understood that Lydia's routine was to begin with a glass, some ice retrieved from ice cube trays in the freezer, the opening of an upper, kitchen cupboard door, and reaching for the squat, cut glass bottle of Crown Royal or the tall, brown bottle of Canadian Club. Fill 'er up, drink 'er down. And how that would feel, one round after another.

I didn't know anything about Lydia's quiet existence with her husband, whom I never saw, and a son who was old enough to live on his own. Not until the silence was broken when the sirens shrieked and the darkness was shattered by the flashing lights of the fire trucks dispatched from the station on the south side of St. Clair.

Chapter 4

Fire & Snow

I saw the world through the triptych window in the living room. The middle window and its smaller, flanking ones provided a vista that shaped my understanding. They were a constant source of information. They were my eyes. The middle one gave me straight-ahead perspective, the two others, my peripheral vision. Across St. Clair and down Hennrick—the street opposite and perpendicular—I could see the fire station almost at the corner and picture my schoolyard, which I knew was at the end. I could just make out Atlas on my left and the beginning of the synagogue on my right. Traffic going east and west on St. Clair was all mine to behold. I could be summoned to the window whenever I heard the roar of streetcars in both directions and the plaintive clang of their bells signaling an injustice, only to witness a thoughtless driver in their path, who scoffed at their ding-dong nursery rhyme sound. Some threat.

I could see vehicles parallel-parking in front of the store, people getting out and getting in. It was from this vantage point that I learned to identify makes and models of cars. Most exciting were the new ones I would first see advertized on TV, especially the Pontiacs with their flashy names: GTO, Parisienne, Laurentian, Grand Prix, Firebird, and Camaro. Then, sure enough, I would spot them from above moving along St. Clair and I could point out the changes in style, like the new shape of the lights since last year.

An invisible Rapunzel to be sure, too insignificant to be rescued. No one knew where I lived, or that I lived. Our door, adjacent to the front door of the store, was as inconspicuous as it was inconsequential. No one noticed it, their attention commanded by what lay beyond the glass in the display case. Even the address shrank our entire existence into the appended afterthought *A*, the second floor decidedly second-class compared to the weighty, three-digit number of the commercial enterprise on the main level.

I referred to myself as living above a store, as if who I was depended exclusively on my association with it. Even then the assumptions would continue. "Oh, then it's your store, your father's store," as if it were the only logical reason to live upstairs, like Henry when he lived next door above his father's glass business. Otherwise, families belonged in houses, didn't they? But no, it wasn't that simple. Whose store was it? And what did my father do for a living? More questions to add to being an anomaly.

Did I exist? If someone were coming over for the first time or, like the Eaton's truck driver, delivering something, I knew I would be in for the long, frustrating interlude, awaiting discovery. Watching from the living room window, I would see the truck pulling up in front, the driver stepping out holding a package, and then disappearing underneath. I could imagine him coming up to the street number, seeing the store, being confused, looking at the door beside, and immediately dismissing the notion that this "other door" could be of some value. How could an entire household reside behind a door that seemed to lead nowhere? The Eaton's driver wandered around, perhaps stopping someone on the street who would be of no help to him, until he thought of asking at the store. Finally, the doorbell would ring.

The same problem occurred with any new postal worker. Misplaced mail, mostly ours, going to the store instead, having to rely on the store owners and salespeople to redirect our letters, a gesture not exactly a priority for them, and this at a time when correspondence by mail was the preferred, if not the only method of getting in touch with those from afar. That unassuming *A* held the key to where I was, yet it was constantly underestimated. Maybe I wasn't as doomed as I would be finding myself alive in a coffin that was nailed shut and buried, but the feeling was similar, in that my presence was not generally known, or worse, not expected. Less macabre, it was like a two-way mirror I could see out of, but no one could see in.

And so I reacted to the world and kept up with the news, having scuttled the hope that I could affect my environment.

28

Sounds were amplified on the second floor, and I could be alerted to anything, from a commotion, to two people having a conversation on the street. Sometimes it was hard to tell which was which. Any noise that couldn't be confirmed with a visual, because it was outside the window's range despite my best efforts to try angle after angle, felt threatening. But even noises in plain view could be dangerous if I were spotted watching, like the unfortunate witness who would become a casualty so that criminals could get away with their crime.

The layout of the flat added to the unease. I lived on a line, it seemed. The front and back entries of the flat were on the same linear plane; our rooms were dead ends off the main street and felt like little traps. The back lane, so vital in the day, was the scene for a perfect murder at night. St. Clair, all abuzz with its daily business routine, changed at night, attracting hooligans loitering, hollering obscenities, and disturbing the peace. I was vulnerable.

Nighttime was the enemy.

I wasn't sure if I couldn't sleep because of the noises, or that I couldn't sleep in anticipation of the noises.

And there *were* noises. A thud followed by the sound of glass shattering late at night paralyzed me. I was too terrified to see what happened, and more terrified that my parents wanted to have a look. Finally, after about an hour of listening to the silence, my father went down and confirmed that the front glass of the store's display case had been broken, and items stolen. Police questions, store owner awakened and requested to appear, statements that didn't help, thieves long gone, and lingering fear for me.

My usual routine at night was to lie in bed afraid, ears attuned to any sound coming from the front and back of the flat. Each sound was immediately processed for familiarity, and the fear would ebb and flow as information was gathered to ascertain the sound's benign or malicious properties. Familiarity would not necessarily bring calm. Especially with respect to one sound in particular. It was a sound that came almost exclusively at night. And very often too. But I never got used to it.

It would begin slowly, like a stirring, like the breaking into consciousness of that which can no longer be denied, the way we

29

begin to live our nightmares. Moaning, then wailing, then screaming. The sirens. Somewhere there was a fire. That help was on the way was a distant second to the picture in my mind of someone in a life-threatening situation, maybe me. The fire engines were manned and maneuvered, turning right to get out of the station, their sirens' sound rising and then falling as they paused briefly at the intersection before going left or right onto St. Clair.

When a direction was chosen and the trucks picked up speed, the searing sound would expand with the full range of tiers of increasing intensity. I held no stock in the fact, nor did it appease me, that the fire station was across the street in such proximity. Quite the contrary. All it meant was that I was in a state of poised dread, an "Ask not for whom the bell tolls, it tolls for thee" frame of mind, until I was cleared of being the alarm's intended.

Straining to process the loudness of the sirens, to find out in what direction the engines were headed, was stressful for me. I knew that there was a critical point when the volume could either increase or not, the former signaling danger, the latter that I had been spared. Only the definitive receding of sound would quiet me lying there in the dark, still listening to the slow fade-out that distance would bring, engines speeding towards a destination far away from me. But when will it be my turn?

My mother had beaten the odds in the face of mortal danger. Sixteen times she confronted death and sixteen times she lived. If a cat has nine lives, then my mother had almost twice those chances.

Roll call. The Nazis have their own version of downsizing. Their "pink slips" of termination are terminal. Everyone is summoned to appear before the foreman of the labor camp, who will whittle down the ranks. He points, a woman comes forward, and he says one of two words, "Links" ("Left"), or "Recht" ("Right"). The word is uttered with quick precision. His decisiveness is so instantaneous, he either has a finely honed ability to assess and then direct whoever is before him, or the decision is of such unimportance it becomes an act of whimsy. There is no arguing with the verdict, and there is a substantial difference between Door #1 and Door #2. Sometimes "Left" means you can show up for work tomorrow, and sometimes it means that your services are so permanently not needed that you are treated to whatever efficient means there are of dispatching you from this world. The criteria for who stays and who dies are never the same.

Sixteen times, the woman who approaches is my mother. One time she dares to presume upon the foreman's reasoning. The woman before her, ordered to go one way, is, in my mother's view, very similar to her, so to be helpful to the selection process she follows the woman, almost in a daze. The foreman notices and is angry. "Where are you going?" he remarks sharply to my mother. She tries to explain. "I didn't tell you to go there. You, go there!" He points in the other direction. My mother can only obey. She is sure that her apparent insubordination has sealed her fate. But the group with the other woman is never seen again.

My record for beating the odds wasn't as exemplary as my mother's. Each time I heard the fire engine sirens, I held my breath, and each time the sirens waned, I sighed. And that happened every single time, except twice.

The second time would happen more than a decade later. The first, there it was...the crescendoeing sound and my attendant worry. As always, the fire engines paused before turning one way or another onto St. Clair. Soon I would begin to hear the diminishing tones that signified the end of my troubles. But the sound levels remained loud and then got even louder. Wherever the fire was, was close. I rushed to the front window, looked out across the street, and saw nothing. Then I tried to see out of one of the two smaller windows...still nothing. The sound was all around me. Frantic, I ran down the hall and immediately caught sight of the intermittent, red pulse of the beacon through the upper pane of glass in the back door. I reached the door, moved the little curtain aside, and saw that the engines had pulled up outside Lydia's.

It had been a quiet, frigid winter's night, a night to be in bed, snug. That had been Lydia's and her husband's thinking too, as they drifted off. The evening's events before were typical for them—perhaps drinks and smokes. One last cigarette before bed, butting it out, they thought, and then fast asleep. How the cigarette toppled out of the ashtray, how an ember managed to fall onto something and remain there long enough to begin to sizzle and smoke and spread, can only be surmised. Lydia ended up in a hospital bed and was treated for smoke inhalation and serious burns to her limbs, her husband on a slab at the morgue.

Lydia was never the same after. She wore the housecoat she had worn that night, though it was badly singed, and, perversely proud, showed me the burns she had suffered on her legs, scabbed and scarring against the pallor of her skin and the tiny, blue veins that ran just underneath its thin layer.

Chapter 5

Clothes Make the Man

I was excited…. Going out anytime, anywhere, was an infrequent and welcome pleasure. My parents had been invited over to their friends' house, which was up the street about a block and a half on Atlas. I got to come along.

I watched my mother getting dressed. Her ritual was unwavering. After washing her face and brushing her teeth, the methodical donning of attire was about to begin. She removed a champagne-colored, satin garment from the top drawer of her dresser. It had been made for her here, like it would have been in Poland, first measured by the seamstress, and then sewn to fit exactly two sizes too small, in the spirit of non-surgical breast reduction.

The "stunyik" was more than just a bra; it was a feat of engineering, a private matter that was shamelessly publicized by Jane Russell and Howard Hughes. The large, tent-like forms harnessed my mother's breasts and wrestled them into submission, while the long line-up of tiny eyelets and hooks reinforced the bodice from the middle of her back to her waist, ensuring containment.

My assistance, where she could not reach, was a necessity, "Vist a zoy git zine?" a polite, formal request along the lines of "Would you be so kind?" I was aware that she would never have asked me if she could have done it herself, and so the preamble felt at once apologetic and sadly helpless. This was her own turmoil, for I was very eager to oblige. I thoroughly enjoyed the feeling of hooking the eyelets one after the other and noticing how the formerly lifeless garment in the drawer began to take its shape and fulfill its function.

Next was the garter belt, worn under panties, with a few eyelets at her waist she could do up herself from behind, and flapping rubber tongues at the front, flank, and backs of her thighs. She sat on the edge of her side of the bed, began to remove a cellophane wrapper, and unfolded two, two-dimensional, diaphanous stocking legs, separating the first, and then the second, from the cardboard insert.

Carefully bunching the delicate garment to reduce its length, so that the entire stocking would clear the foot, was crucial in order to avoid any wayward, hardened skin points or sharp toenails, which could snag or rip the nylon and produce a run. Toes first, then heel, she fed and released enough material through her fingertips to keep the stocking at a specific tension, not too taut to tax its fragility, but not too loose. She made her way past her shin, over her knee, and around her thigh, until she reached the rubber tongues. Beginning with the front one, she pulled the material into place, affixed the steel, u-shaped fastener over the tongue, securely sandwiching the beige, transparent fabric.

Stocking feet squeezed into pumps with thick heels. A dark blue skirt and silky, white blouse with blue and green flowers lay inanimate on the bed. Skirt first, hips twisting this way and that in an opposite motion to the skirt as it slid up her body. There was a sizable *V*-shaped space that emerged, which the zipper must eliminate. Pulling the tab at the waist and doing up the button helped change the *V* to an *O*. Tugging at the bottom of the zipper narrowed the *O* and allowed the zipper to move more freely up its teeth. My mother then applied her Ban Roll-On deodorant over the thin, long hairs of her armpits, not shaving there a practice that European women favored, and North American women shuddered at.

She approached the bed, held up the blouse, and unbuttoned it, so that she could put one arm in and then the other. I helped because I wanted to, holding the opposite arm and shoulder until she was ready for that side. She buttoned the blouse beginning at the top. At her breastbone, where the fabric gaped, she had already remedied the situation by sewing in a tiny grommet, which she now snapped into place, making no one the wiser. I elected to button the cuffs for her, and she let me.

It wasn't easy to help her when she could help herself, but I did have two responsibilities—performing tasks she couldn't possibly manage on her own—which she didn't object to. It was a nice reversal of roles, my assisting her this way.

"Kenst du mir einfadeln?" ("Would you thread this for me?") she would ask, as she took out her sewing box and lifted the lid to reveal an assortment of colored threads wound around two kinds of spools: the home-use version—small, squat, wooden—and the commercial version—large, conical, pressed cardboard—which was acquired from my father's workplace. There were yarns for knitting, a special, mushroom-shaped wooden object used for darning socks, with a stem that screwed into the mushroom top, needles in a range of sizes suited to pushing through a variety of fabric weights, a stainless steel thimble, tiny scissors to cut the thread when the job was done, and scads of buttons, singular and matching. She squinted painfully, chose a needle and thread, and handed them to me. Her eyes had suffered irrevocably from the years of welding in the slave labor camp. Every time she opened the sewing box, she would be reminded of it. And she sewed often.

My other responsibility was as chief sniffer. She had been born without a sense of smell, though her taste buds were not affected. Thus she relied on me to confirm what had gone bad, or not, and the ability to make the distinction was prized so highly by her, it was as if I had a rare gift, which she could not stop marveling at.

I pondered the implications of her not being able to smell anything. Of course, being young, the first thought that came to mind was that at least she was spared the choking effects of inhaling putrid, anal emissions, but after the blushing joke had worn off, I felt sorry that she also never knew what roses smelled like, or onions frying, or fresh laundry just harvested from the clothesline out back, dry from a sunny day.

But generally, it was she who could always be counted on to care for me, making me tea with lemon and honey when I had a cold, and reading aloud fairy tales, which she did very well, despite her heavy, Yiddish accent. Her standard method of checking if I had a fever was to bring her mouth to my forehead and ascertain, in this affectionate and accurate way, our relative body temperatures. She never feared catching anything from me, believing on some level that a cold was a pretty minor setback in her life, compared to literally courting death in the labor camp.

Maybe she felt somewhat immune to my germs, being as close to me as she often was. Her manner, however, could be rather abrupt. She would hug me quickly and hard, give me a strong kiss on the cheek, smack her lips, and insist that she had just drunk the finest champagne or wine. If I had the flu, she made me "Vojon-keh"—a simple recipe consisting of a little butter, boiling water, "challah" (egg bread) torn in pieces and tossed in, salt, and several chopped cloves of garlic—to stimulate my appetite. It worked.

For the "evil eye," she had a remedy as well. She got out my father's fedora, though I got the sense that any hat would do, passed it over me three times, then spat three times, and repeated this entire sequence three times. An abbreviated version of this was spitting three times, should anyone utter a phrase that could tempt the evil eye. Any suggestion of harm or hubris could provoke the demon.

Meanwhile, I was her lady-in-waiting, and I did enjoy watching her elaborate primping.

She went into the bathroom and swung a towel around her shoulders, and while she combed her thick, dark hair, strands fell on to the towel. The towel was folded, hairs captured and then disposed of. The round, brown, tortoiseshell, plastic compact was brought forth next, and unhinged. A puff of powdery sweetness, like a blown kiss, was in the air. The round, satin pad was moved lightly in a circular motion to catch the powder. She lifted the pad and distributed the powder on her forehead, nose, cheekbones, and chin, in that order. The pad was returned to its pretty housing. She reached again for the comb to smooth the contour of her eyebrows, which had never been plucked. One preliminary pass through, and then she placed the comb perpendicular to her forehead, using the edge of the teeth to outline the top of her brow, making sure no hairs were sticking up.

Almost done. Lipstick. The shiny, red/pink stick with its crayon-like texture was carefully applied to her upper lip, which was pursed in the shape of the top of a heart. She applied the stick to one side and then the other in a quick flick. Now she stretched out her bottom lip so that the skin was smooth and the lipstick filled every crevice. Top and bottom lip were pressed together and offered up to the mirror for adjudication; mirrored reflection looked good. Finally, a few splashes of Yardley cologne—fresh floral scent—and she was set.

My father was already wearing dress pants, a dress shirt with an undershirt, and a sports jacket, and had come to retrieve his shoes from one of a few shoe boxes high on a shelf in the bedroom closet. Shiny brown oxfords. He held them both in one hand, a shoehorn in the other. He set them down before him, and with the help of the shoehorn wedged each heel into a shoe, a gasp of air escaping when his heel reached the insole. Then he tied his laces one loop at a time so that each loop was knotted separately, a method I have never seen anyone else use.

They stood before me, and watched me watching them. They looked presentable, and they thought they did too. They could see that I approved. What they couldn't see was how ashamed I was the rest of the time.

They had "good" clothes, and clothes for wearing "around the house." My father's transformation was not terribly dramatic. When he came home at the end of the day he put on a pair of pants that had worn themselves into the "around the house" category. He sported just an undershirt in the summer, or another old shirt if it was colder. He looked a little worse for wear, but not destitute.

My mother, on the other hand, stretched the limits of propriety. The housedress was her preferred "dressed down" choice of attire throughout the week, with the exception of Thursdays. Mondays were washing days. Tuesdays, ironing. Wednesday morning was shopping, so Wednesday afternoons were a curious hybrid of housedresses and lipstick. Thursdays were cleaning days. Fridays, cooking and baking. This regime never, ever changed.

The housedress could be bought in any bargain basement store for a song. Its fabric was stiff cotton, which softened over time and then disintegrated. There was quite a range of patterns and colors of housedresses to wade through at the store. Both tiny and huge floral prints, and loud backgrounds of green apple and orange, promoted the image that housedresses wished to present: garish and gaudy. But they were "easy to wear"—sleeveless, knee-length, with a zippered front. Very popular with anyone who was known as "Mama." Would June Cleaver ever find herself wearing one? Decidedly not.

My mother's housedress was embarrassing enough, but what she wore on Thursdays was downright mortifying.

In the peripheral way children get a whiff of their parents' plight, I knew that housework was hard. She always complained about being "hot." "Siz heis!" ("It's hot!") she hissed irritably. The phrase sounded like sizzling oil in a pan. To combat her body heat she hiked up her housedress and stuffed the excess fabric into the front of her worn and virtually transparent nylon underpants. Legs completely exposed and unshaven, the bib of her housedress soiled and torn, stretched-out cotton bra, breast skin bulging out through the slits produced by weakened material, a number of safety pins attached to whatever fabric could be brought together, she was a walking pin cushion.

I was now perversely grateful that no one knew where I lived, reneging on my deepest fantasies of spontaneous visits, easy introductions, and impromptu supper invitations extended by my gracious parents to my friends, "for there was always room for one more." Not in this place. My mind reeled. The lofty images of Laurie Petrie and June Cleaver were dashed by my mother's stubborn self-determination and brutal realism.

The best I could do was to become the director of a rehearsal called "How to act when my friends come over?" My parents indulged me. From their point of view, the silliness of the exercise compromised their ability to play their roles effectively, but I had no choice regarding the cast. I was costume mistress, dialogue coach, and I also played "the Daughter." For the most part we did okay. But I knew the truth, and it burned most of the time, whenever my existence was strenuously poised between embarrassment and pretense.

Tonight, however, was sublime. We were going out, my parents were dressed in their good clothes, and I didn't mind being seen with them.

Chapter 6

Sponge Cake

As soon as the three of us turned the corner to go north on Atlas, the din of St. Clair Avenue faded, as if someone had turned down the volume. Within a few minutes we were on my parents' friends' short walkway.

There was an ambience on front porches, especially on a summer evening. You felt it as soon as your foot hit the floor and elicited the hollow, warm sound of the wooden planks. The rotund, white posts on brick pillars, the curved, white spindles along the front and sides, and the green railing that defined the outdoor enclosure, slowed and contained the air in contrast to the wind tunnel on the main street. A vantage point, a perch, partially hidden, yet still a part of it all. There was no porch where I lived. The only vantage point was the living room window where, invariably, the strain from looking out resulted in a series of nose prints on glass panes. Here it was just three easy steps up to the porch and you were there in an outdoor room, floating at first, and then respite as you beheld the view. Not like the apartment with its twenty-step hike as soon as you entered, leaving you winded.

We walked to the front door, which was protected by an aluminum screen door, whose resistant mechanism required someone to lean on it and then bend forward. The heavy, oak, front door had a leaded glass window near the top, covered by a sheer curtain creating willowy shapes. This door had a brass knocker, but others had ding-dong bells, which sounded pretty and friendly. At our apartment you would knock yourself silly using a knocker, because no one would ever hear you. As for a ding-dong bell, that too would fall on deaf ears. No, ours was a not a bell, but a buzzer—the loud, blaring version, like the affronting, derisive, punitive sound following a wrong answer in a game show.

41

We saw the hostess heading towards the door, and then it opened. She ushered us in, and I was given a special handshake befitting a youngster. All the lights were on. Sparkly front hall, mellow, tall, table lamps in the living room with their large bases and barrel-like shades, glittering dining room chandelier, large, bowl-like kitchen fixture. I was thoroughly excited and had the living room to myself, while my parents and their friends took their seats in the dining room. I had been waiting for this moment, to be alone with the one, enticing item that made this visit so worthwhile: the candy dish.

It sat on four feet like an oversized sugar bowl, intricately cut glass with a delicate handle to remove the lid. All houses had them. They adorned rectangular, wooden coffee tables and were the most important piece in a presentation that might also have in-cluded an ashtray and a souvenir from Israel with its design and font in the style of Chagall, the Jewish Picasso. I stared at the dish while I sat on the silvery, ivory, jacquard pattern of the sofa fabric forever protected from soil and the ravages of time by its plastic cover. The exposed skin on the backs of my legs stuck to it, but I was not concerned. The sofa was long and narrow, and at the ends of the fabric arms were what look like wooden fists or the scrolled tops of cellos.

Two chairs in the same style sat kitty-corner to the sofa, a side table filling in the square between. Behind me, on the wall, was the proud example of our hostess's craftsmanship: a needlepoint version of Paint By Number depicting one of the many Renoirs that were subdued enough in subject matter to be framed and displayed by those who firmly believed they now had "art" in their homes.

I was waiting for either the host or the hostess to offer me a candy. I saw them busying themselves moving back and forth from the dining room into the kitchen, sorting out who was drinking what. Everyone was having "kaveh," coffee, the men a little schnapps as well, Canadian Club, or VO. Plates, napkins, cutlery were distributed for cake and fruit. All this was bad news for me, as my agenda was clearly not making the grade. The last opportunity to be noticed would come after the food was served, before they ate, but more importantly, before they launched into the inevitable "discussion," which immersed them irrevocably into a vortex of the Jews, the Nazis, the Americans, the Russians, and the Israelis. Once they started in on all of that, I was finished.

Time was running out. I made movements to catch the hostess's eye. Though she couldn't read my mind, it was possible that my persistent staring at the candy dish, and back at her, would be picked up. I knew it wasn't polite to ask, but was putting me through this excruciating suspense supposed to be civil?

"Peril, have some candy." Sweeter words were never uttered.

I lifted the lid off the candy dish and set it aside. It would be a while before I put it back. There they were. Assorted flavors. If I were very fortunate, the dish would be filled with wrapped toffees or chocolates. But, more often than not, it would be the soft-center, fruit-filled candies that I saw before me. They were wrapped individually, like tiny, oblong presents, their tabs sticking out like wings supported by the folded paper underneath. Each one bore on the top a picture of its flavor—a couple of nesting strawberries, oranges, lemons, grapes. I reached for the strawberry. I unfolded the paper and then the wax paper that lined it. Depending on the candy's freshness, the wax paper would come away easily; otherwise, you would have to peel away the bits that might have adhered to the coating during the unveiling. This batch seemed fine. I popped the candy into my mouth.

I'd developed an approach that required patience and restraint. The goal was to first suck the coating away, and then to relish the chewing of the jam-like, fruity center. This was not as simple as it sounded. As the coating thinned, it could become brittle and break before it was time. That was what the next candy was for. Practice makes perfect. At some point I had to shift away from refining my technique, to consider the ethical dilemma of looting the candy dish, since the hostess's offer also carried with it the unspoken caveat of a respectful limit. Translation: more than one candy was acceptable, but four was stretching it. I was already on my second one and knew that after the third I would be teetering on the brink of bad manners. But another factor was how many candies were in the dish to begin with, and whether a fourth would be missed. Rather than reminding myself of candy dish etiquette, I was thinking about how to get away with the impropriety of taking more than my fair share. This went under the category of feeling badly only if you got caught, not for having committed the crime. No harm in just thinking.

I decided to leave morality for the time being and go over to the dining room table to see what was going on. My mother welcomed me and put her arm around my waist. "Would you like a piece of cake and some fruit?" the hostess asked. Of course I would.

Marisa, the hostess, grabbed me by the wrist and said, "I've got you now; I'm going to steal you away from your parents!" Curious the ways in which adults enjoyed pretending to torment you, as if it were a perfectly reasonable way to joke with children. She purposely blinked both eyes to let me know she was kidding. Like I was that stupid. Actually, I was mesmerized by her mouth.

On the tip of her tongue was a growth. Her lower front teeth were shorter than the ones at the back, so there was always a space when she closed her bite. If I were lucky, I'd catch a glimpse of the wart when she pronounced certain letters. It helped that she loved to speak slowly and deliberately, as if she were dictating and I was writing everything longhand, or learning how to lip-read.

I listened to her carefully, while staring at her lips. She spoke to me in English, switched to speak to everyone else in Polish, then Yiddish, and back. A multi-linguist, some might have thought. Seemed to me that she was showing off. I didn't care. Now where was that wart? I had the best chance with *l*s. When she placed her tongue between the top and bottom teeth, the wart was in full view. With other consonants like *c, d, s, t,* the wart was maddeningly up against the backs of her teeth. If she were Greek or Spanish, I'd be in heaven with all those "*th*s." There are lots of "*th*s" in English, but my parents and their friends found this sound troublesome to pronounce. The best they could do was "tuh," so they would say "tree" instead of "three." With wart sightings being chance occurrences, I diversified into other areas of Marisa's look, and found much there.

Her hair was jet black, combed flat and behind her ears. Her hairline began well back from a shiny, round forehead. The first ridge of waves rippled immediately, followed by many others in close succession, ending just above her shoulders in a mass of frizzy curls. Her eyes were black, like the sultry, plaintive, Polish love song, "Ochee Charnee" ("Black Eyes"). Aside from being the same color, Marisa's eyes seemed far from what would inspire anyone to break into bouts of amorous yearning. Her eyes were small and intense, her eyebrows black and bushy, her brow furrowed. Or, to put it in the simple way in which children characterize adults, she looked mean.

She wore lipstick on her thin lips, a deep, dull, corporate leather red, the two, sharp peaks of her upper lip looking like a capital *M*. This didn't add to her "warmth." Her earlobes hung stretched out of shape like Dali clocks; the piercings were not the barely perceptible holes, as one would have expected, but slits, and her earrings were an orange-gold in color, shaped like a treble clef. A small orb of onyx dangled at the bottom of each hoop, vibrating and jiggling when Marisa spoke or moved.

I then turned my attention to Marisa's husband, Walter. He was a man of fewer words than his wife, and spoke at normal speed instead of in slow motion. He seemed straightforward, attentive, and generally good-natured. He sat at the table looking very relaxed, leaning back so that his shoulders slumped a bit. His face was what intrigued me.

Beginning from the top of his head, his face expanded as it got towards his jawline and neck. The front of his face was tiered. The first tier was produced by his bulging eyes bringing the line out from his forehead. His bulging eyes rested on the next tier—the bags under his eyes—which rested on his ample cheeks, which rested on his jowls, which had added support from a large, fleshy, bottom lip, and bottom teeth, which protruded beyond the top ones. When he spoke, the only movement in his face came from his chin, like the hinged and unhinged trap of a ventriloquist's dummy. Overall, he looked a lot like a bullfrog.

I finished my cake and had some ginger ale, so I was just as happy to go into the living room and watch TV. It didn't take long for the voices in the dining room to rise like a tidal wave and crash. My mother's voice was the loudest and most authoritative.

"Ah voos reds du!..." ("What are you talking about!..."). She was irritated and dismissive.

Someone had just made the fatal error of commending the Americans for what they did during World War II.

"The Americaneh!" ("The Americans!"). She was disgusted and mocking. After a pause, she ramped up for her assault. She was trembling and yelling. She cautioned them against feeling too sorry for the Americans. "Da Americaneh hobben gemacht shvereh millionin" ("The Americans made heavy millions") was what she said; *while the Jews were being incinerated*, was what she implied. Her mantric point was to compare the way the Russians fought Hitler, suffering staggering losses and numbers of wounded, while the Americans came in at the end of the war and, in the meantime, converted all their factories to produce war machinery, thereby amassing huge profits. After the war, the Americans offered safe haven to Nazis. The "West" demolished the concentration camps that were in West Germany, while the East Germans left the blight for all to see, lest the atrocities be forgotten.

Marisa and Walter were visibly uncomfortable and quiet, because the Cold War was on, and no one dared talk about how much they admired Russians. Then, one mention of the Israelis, and my mother discharged the next part of her tirade. She condemned "the Zionists," as she called them sarcastically, for their part after the war and during the anarchy and chaos around Israeli Independence, when, she claimed, unscrupulous Israelis took advantage of their fellow Jews.

No one wanted to touch that topic with a ten-foot pole. In fact, the current political climate was diametrically opposed to my mother's views. If everyone was flying SSE, she was going NNW. If the Americans wanted to protect Jews now, so went the prevailing view, far be it from Jews to complain, and the Americans were pro-Israeli. Nor would Jews talk about how Jews treated other Jews. "There was enough anti-Semitism out there without giving the goyim more to hate about us" was the thinking.

My mother was isolated even from her peers. My father's tacit support of her was hard to read. After a while, she calmed down, more from the futility of talking than from anything else. She

46

was still left with the horrific memories, the outrage, the injustice, and the sting from the lack of response from others who had lived through it. Who else would have understood, if not them? And what could she do with all that disillusionment?

It never went away.

A bit of it dissipated in the mundane exchange about who made the better sponge cake.

"A zoy vie a kliskel!"("Like a dumpling!") my mother blurted out with a shudder, when we got back to the apartment. Marisa's version was squat, compressed, a deep yellow, oily, and heavy, and, according to my mother, it loitered in her digestive system like a lead weight. My father concurred, which delighted my mother. Both of them feigned stomach aches. We all laughed.

In fact, my mother's sponge cake did bear all the hallmarks of perfection: tall with the expansion of expertly beaten egg whites; pale-yellow in color; light and fluffy in texture, with a hint of lemon on the nose and palate. Small comfort... There was still every single night to contend with, and all the tricks the unconscious liked to play on drifting brain waves. The anticipation of fitful sleeps and violent nightmares wasn't an incentive for bedtime. My mother armed herself with big, thick books, sagas mostly, and read well into the night, or until she successfully obfuscated her thoughts long enough to get the first leg of the sleep trip underway. My father had to work hard the next day and needed his rest. His strategy was to keep his nose to the grindstone, steeling himself against the past with a commitment to provide for his family in the present. My brother was "out" at night, the status quo for a teenager.

The visit was over, and I felt deflated. I was back in the apartment at nighttime and afraid of the dark. I faced it with no strategy, except to listen and wait for something awful to happen, or until the first streaks of dawn leaked through the narrow space between the window and the blind in my little room, and it was safe to go to sleep.

There was no place that was home.

Chapter 7

Tenants

I was always particularly dejected after going over to someone's home.

"Why can't we live in a house like normal people!" I said with exasperation.

My parents looked around the kitchen as if they were aware of sounds, but not sure where they were coming from.

Then my mother turned on me.

"Do you want to live with tenants?" she countered. "Strangers living in the basement! They can steal from you, or get drunk, smoke and burn the house down! You don't know who you're taking in."

My mind wandered for a moment to Lydia, and the memory was haunting. But I came back.

"Then what about Hanna? She has tenants." She was a friend of my parents, who lived in a bungalow in North York with her husband and children.

"Hanna!…Hanna ist meshigeh fa gelt" ("Hanna is crazy for money").

Did somebody change the subject, was what I thought to myself.

I did know that, when we first moved into the apartment, we rented out a room for a spell, and the fact that we didn't have to rely on the extra money anymore, or put up with the trouble, was a sign of progress for my parents.

While my brother and I were still young enough to share a bedroom, my parents surmised that they could rent the other bedroom, fully furnished, to a single person.

So strange to think that there could be anyone in the world who would want to rent one of three bedrooms in a small, five-room flat and live in the midst of another family's existence—parents and

49

two children all sharing one little bathroom. But there were two individuals who signed up for just that experience.

One was an odd, older man, "a bachelor," the term used to whitewash the anomaly of a male who never married, pretending that he chose instead to date in perpetuity. He wasn't exactly a suave James Bond or debonair Cary Grant. He was a short, balding, plump fellow who looked like Laurel's jolly counterpart, Hardy. But the similarity ended there, as I discovered. Going on the strength of the comic persona I had seen on TV, I imagined he would be like Ollie, lively and funny. But this individual was as humorless and ill-tempered as they came, with no interest whatsoever in children. So he kept to himself as much as he could in the confined space that four others occupied. Aloof and unresponsive and haughty, though what he had to feel superior about was completely unfathomable, both visually and interpersonally. He didn't stay long.

The other tenant was a young woman, probably just out of high school, pursuing her vocation. The Yiddish term for her was "shiksa," a gender-specific, derogatory word combining "low-class," "of dubious morals," and "non-Jewish." She worked from nine to five as a secretary, in one of the big, downtown office buildings in and around Bay and College, for a company like Bell Telephone. She was slim, pretty, and stylish. Her name was one of the many first names male teenage idols popularized in song, be it Donna, or Brenda, or Sherry.

She had bangs, and shoulder-length hair in a flip, sometimes teasing the top half for height and letting the rest fall, or teasing it all and wearing it up in a French twist. Tight, V-neck sweaters, full, knee-length skirts, heels or flats, and the trademark heart pendant with initials and their cryptic meaning engraved in a feathery font and worn to the cleavage on a silver chain. If you opened it discreetly, you would find a photo in each of the halves, which were separated by a thin, mirrored divider for security, revealing what was dearest.... A steady boyfriend was best.

Her undoing was that she harbored something my mother found unforgivable, highly offensive, and definitely not part of the tenant agreement. Not booze, not men, but a kitten. Out they both went.

50

The couple and their little daughter living next door were tenants. They rented the flat above the very classy menswear store, Zaks. Somehow, I was invited to come over to play with the small girl. It was a sign of children's loneliness, when they befriended someone clearly younger than they were, ostensibly because there was no one else around. Such was the nature of my friendship with Darlene, who was four years of age to my nine, a world of difference.

Playing with her was a voluntary act of deference on my part, coming in at her level, our relative experience of one another like the point behind the phrase "one's man's poison": hanging around someone older—her coup—and having to play with someone younger—my ignominy. But it did pass the time. Patty cakes and hide and seek, milk and cookies, were all easy enough to tolerate, and watching her getting ready for bed, wearing her cottony, soft pajamas with depictions of little lambs upon tufts of grass, fluffy clouds overhead, the inspiration for restful slumbers.

She dutifully brushed her baby teeth, still trying to master the quick wrist action of going up and down, and then across and back, without getting confused. Her mother gently reminded Darlene to say her prayers, and Darlene would kneel by her bedside. In her pixie child's voice, as if helium-induced, she would utter the most alarming words:

> Now I lay me down to sleep,
> I pray the Lord my soul to keep,
> If I should die before I wake,
> I pray the Lord my soul to take.

Then the lights would be turned off in her room, and the door shut. She was all alone in there, and it didn't bother her. For me the prayer helped reaffirm that I had good reason not to go to sleep. Maybe Darlene was too young to think of the meaning of the lilting rhyme, but there was no way I was going to risk dying before I woke up. For me it was lights on, door open, ears cocked, and eyes vigilant.

But Darlene survived, as I discovered when I returned to play the next day, and, for the duration of our acquaintance, I learned a thing or two. It occurred to me that I was the fulcrum between two extremes of womanhood—the recent toddler-graduate side of Darlene, and the all grown-up side of Laura, her mother. I was able to relate to Darlene, having lived through the phase she was in, and to project upon my future by studying Laura. There were already many images of being "grown-up," on TV, in magazines, and particularly in movies like the *Gidget* series, or in the "bikini-clad teenagers on the beach" genre starring Frankie Avalon and Annette Funicello. Laura, as a married woman, was just barely out of her teens, still wanting to look her best, if not for herself, then for her husband Sal.

I'd seen Laura all made up, and not, a truly lived experience of "before" and "after." She looked a lot like Ann-Margaret in her *Bye Bye Birdie* days, and was a very good specimen of "thistle, shamrock, rose entwined, the maple leaf forever," hence, quintessentially Anglo-Canadian. She would sit at the altar of femininity, the vanity, on the delicate, matching wooden bench with its floral, upholstered seat, and gaze at herself in triplicate, the gracious middle mirror, and the two smaller, adjustable, attendant ones for side views, to ensure optimal circumspection in the process that would transform her from plain to glam.

Designed with two banks of drawers and a lowered, middle section to accommodate the bench, the vanity was especially suited to housing an array of beauty accessories: rollers, clips, pins, combs with long tails for separating hair sections and for teasing, and hairspray for the final touch. A series of brown, plastic cases of various sizes, for specific products like shadows and blushes and powders, different shades of lipsticks, assorted necklaces, earrings, bracelets, and rings, even bras and panties could be found on its surface. The vanity was also featured in movies, making its appearance as a precursor to love scenes.

Take: Woman in a slinky nightgown, hair tumbling down from an updo, the mandatory sterling silver grooming set of three items before her, which includes a soft-bristle brush, comb, and hand mirror. Every vanity seems to be furnished with these beauty aids. Perhaps it's part of a woman's dowry, a symbol of a tacit edict that she be well versed in the art of seduction, because that is how she can best attend to her husband. There she sits at the vanity brushing her tresses, her long, voluminous hair swept around to one side so it spills down past her shoulder and over one of her breasts. Man approaches from behind; the camera shot is through the mirror. He is unjacketed, white dress shirt, top button open, bow tie hanging like a monkey from a vine. He leans forward to kiss her at the exposed curve. Her swan neck lengthens, and her eyes close in a swoon.... Cut.

In the real-life version, Laura has taken her seat at the vanity, hair still in rollers to get the most curl possible. Her face has been freshly washed. First step, moisturizer. There were three competing brands at the time: Noxzema, Nivea, and Ponds, all with compelling ad campaigns to entice you, each Siren whispering different slogans. Whether you used Noxzema, inspired by its sexy "Take it off. Take it all off" ads, or you yearned to look like the "Nivea girl," or you had decided to be on "The Ponds Seven Day Beauty Plan," these products did pretty much the same job as you slathered them on your face and hoped that you could forestall the inevitable aging process, which was, and has always been, the arch-enemy of women. Any one of these names could be spotted among the many bottles and jars playing cameo roles in a woman's beauty regime.

On her now moisturized, fair, luminous skin, foundation was applied evenly and blended to avoid the terrible embarrass-ment of creating a mask if your jaw didn't match your neck. Im-perfections were hidden, darkened circles under eyes disappeared, and the canvas was ready. Time for color.

The trend in eye shadow was blue, green, or purple. With Laura's eyes being a pale blue, she could choose from any of them. Blue. A generous amount was rubbed on the lid and brought to the outside of the eye. Another color, like grey or brown, went on the crease to create depth, and finally, a light shade—white or beige—was applied to the eyebrow bone for greater definition.

The eyebrows were next. Their shape was perhaps an important clue to which era we were in. Thin, pencil-like arches identified the times from the '20s up to the '50s. Bushy eyebrows, made famous by Brooke Shields, defined the '80s. The '50s and '60s were a hybrid of the two—a tuft of hair in a loop, narrowing to a tail.

If, from birth, you had the misfortune of an eyebrow shape that was not in style, you could simply pluck until the shape was more or less there and draw the rest with an eyebrow pencil. That was the case with Laura. She had a few hairs left to guide her as she created the outline of the loop and, with a light brown pencil, which matched her auburn hair, she drew a generous arc just above the bone of her brow and then colored in the loop. The artistry of this part of the process lay in one's ability to create the exact same shape for both eyebrows. Not easy.

Liquid eyeliner was next. Hands needed to be as steady as a brain surgeon's. For those with greater talent, the line would begin thin, then fatten as it moved towards the center of the lid and just beyond, then thin out again until the end of the eyelid was reached, whereupon one had the option of drawing a little tick, or not.

Finally, there was mascara. Training yourself not to blink when a foreign object was moving towards your eye—one of the most vulnerable parts of your body—was a laudable example of mind over matter. The mascara wand with its tapered brush was held parallel to your eye and combed onto your eyelashes. All the while your eye was opened as wide as possible and held perfectly still, even though blinking was an involuntary reflex. The goal was to emphasize each eyelash without creating clumps. Also easier said than done. An eyelash curler was optional. Some unlucky ones who used it may have discovered, to their horror, that when the device was closed on mascara-hardened lashes, some hairs simply snapped off. The remedy? False eyelashes.

Eyes done, now back to the finishing touches for the face. Taking out the large brush for blush, from its own special case, meant the hard part was over. Color was more important than technique here. If you had peach undertones in your skin, you had to choose a blush that was more orange; with pink undertones, more blue/pink. Otherwise, disaster. Loaded up brush was then applied to the cheekbone, and blush blended out towards the temple, down towards the hollow in your cheek, no farther. Powder to set the whole face. And now for hair.

54

Big hair was the coveted look. Huge rollers were essential for volume. As Laura removed the rollers and clips, heavy, pipe-like curls fell onto their sides like Slinky toys. She then teased it all so she looked like an electrocuted cartoon character. Between smoothing and maintaining height and applying hairspray for support, the desired shape and hairdo would emerge. A final, generous spritz of hairspray secured the result, although to the touch, the hair felt a little crispy. On this day, Laura would wear her hair half up and half down. After getting dressed, she resumed her seat at the vanity in order to put on lipstick; anything from a ghostly white to a shimmery coral was right in vogue. A dab or two of "Evening in Paris" from its tear-drop-shaped, silver-capped, indigo glass bottle, wet behind each ear and at the cleavage, and voila!

The results were spectacular, though very time-consuming, especially as a daily routine. But not worth the effort, as it turned out.

The prevailing view at the time suggested that the key to marital bliss was a beautiful wife, all dolled up, greeting her husband at the end of what, for him, had been a long, important day at "the office."

Sal *did* work hard. And they *were* a striking couple. She with her Anglo, Irish, Scottish roots, pert features, fair complexion; he a mix of Bobby Rydell and Frankie Avalon, olive skin, thick, dark, James Dean hair, Italian background, quiet, but with a sullen attractiveness, the knit brow from the stress of providing for the family, which only the love of a good woman could assuage.

I met him briefly a couple of times, the kind of fleeting moment that precludes eye contact. It was not surprising that a grown man with a lot on his mind might hurry the perfunctory introduction to the kid next door, there to play with his four-year-old.

For a man with little to say, he certainly made up for it at night. That was when I would hear him. And her.

Their flat was a mirror image of ours too, but the reverse of Henry's. Starting from the far side of Darlene's flat and moving across, the layouts went like this: bedrooms, hall, then our hall, and our bedrooms. Even with two halls, and a lath, plaster, and brick wall separating Darlene and her parents' bedrooms from ours, you could hear surprisingly well.

His raised, reproachful voice would come through first, then an anxious explanation from her. More indignation from him, and then her apologetic crying. Now he was yelling, and she was trying to say anything to calm him, which inflamed him further. It was only his rage now, a few thrown items that didn't do the trick, until he found catharsis when he struck her hard. A shocked, brief scream, a slammed door, and then choking sobs, which ultimately died down.

Now I understood Darlene's impassioned pleas at the side of her bed. Better for Jesus to take her than to face what might befall her if her door flung open. Barring that, the darkness protected her, the closed door setting her apart from the turmoil just beyond.

The next day, Laura would sit before her vanity, using the arsenal of beauty tips to face a most challenging problem.

There were things to do outdoors today, like buy groceries, take Darlene to the park. Too soon for the deeper greens, magentas, and plum purples to appear. They would come in the next couple of days. Right now there was redness and swelling.

A cold facecloth to her eyes for ten minutes minimized some of the puffiness. Laura knew the tricks of the trade, how to hide unwanted blemishes, dark circles. This was just a simple case of lateral thinking. Green combats the red…. Laura used her green eye shadow, then added foundation and a bit of powder. It would have to do.

Large sunglasses that Jackie Kennedy made famous, and a kerchief for those flatter hair days, tied under the chin and around to the back of the neck, was the look. All the girls were wearing kerchiefs, from the Audrey Hepburns and Sophia Lorens, to the devil-may-care girlfriends riding on the backs of motorcycles, bangs dancing in the wind.

St. Clair was the home of the motorcycle gang, the Black Diamond Riders, the BDRs, on the south side across from the synagogue, an ironic counterpoint. They left the clubhouse in a pack, motorcycles lined up at the light, engines revved up and panting. I would see them on my way home from school as I crossed with the green light.

Beefy bad boys and their pretty, kerchiefed passengers, preparing for the heady speeds. They took off in a spurt. The tied ends of the girls' kerchiefs stuck out like pointing telltales on sailboat stays, while Laura's fluttered and fell, fluttered and fell, as she mingled with pedestrians on St. Clair. Got her chores done, pushed Darlene on the swing, was home in good time to make dinner and hunker down, to be holed up in the apartment for a few days if need be, and await the colorful, tie-dyed effect that would span both eyes down to her cheekbones.

Darlene was too young not to believe the lame reason why her mother's face looked like a psychedelic poster. Sal came home later than usual, to avoid the visual results of his violent outburst. Laura made sure she was in bed, eyes closed in the dark, and the week that ensued underscored the adage that time heals all wounds, as the deep colors faded like jeans, and covering up became easier and easier. No one would be the wiser, except for us next door.

"Er shlugt sie" ("He beats her"), my mother said with contempt. I picked up the subtle implication that she wasn't surprised at all. This just reaffirmed the poor opinion she had of goyim, their violence and machismo in general, as if Jews were immune.

It disturbed me to imagine a man hitting a woman with such force. The strong harming the weak. I felt so sorry it hurt inside, making me feel that sadness was an abyss that could only become deeper and deeper.

My mother didn't seem sad for them, but sure about them, as if she would never again be blindsided by the cruelty of the world.

After all, they were tenants, like some underclass with inherent flaws.

Then it occurred to me....

All that sh-sh-ing and finger-wagging—couldn't do this, couldn't do that—because of the store downstairs, having to be quiet during the day, my mother scolding me through clenched teeth when I made noise.

"They'll hear you in the store, and then what!"

"Then what!" sounded frightening enough. Who brandished that kind of power? Who could dictate behavior by instilling terror? Who made the rules? Landlords, of course. Now I realized why my mother was petrified. It was because we'd be kicked out if the noise from our flat disturbed the patrons in the store. So the criticisms, the bitterness, the insults about tenants, were hypocrisy. I had caught my mother calling the kettle black.

"You're always saying bad things about tenants," I asserted. "Well, it's because it's true."

"But we're tenants too. I guess that doesn't make us much better than them." There, I had said it, proved her wrong.

"What are you talking about?" She looked upon me as an annoyance.

"We're the tenants, and downstairs is the landlord, and that's why I have to be quiet all the time!" I finally had her.

She laughed and laughed.

"Oy, Peril, Peril," she shook her head.

"What?"

"*We're* the landlord, and downstairs is the tenant!"

58

Chapter 8

The Ceiling's the Limit

The businessman downstairs, *our* tenant, called the shots.

And for the eighteen years we lived on the second floor flat of the building *we* owned, my parents were afraid to raise *his* rent. When we finally did sell the building, our tenant downstairs was paying half the competitive rental rate for any store in the vicinity.

My parents could have sorely used the extra cash, and would have been well within their rights to increase the rent incrementally over time. But this commonplace landlord conduct felt so foreign to them, and so treacherous, that only disaster could follow if they stopped believing in the devil they knew.

"But why can't you raise his rent?"

"Because he'll move his store and then we won't be able to pay the mortgage and we'll end up on the street!" She glared at me as if I had suggested we consider complete ruin as a solution.

Truth was, even after the mortgage was paid off, the rent stayed the same.

So I was constantly reminded to pipe down during the day, and I'm not sure that I wasn't especially loud sometimes, because of my anger and frustration with the unyielding defeatism of my parents' position.

Not disturbing the status quo, and abiding by her oft-repeated phrase, "Don't rock the boat," informed my mother's inactions. Being the squeaky wheel that got the grease was fatal in her mind.

Work days are very long in the ammunitions factory, and there is no going home at night. Slave labor is not a metaphor. My mother is forced to be a welder, not because a mentor has spotted that she has some affinity for the skill, nor to boost the number of women in the trades, nor to emulate Rosie the Riveter helping the

59

boys overseas fight the good fight. It is a corrosive activity. Having to make the very weapons that will kill Jews like herself implicates her, and translates into a subtle form of soul destruction that will only get worse with time.

Productivity is high, even if morale is barely perceptible. Occasional reminders of the importance of doing a good job purge the atmosphere, making the laborers particularly grateful for what little they have. The foreman doesn't bother with meetings or warnings. When it comes time for a performance review, he simply picks up his rifle and shoots dead anyone who he feels isn't pulling her weight. Works like a charm. And those who are still alive make feverish mental notes regarding the odds of survival and what is their best shot.

Some, through no fault of their own except being beautiful, catch the attention of those in charge. Others "offer" themselves, based on a delusional belief in a fair exchange. The form of "special treatment" these women receive doesn't necessarily increase their chances; their strategy may even backfire. Whether the bosses get bored, or, perversely, find to their horror evidence of a misguided feeling of affection for the enemy, the results are the same: the elimination of the offending presence.

With a steady stream coming in to replenish the supply of laborers, and a dictum to permanently reduce numbers, my mother's work day is the only proof of her existence. Though she is good-looking, she does not stand out, her work is acceptable, she never complains, is never effusive in her greetings. She even stops menstruating while she works in the labor camp, as if her body has concurred that being as inconspicuous as possible is as good a strategy as any.

Can't argue with success. The rent check my mother received from the tenant passed seamlessly to the mortgage-holder—no waves, no surprises, no exceptions, no privileges.

I dreaded that things wouldn't change, that I was trapped in this flat, living on a short, thin transit line called the hall, with tiny, dimly lit stopovers known as bedrooms. We would never be like Henry and his family, who moved on, or like Hanna in a bungalow, or Lydia with a yard. Even Darlene, Sal, and Laura bought a house farther west on St. Clair on a quaint residential street where children played safely and unwittingly. And so I kept coming up with ideas appropriately forged by age and context, one way or another to make life a little more palatable.

Resourceful and impecunious were the strict conditions I had to work with. It didn't look like much, but I got a great bang from the buck I didn't even have to spend. There were a number of household items that had always been there, had preceded my arrival on the scene. Whatever we had, however small, was not taken for granted and not replaced unless it was broken and irreparable. One such thing was a simple mirror measuring about eight by ten inches. Framed in rustic beadboard and painted white, it was helpful for those hard-to-see places like the back of your head, and portable if a stationary mirror wasn't handy.

This mirror opened up to me another reality, somewhat like Narnia beyond the back of the wardrobe, but much closer to home.

It was by chance that I increased the angle from ninety to one hundred and eighty degrees, pivoting the mirror, so that instead of holding it parallel to my face, I held the mirror parallel to the floor and facing the ceiling. Suddenly the view was transformed. The world was white and smooth, plaster looking like icing on a huge slab of wedding cake. Doorways became architectural features, reversed arches encased in glossy wood against the matte pallor of the ceiling paint.

I traversed the flat in this way, bedazzled by the beauty of things upside down. I sidestepped the light fixtures, the kitchen one looking like an orb on a stick, stepped over the arch between the kitchen and the hall, and continued. Because the hall was narrow, I had to squeeze past the first light, a glowing mound of a spaceship, and then turn into the bathroom.

It now appeared as a small, unencumbered vestibule, perhaps an anteroom of sorts. A far cry from what lay below the mirror—objects like the sweating toilet, chipped porcelain sink with separate faucets dispensing water that was either too hot or too cold, forcing you to move your hands quickly from one to the other, hoping for a tepid average instead of the scald and freeze you actually ended up with. Finally there was the cast-iron bathtub and its cave-like underbelly evolving over time in an environment of moisture, hair, dirt, and grime, a perfect breeding ground for things that crawled.

Quick turn, back out, and over the threshold into the hall, past the other spaceship, and over the next threshold into the first bedroom. Soft, white surface again, and, at the center, a square, origami-like shape, frosted from the incandescent light. Back out to the hall, into the next bedroom, always stepping over the foot-high retaining walls created by the door frames in reverse, until I reached the two last rooms, one in tandem to the other. These felt spacious and luxurious, especially when I stepped over the double archway, a plaster bulkhead painted beige, which bridged the two white surfaces of the two spaces.

Something fascinating about ceilings... Blank canvases, the recipients of artistic expression, wind-swept clouds and heavenly blue skies, cherubs in motion, acts of creation in a single finger-to-finger conduit. For me, the blanker the ceiling, the better.

I must have looked a sight, walking robotically and systematically throughout the flat to see how the dearth of my living situation could be transmuted into another perspective so sublime. But no one noticed. I knew, because if someone had seen me, it would surely have been accompanied by a derisive comment, and I would have felt ashamed.

I also knew I did this often— pulling out the mirror, walking around—and the activity never lost its ability to delight me.

Chapter 9

God, Part I

Was Darlene on to something...or not informed of the other options?

It wasn't as though there was an official time for parents to tell children about God, but practice suggested that the earlier the better. A weighty philosophical and existential notion, God. Who knew what would happen if you left it to the scrutiny and investigation of a developed mind?

Was it the frustrations and insecurities of parenthood that invoked a Higher authority? Was it guilt for adult loss of faith, or fear that children would otherwise fall into an immoral quagmire, that compelled parents to play the God card? Was it because there was no fun answer to why Fluffy, the family cat, who lay inert and stiffening, had to be removed from the household **FOREVER**?

And so, innocent-minded children were treated to the notion of God by their parents, whose knowledge on the matter was above suspicion. My parents were no exception.

This was the basic Judeo-Christian drill:

God knows all…children become wide-eyed.

God hears all…children think, "Hmmm, a direct line that is never busy."

God sees all…children balk, "Even when you're going number one or number two?!"

And the kicker:

There's heaven when you die and you've been good, *or* **HELL…if you've been bad!**

The machinery for imbuing me with a religious sense was strategized on several fronts: Hebrew school, social and cultural activities, and attending synagogue to observe the Sabbath. And it all happened under one roof. The east end of the synagogue building housed the sanctuary, the Rabbi's study, and the school office, while the west end contained all the classrooms on its first and second floors and the gymnasium in its basement. Hard to believe that the bustling synagogue entrances on St. Clair and the quiet "schoolyard" at the back where I played ball were one and the same building.

As among other ethnic groups concerned about the retention of culture now that they were on Canadian soil, Hebrew school took place after regular school, for a few hours three times a week. We were given primers, the Hebrew equivalent of the Dick and Jane series. Big print, two to four lines per page, with a large illustration.

It was funny at first, being told that you're supposed to read Hebrew from right to left. But that novelty soon wore off. The other weird thing was the dots and lines under the letters, which indicated what the vowel sounds were. The basic Hebrew alphabet consisted of consonants; even "aleph," our English *a*, was silent.

So we learned how to read and write much like we did in Grade One, and that was where the parallel to public education ended.

It was a mystery where the "Hebrew teachers" came from. For the most part they seemed like a sorry lot. With demand being high and supply at a low, the job attracted many eccentrics, to use a euphemism. The best word to describe the environment in the classroom was "mayhem." Why the students so flagrantly disrespected these poor souls at the front of the room, was elusive. None of us took it seriously, somehow sensing that there would be no real consequences, Hebrew school not likely to be a crucial entry on a future résumé. The only time there was peace and quiet was when we had tired of making trouble for them.

Maybe we were just hungry. Hebrew school began around 4:00 p.m. and ended around 6:00. Between 3:30 and 4:00 was just enough time to go to the variety store and fill up a little paper bag with goodies. My favorites were Lik-M-Aids—long straws filled with tart powder that would stimulate your salivary glands upon making contact with your tongue; Double Bubble gum, wrapped in a waxy joke; Jersey Milk chocolate individual squares; strawberry marshmallows; and Tootsie Roll pops.

Sneaking the bag into the classroom was the just the beginning. Our desks with their welded seats had a generous space underneath the surface for books and writing materials. Our teacher didn't seem to notice that our arms and hands were never visible, never folded neatly on top; that when she turned her back to write on the blackboard, students would pop something into their mouths and chew quickly, then stop abruptly when she turned to face us.

The biggest fear was being asked a question when you had a mouth full of candy. Those with good technique could herd and then sequester the mound to one side and as far back as possible, while speaking from the forward part of the mouth. Took practice, but was entirely possible. How the room didn't reek of intoxicating sweetness, as young teeth broke open and released essences of artificial flavors into the atmosphere, was a wonder. The collective glycemic index must have skyrocketed sometime around 5:00, and then plummeted soon after. Could account for our listlessness at the end of class. Teachers probably thought they had finally gotten through.

They had, on a level….

With time, the tentative hyper-consciousness of forming the sounds and adding in the proper vowel as we read aloud gave way to evenness of articulation. As incentive to keep reading in Hebrew, we were told that the scholars could read it *without* the aid of the dots and lines; in fact, there were none in the literature. Impressive. Then the primers got thicker, the print smaller, the illustrations shrank. I guess we progressed.

The stories that delivered the text were biblical. Stories of courage, faith, danger, love, sacrifice, betrayal, tragedy, miracles. A cast of characters: gullible Adam and sultry Eve; Abraham, the original recipient of a not-so-funny practical joke—"Go kill your son…just kidding"; the nautical Noah; the reverse psychology of Solomon; the story of Ruth and Naomi—a touching vignette meant to melt the stereotypic ice between mothers-in-law and their daughters-in-law; Queen Esther, with its sexy themes fit for a television series; and finally, the winner of the best magic trick with his sensational parting of the Red Sea, Moses.

My indoctrination proceeded, honed into the precepts that Moses brought down from the mountain, the Ten Commandments. While some of the imperatives were lost on me, like "Do not commit adultery," and "Do not covet thy neighbor's wife," the one about not using God's name in vain reverberated within me. It was unsettling and scary. What was so wrong with saying "God"? What would happen if you did? Seemed like a small indiscretion compared to "Thou shall not kill," but even asking seemed sacrilegious. With so many "G-d's" in print, and the plethora of "Oh my goshes" coming from the American Bible Belt, I felt alone with my insolent inquiries and went against another, perhaps more important, "commandment": "Be yourself." There would be time enough for that. At this point, I just followed the rule and tried not to ask questions.

There were provisions in place to keep you on the straight and narrow. If you wanted to say "God," there was a substitute, "Ashem." The real word was "Adoneye." So, for everyday usage, it was "Ashem," and for special occasions, the Sabbath being one of them, it was "Adoneye." Even when it was permitted, I couldn't help but feel apprehensive. If God was so particular about when and when not to use his name, he wasn't going to go easy on much.

Though nowhere to be found in the Ten Commandments, word got around among us children that it was a sin for Jews to say "Jesus Christ." Spread like wildfire. So when our public school teachers began the morning with a ritual, which was deemed politically incorrect sometime in the future, asking us to bow our heads for the Lord's Prayer and close our eyes, there were at least five pairs of eyes that peeked and five mouths that didn't say a thing. At Christmas, it was customary to congregate in the halls to sing carols. Such a joyous time for all good Christians, singing out, but we anxiously anticipated the lyrics, lest we say...well, you know.

Hark the herald angels sing, glory to the newborn king/ Peace on earth and mercy mild, G-d and sinners reconciled/ Joyful all ye nations rise, join the triumph of the skies/ With the angelic host proclaim, **MMMMMM** *is born in Bethlehem.*

Or, **MMMMMMMM** *loves me, yes I know, for the Bible tells me* so.

Or, *Away in a manger, no crib for his bed, the little lord* **MMMMMMMMM,** *laid down his sweet head.*

"Deck the Halls" was safe.

Irreverent Jewish boys would taunt us with their made-up lyrics to "Jesus Loves Me," singing, *"Jesus loves me, yes I know, Rabbi Moses told me so,"* but we held fast.

To ensure my adherence to the rules, I was lucky to have befriended a few girls who were more religious than I was. Kind of like having a sponsor if you were in AA. I spent a lot of time with them at public school, then at Hebrew school, and on the week-end—Saturdays at two different synagogues. The customs were quite clear, especially around the Sabbath. No lights could be turned on, or stoves; no driving was allowed, or any activity that could be perceived as "work." The Sabbath would begin at sundown Friday and end at sundown Saturday.

I often broke the Sabbath at a friend's house, enjoying a delicious cold supper on Saturday night, because their stove would not be used all day. Mounds of chopped egg, tuna, and a mixture of salmon and egg (my favorite); creamed cottage cheese; platters of sliced tomato, onion, and cucumber; and fresh "challah" or buns. My friend's father always wore a "keepa"—a skull cap—or his fedora; his wife, a wig. My father would make jeering remarks about the "Hasidim" (the orthodox ones) with their "kupelishes" (literally, hats, but his point was to criticize them for believing in a rule that required them to cover their heads), his scathing opinions serving as a counterpoint, but not a deterrent, to my foray into the rank and file of pious Jews.

In most Jewish homes, the beginning of the Sabbath on Friday night meant an elaborate meal, white linen tablecloth, silver flatware, patriarch at the head of the dining room table, family around him. Blessings for the wine and bread uttered in a kind of *"Sprechstimme."* Whether in Forest Hill, Bathurst Manor, or York Mills, chicken soup was the staple first course, followed by brisket or roast chicken, potatoes, and vegetables. When salad, and dry red wine from France instead of sweet Manischewitz, appeared on

Jewish tables, it was a sign that European Jewish ethnicity had coalesced with North American culture.

In our small kitchen, pots were on the boil by mid-afternoon. My mother told me that turkey was better than chicken for making chicken soup. The first step was to scald the meat in order to eliminate the scum. Turkey legs, breasts, necks, and gizzards were loaded into a large bullion pot with cold water to cover. As soon the water boiled, the pot was removed, the water discarded, the meat rinsed, and then reloaded into the pot along with whole onions, carrots, celery, parsley root—*not* parsnips—and plenty of water. As soon as the water boiled, any additional scum was spooned off. It was crucial to turn down the heat to a simmer at this point, otherwise the broth would cloud, which resulted in chicken soup failure. Kosher salt was added to taste. The lid was adjusted so that it remained slightly ajar, and then two-and-a-half hours later you would have a clear, delicious broth.

On another burner was an odd-shaped pot that was special enough to be brought over from Israel when my parents immigrated to Canada. "Why replace what you already have?" was the thinking, I guess. Embossed with Hebrew script, presumably from the company that manufactured it, it was a small, but tall, saucepan, with an uneven bottom, black with use. In it my mother boiled "boondlech" (lima beans). And finally, about a half-hour before we ate, my mother boiled noodles. She drew heaping handfuls out of a long, white paper bag with a plastic window, through which you could see the product—extra fine egg noodles made by Lancia—which she then put into salted, boiling water. That was on the third burner. On the fourth, in a small saucepan, was a serving or two of boiling rice, my mother's choice for an accompaniment to her soup.

Sabbath candles, stubby and white, came ten to a box, and were stored under the kitchen sink amidst Ajax cleanser, a petrified cloth, and rusting spools of steel wool looking like clumps of gray hair. My mother removed two candles and put back the remainder. A humble, squat, iridescent, amber glass, two-candle candleholder appeared. She placed the candles in the round molds and lit the two with a toothpick from the stove flames. She covered her head with a kerchief, made two circular motions with her hands as if she were assembling the air and gathering it to her, and then brought her hands towards her face, but not touching it, fingers bent slightly. She said something under her breath, which I couldn't catch. It looked like she was weeping, but when she raised her head moments later, she seemed perfectly fine. Then the candleholder was moved to the counter beside the sink, leaving the candles to burn until their wicks expired, as was the custom. One time, the forgotten flames almost caused a catastrophe. After that, the flames were blown out, tradition falling in priority well below safety.

We sat down to eat after my father came home, which he did faithfully every day at 5:30 p.m. The table was never set. My mother grabbed forks, spoons, and knives in uneven numbers and deposited them in a mound in the middle of the table. The cutlery didn't match. Some of them looked like they were purchased at the local hardware store, some were acquired. What stood out from the group was a spoon, quite a bit larger than a soup spoon, which my mother liked to eat with—a utility spoon made of aluminum, another Israeli import. We affectionately called it the "lefeleh," meaning "little spoon," an ironic comment on the spoon's size, and perhaps an oblique jab that alluded to my mother's volubility.

No napkins, no dinner plates under soup bowls, no ready glasses within your reach. A stack of sliced "challah" was set on a plate near my father, who seemed to be the bread-eater of the family, as well as the breadwinner. The table leaned against the back wall, so no one could sit there. My father sat at one end, my mother and I in the middle, and my brother at the opposite end. My brother's presence at the table became more and more infrequent as he got older. There was no understanding by either of us that Friday night dinners were sacred and that our attendance was expected. This was vastly different from any other Jewish family I knew then and well after.

Our Friday dinners were really only one course—soup. My father liked his soup with plenty of noodles, and "boondlech" piled high. I liked a small portion of noodles only, my mother rice only, my brother a small portion of noodles and "boondlech." My mother ladled out the broth one bowl at a time. If you were still hungry, you could fish out pieces of boiled turkey, which were sitting in the broth, and some of the carrots and celery used for flavoring. And that's as fancy as it got until my brother, like Marco Polo after his visit to the Orient, brought back to us manners and the proper way to set a table, which he had witnessed as a guest at friends' houses. At our table, when we were finished eating, no polite children asked, "May I be excused?" like Wally and Beaver did. Nor did we automatically pick up our dishes and take them to the sink. We just got up and left.

My brother was "going out," a term used by teenagers, which to my ears sounded adventurous and bold. The words were non-committal in the information they imparted, or rather didn't impart, and indicated that further questioning would not be entertained. When my mother called after him, "When are you coming home?" he evasively offered, "I don't know." He knew that no answer he could possibly give would calm her. She would worry in any case. If he had said "Midnight," then before midnight, and for the excruciating minutes after, she would be restless. Not knowing when he was coming home meant that she would guess, then the guess would be like knowing when, and if he didn't appear at the estimated time, thoughts of how tragedy could strike him would start to assail her.

I had "things to do" on Friday night too....

First was taking a bath. Our claw-foot tub wasn't considered an antique at this juncture—the serendipitous find for a gentrified home—but a symbol of being "have-nots." I calibrated the desired combination between the hot and cold water of the two faucets, and then checked intermittently as the tub filled, lest it overfill, which had happened. It didn't take long for the humidity to eclipse the ambient air in the small bathroom, creating a sauna-like atmosphere, with no exhaust fan to dissipate the moisture.

As a mecca for microbes, it was second to none. The walls, with their sickly, orangey-pink, high-gloss paint, sweated helplessly, the mirrors a fog. Privacy was out of the question. My parents were disproportionately worried about a locked bathroom door. Their concern was contagious. What awful fate could befall me, if I were on one side of the locked door and my parents on the other, loomed ominously in my mind. I settled for being unsettled, exchanging my right to privacy for my hypothetical safety, by leaving the door unlocked. I guess they thought I would drown, and I couldn't seem to refute the possibility, however remote, having been treated to the impressive fact one day, by a schoolmate more worldly-wise than I, that a person could drown in a foot of water.

I stepped into the tub and watched the water level rise as my body mass displaced the liquid. I could feel my arms floating involuntarily to the surface when I relaxed them. The back of my head was submerged, water trickling into my ears, my hair an aura of seaweed. For a few minutes I felt quiet and calm. But my back was to the closed door, and I knew that if I lingered too long, a frantic voice, lips almost touching the door frame to ensure that she was audible, would call, "*Peril!*"

If, by chance, I were dunking my head and couldn't hear her, the door would open. Giving her a play-by-play would be giving in to her demands. "Okay, now I am about to shampoo my hair, and then after about five minutes, I'll be rinsing out the suds. That should take another ten minutes...." It wouldn't have helped; she was inconsolable. The only option I had left was to get angry, which, surprisingly enough, mollified her. "Would you leave me alone!" I was alive, obviously.

So I bathed with trepidation. And then there were other issues. When I was old enough to realize that washing with soap, shampooing, and rinsing in the bathwater made the water "dirty," evidenced by the suspicious, dark, foamy ring, I had to come up with an alternative to the shower we didn't have. The answer was the "tepull," the white enamel chamber pot from an earlier, non-toilet trained era. I let out some of the water to make way for fresh, used the pot to rinse my hair and then the rest of my body. Mission accomplished.

The bathroom was unusable for many hours, a humid vacuum that stole your breath away.

I couldn't pinpoint exactly when it first occurred to me that I had to "do my hair," but it was to become a lifelong habit and chore. The picture I had in my mind was either the flip of Patty Duke on *The Patty Duke Show,* or the pageboy of her English cousin, Cathy. I thought I had the means to accomplish it. Spongy, pink rollers with their plastic traps were meant for wearing overnight. My thick hair would be damp the next day and bear the mark of unwelcome ridges from what seemed like a clever design that eliminated the need for bobby pins.

I had to wake up early and felt a dull, achy discomfort, my stomach's way of protesting the injustice of sleep cut short. My skin crawled as soft flannels were removed and hard cottons donned. Wanting to look grown up had its privileges and trials. Wearing stockings made my legs feel like they were suffocating and cold, and the rubber tongues of the garter belt, which secured the silky material, rubbed mercilessly the same spots at the top of my thighs, which then alternated torturously between feeling sore and itchy. Pointy shoes cramped my toes. But the overall look was fetching.

Saturday morning...Sabbath in the synagogue. Adults prayed in the main sanctuary. "The young people" congregated in the gym for Junior Services. It was a good idea, separating us from the adults. We weren't on the same wavelength as the men, with their austere devotion, bobbing rhythmically as they stood and sang, their "tallises" (prayer shawls) draped variously about their shoulders, their "sidoors" (prayer books) cupped in their hands, the square, navy, velvet prayer shawl cases with their silver, embroidered Stars of David lying beside them on a seat. Or, even more so, the sad individuals who stood abjectly for "Mourners' Kaddish," a sorrowful prayer for those who had lost loved ones.

My intentions for Junior Services were of a particularly lowly variety. There was this boy....

Wooden chairs were set up on the gym floor in two sections, with an aisle down the middle facing east, basketball nets at either end easily ignored. My hair always got caught around the bolts that held the wooden back to the frame, so when we were asked to stand, which took place at a number of intervals during the service, a few hairs would be yanked out of my head each time. I would get a reprieve from this one day, when plastic molded seats replaced the wooden ones.

Our voices rang out in one range, except for some of the boys who had crossed into manhood. We went through the many

72

prayers and songs, stood, bowed, and sat at appropriate times. I prided myself on having memorized a lot of the liturgy, and demonstrated my proficiency by closing the "sidoor" and looking around while I confidently recited long passages in Hebrew, like the men in the main sanctuary whose scholarliness and deep faith were second nature to them. I was just showing off.

The high point of the service took place when the precious Torah, with its charming, fitted, velvet clothing and numerous gold accessories, was undressed, and its scrolls turned outward to find the spot for the day's reading. After this, the sacred object was dressed and carried like a toddler down the aisle.

The service concluded when we sang "Adon Olum," a jubilant melody, which looped unceasingly, much like the tune "This Is the Song That Never Ends." I sang with great exuberance, moved by relief that the tedium of the service was over and that socializing and munching were about to begin.

We crowded around the white linen-covered tables for "kiddish," a snack after prayers. For us young folk, "kiddish" consisted of assorted cookies and loganberry juice instead of the adults' honey cake and wine. Large, heavy, plump glass jugs containing the juice waited to be lifted and dispensed into small Dixie cups, whose pleats folded in sequence and fit into the rim. The cups were fun to pull apart, ending up looking like saucers. Inevitably there were spills, indelible purple stains, which spread briefly and permanently into the white linen tablecloths, or worse, if the juice got on your clothing.

Cookies were a version of shortbread, minus the butter, neutralized from being either meat or dairy. Instead they were "pareve," making it permissible to eat either meat or dairy afterwards, rather than having to wait many hours to switch. Eating them together was a big no no. Dishes like lasagna were definitely out. The cookies were so delicate, they could crumble under the slightest pressure. The rosette shapes came in two varieties: either the ones with a blob of candied fruit in the center—usually a red or green maraschino cherry—or the rosettes that had chocolate sprinklings on them. A third choice, plain and round, half dipped in

73

chocolate, looking like eclipses of the sun or harlequins or yin/yangs, was my favorite.

All the while, juice and cookies in hand, I had my eye on one boy, who held the office of "The President of Junior Services," the preteen equivalent of heading up a successful company. He was also awarded the highest accolade a preteen girl can bestow: he was cute. Glances in each other's direction swept over a number of people, like casting a wide net that catches a lot unwitting fish. It was clear on a gut level that there was interest on both sides, but propriety made it difficult to be sure. What could be offered at this age anyway? We went to different schools, so progress was confined to the exchange of a line or two of greeting on Saturdays in the presence of his friends and mine. Everyone filed out of the gym sometime between 11:30 and 12:00 noon, and we went our separate ways until the next week.

For a time, I accompanied my religious friends to another synagogue for afternoon activities. We walked east along St. Clair for about twenty minutes to Vaughan Road and turned north at the corner. The recessed building was nowhere near as large and elegant as the one a few doors down from me. And the people who ran things there were orthodox Jews, rather than conservative.

What I remember most is singing a variety of Hebrew songs and learning to dance Hebrew dances. Especially dancing the "hora" to "Havah Negilah"—fast, upbeat tempo, a favorite at bar mitzvahs and weddings. Holding hands with other girls in circles, or with partners, and noticing whose palms were sweaty and wondering why sometimes mine too would be sweaty and at other times not. Fancy steps, foot over foot, behind, then in front, rushing with arms held high towards the center, and then dropping them down as we inched backwards to increase the size of the circle. Turning and going in the opposite direction, making spirals and concentric circles, our skirts swinging and lifting with air. Melody building and building to a fever pitch. The exertion of singing while dancing leaving us flushed and breathing heavily.

Afterwards, in the fall or winter, my friends and I walked back home in the failing light of day, or, in warm weather, with hours of daylight left, which made the Sabbath a long one. When they asked me to sleep over I would stop off at home to get permission. The conversation with my mother was always heartrending, as if I were saying goodbye to her forever.

"Can I sleep over at Nina and Marsha's?" I would ask.

"No!" my mother would say, instantly and forcefully.

Somehow I knew that her strong, negative response was disproportionate to the question.

"Please?"

"No." The intensity had abated slightly.

"Please, *please*? We're walking there together and they'll walk me home tomorrow." I offered this as solace.

She hesitated. Perhaps she was reviewing the possibilities of something going terribly wrong at their house. A nice Jewish family, homebodies. The scales tipped in my favor.

"*Please, please,*" I said more excitedly.

"Okay." She gave in.

"See you later."

It was as if my mother wished she could hang on to me with all her might, but I pushed hard enough against her to break her grasp, taking her aback, because in her mind she feared she wouldn't be able to protect me from what lay in wait.

There was a time she had had complete faith that the words "I'll see you later" meant just that.

The instructions for everyone to report to the train station spread rapidly. There is nothing in the news that suggests they shouldn't comply. So they walk there together, leisurely, my mother, her father, and her brother. At the station there are personnel organizing people this way and that. It's just a short train ride my grandfather and uncle have to take for processing. They'll be back for supper. My mother can go home.

"We'll see each other later."

They all agree that they can project this plan with certainty. That the world in which they live holds the promise that everything is just as it should be and as it seems. No other possibility is even remotely within their imaginations to consider. Least of all, that this is the first leg of the trip to her father's and brother's deaths.

75

But that's what it turns out to be, as they miss supper, don't come home that night, or the day after, or ever again.

I was so looking forward to being in an actual house with three floors and a large family. Toothbrush and a change of clothes, and we continued on. Nina and Marsha were sisters, one older than I, the other, younger. Our differences held us in separate orbits, because of our ages and relative experience, the older one clearly more educated, to whom both of us deferred on certain matters, the younger one more carefree and wanton, making the most of her disadvantage.

As for the rest of the family, they were peripheral attractions. The father was a kind, portly, pious man who was technically the head of the family, but who considered closely his wife's opinion. She seemed tired and exasperated, what with taking care of the baby—the youngest, a boy—and managing the raging hormones of the eldest—a teenage daughter who had to reconcile the sex appeal of the times, Beatlemania, tight skirts and teased hair, with the demure demeanor of what was expected of an orthodox Jewish girl. Nina and Marsha were the middle children. The two of them and I just sat back and watched the sparks fly.

I wasn't much interested in the baby, who, by all accounts, seemed pleasant enough, though feeding, changing, bathing, carrying, minding, comforting him looked pretty strenuous in and of themselves. But it was the eldest daughter, Sara, who intrigued me. She seemed like a caged animal, and though she was especially mean to us, I felt sorry for her. Her ineffable boredom and profound contempt for having to endure our company pained her. Our pathetic unhipness repulsed her. It was Saturday night, and she was stuck at home. "All dressed up and nowhere to go."

We knew what she was up to in her room. We, of course, were far more involved with her than she with us, and like paparazzi with telephoto lenses to witness her privacy, we spied on her. She played her favorite hits on the mono record player which, when closed, looked like a lady's carry-on suitcase, and she posed in the mirror primping, fixing, as if she were imagining getting ready for a date.

She sang the lyrics which she knew by heart, songs like "Leader of the Pack," a tragic love ballad, where a girl falls for a sweet, misunderstood leader of a motorcycle gang. The girl breaks up with him because of pressure from her father, and the devastated motorcyclist recklessly speeds to his death. Playing one 45 at a time, Sara transported herself from song narrative to song narrative, sometimes adding a Dick Clark dance tune, and did the twist or the jerk or the watusi to a frenetic beat.

Piled beside her bed was a stack of *Sixteen* magazines, which validated and created the trends. The articles somehow spoke to her as she fused the images of the pert-nosed blondes on the glossy pages with the lonely Jewish girl that she was. Red hair to their blonde, short and curvy to their tall and svelte, it was a stretch, but didn't deter her from flights of fancy. As for the teenage heartthrobs, they were definitely off-limits, not because of their star status, but because they weren't Jewish. There were no hunks wearing skullcaps in the magazines. Non-Jews way outnumbered Jews at school, and cute boys were almost always not Jewish. Life was sad.

Soon enough, whether we got sloppy, or had started to laugh at what we saw her doing, or just wanted the drama of being found out, she caught us.

"Maaaaaaaa!" she bawled.

Her mother rushed up the stairs, worried.

"What…what is it?"

"They're bugging me!" Sara screamed.

Her mother looked at the three of us and read our guilt.

"That's enough, now go to your room and play there and don't bother your sister. Understand?"

We nodded. In fact, we had seen pretty much everything we needed and wanted to about what to expect when we became teenagers. It all seemed enthralling to me.

We were back in the room shared by the two girls and for the rest of the night we played cards—fish, rummy, and crazy eights. Then pajamas and lights out. In the darkness, with the other two in the room, in a house on a quiet street, I could actually sleep.

Chapter 10

Sundays

Nina and Marsha walked me home at some point after breakfast when time became a muddle, as schedules and routines were thrown into confusion. One could be thankful for Sundays, but not me. If it had felt simply anticlimactic coming home after a sleepover, then only an adjustment would have been required to make it right. But it felt like heading into heavy weather. A long, gaping Sunday awaited me, beginning with a walk through a mine-field.

"Did you have a good time?" my mother asked.

It was a trick question. Answering "yes" could mean that I liked it there more than at my home, which was treachery to my mother, and answering "no" would have been a lie.

"It was okay." So far I played it safe.

"What did you do?" Oh, oh.

"Well, when we got there, we had supper."

"What did you have to eat?"

"Egg salad and salmon together. It was really delicious." Ooops, I had divulged too much. I was a goner now and felt an aching sadness.

"You could have that here." She sounded offended. The comparisons had begun.

"But it was fun with everyone, the whole family." Another bad move on my part.

"Was Mr. Posen there?" she inquired strategically.

"Yes."

"With his 'kupelish' (literally 'hat,' making reference to his being orthodox)!" She said this sarcastically.

My father added, "A bunch of 'Jidlaks' (a derogatory term for orthodox Jews)."

"They're nice people."

"Then go live with them!" she snapped.

There goes the mine.

The rest of the afternoon was lonely and could span many hours. Guessing the time, and being wrong thinking it was later, was a common, deflating occurrence. I would notice a slight disheartening as daylight waned, as if the light had gone out in me, and though day had turned to night every day of my life so far, I was always dismayed by Sunday night's arrival.

Supper was a reprieve and appeared spontaneously, put together with unanticipated ingredients. Tonight was "lockshun" (noodles) and cheese. These were the broad, Lancia egg noodles, not the fine ones for chicken soup. Both kinds were staples in the house.

As for the cheese, it was real, creamed cottage cheese, the curds ground well, but not to the point where it was spreadable and fake like the Philadelphia brand. This cheese came from the original Daiter's Creamery in Kensington Market. A family business, shop in the front, living quarters upstairs, a regular biweekly visit for my father after work on Thursdays.

The first stop was to another family-run business, the Jewish bakery, Perlmutter's. Ebullient and noisy, rye breads, "challahs," pumpernickel loaves, buns and baking everywhere, customers served by one of the owners or relatives. Yiddish dominated the space. Here my father bought a large, flat onion bun essentially the size of a medium pizza, called a "pletzil," and a small rye bread with no caraway seeds, delicious with sliced Chicago 58 all-beef salami and French's mustard.

Perlmutter's had the tastiest, cushiony, icing sugar-coated jelly donuts, chocolate donuts, and granulated sugar donuts, the latter not to be confused with the glazed donuts at Women's Bakery, a franchise that couldn't have been more simply named, evoking the home-baked goodness only your Scottish, Irish, or English mother or grandmother could duplicate, if only I'd had one, assuming there *was* one behind the brand.

What a difference between the two bakeries. The women who were employed at Women's Bakery looked like the Anglo icons of the female-driven work force during the war. They were tall and lean and professionally kind. Their wavy, Myrna Loy hair was always carefully housed in a net to protect the public from strays. Their light orange/pink uniforms, thick hose, and sensible shoes bespoke continuity of service. Even when busy, the store was quiet, almost sepulchral. Customers were staid and reserved. The specialties were white birthday and wedding cakes with white frosting and a variety of contrasting piping of your choosing, and, of course, white bread. My parents had never been there and would have felt totally out of place.

After Permutter's, my father went to Daiter's.

Walking in, one was met by the faint smell of milkiness. All the cheeses were kept cold and retrieved order by order. The proprietor's hand disappeared into the large cooler, bringing out an odd shape that looked like a duck's back swathed in cheesecloth. The fabric was untwisted with one hand, slowly peeled away from the delicate shape to keep it intact, and then placed onto waiting, white, waxy paper proffered by the other hand. Then the cheese was wrapped, weighed, and priced.

There was always cheese in our house. My mother mounded it on her morning toast every single day. And now she would be crumbling it onto the noodles, though, with its creamy texture, half as much was left on her fingers. I liked lots of cheese. The warm noodles and the cool cheese worked well together, neither shocked by the other, but each retaining its own temperature, apart from where the two merged and split the difference. Then my mother would sprinkle on a generous amount of cinnamon and a little sugar. Delicious.

There were still many hours left in a never-ending Sunday. Excruciatingly uninteresting TV news programs were on, like *Meet the Press* and *60 Minutes*. My parents were riveted while they watched, and whatever it was that I said or needed, my mother rebuked with a sudden sting, "Shah!" I felt duped, as if I had relied on something that wasn't there. Sometimes, if their program wasn't interesting, and *Walt Disney* was on, I'd watch that.

At least, on a Saturday night, there was the exhilaration of *Hockey Night in Canada* and the mighty Toronto Maple Leafs rounded out by the likes of Frank Mahovlich, the captain George Armstrong, Dave Keon, Red Kelly, the inimitable goalie Johnny

Bower, the future donut magnate Tim Horton, and Eddie Shack (more donuts). And oh, what a run, winning the Stanley Cup in 1962, '63, '64, and '67. The Montreal Canadiens, with Jean Beliveau, Rocket Richard, and Boom Boom Geoffrion, were a worthy alternative to cheer for during their Stanley Cup wins in 1965 and '66, because it was still keeping it in the Canadian family.

The excitement of the game, beyond the actual, agile moves of the players, came from the enthusiastic emanations of Foster Hewitt. His unique, high-pitched voice, coupled with an immediate reaction time, elevated the most inconclusive moments, such as missed goals, to near-explosions of rapture, second only to the intense climax of his signature line, *"He shoots; he scores!"*

I perked up at 8:00 p.m. on Sunday, with a program running at a close second to *Hockey Night in Canada*. All four of us convened in the living room. There was something for everyone on *The Ed Sullivan Show*. An easy target for impersonation, Ed Sullivan was a welcome guest in people's homes all over the city, and the continent for that matter. His "really big shoe" line was a favorite to mimic, the inflexibility of his jaw causing him to mispronounce "show." His head and entire body moved as one, like a cereal box with legs. And his "shoe" was full of variety. Regular acts included a musical group, a stand-up comedian, and a circus feat.

The American debut of the Beatles had been on *The Ed Sullivan Show*. The four lads burst on the scene. Cute Paul was on the left of the screen, one foot in front of the other, using his guitar as a fulcrum, performing for crazed, screaming teeny boppers, the likes of which poor Ed had never heard. George, with his high cheekbones and deferential manner, was planted in the middle, Ringo bashed the snares, hair flying, and John stood assuredly with his legs apart, moving slightly up and down, singing the main vocals for "She Loves You." Undaunted by the subtitle that had appeared earlier at the bottom of the TV screen, which stated, about John, "Sorry, girls, he's married," the girls continued to shriek adoringly throughout the unprecedented performance.

Perhaps the most fun was the adorable Italian mouse marionette, Topo Gigio. Little did we know we may have been witnessing the first homosexual kiss on television. Topo seemed smitten with the host. The diminutive mouse pranced around and batted his long eyelashes for Ed, whom he lovingly referred to as "Eddie." Topo engaged Eddie in conversation, with the sole intention of cracking that clenched jaw of his and disarming him. When the mouse's overtures were coming to a close, he cooed, "E-ddie...kees me good night." And when Eddie did just that, Topo's heart was aflutter. He hopped, giggled, sighed with pleasure, then climbed into his tiny bed and went to sleep.

Kraft products had the preeminent advertising spot, flogging their wares in commercials slotted between *The Ed Sullivan Show* and *Bonanza*. The Kraft Kitchens were busy coming up with creative recipes that combined as much of the Kraft repertoire as possible. The many ways that Cheez Whiz, Kraft Singles, Miracle Whip, Velveeta, Kraft Dinner, and Kraft Miniature Marshmallows found themselves in a Pyrex baking dish were astonishing.

My mother and father were always aghast at the concoctions and conveyed their displeasure with one derisive word, "Kackari" (literally shit, figuratively crap). Their particular brand of deprecating humor was always hilarious and they ridiculed mercilessly and relentlessly. All of us—my brother when he was at home, myself, and my parents—laughed uproariously.

I laughed until there was no sound coming from my mouth, just the involuntary flickering of my uvula and the spasms in my esophagus, my eyes squinting tightly, tears spitting out, my sides aching with tension as if I'd been tickled beyond any comfort level and was unable to breathe. Just when our laughter became somewhat under control, my mother would get up and waddle quickly out of the room, announcing, "Oy, ich daf guyin pishin" ("I have to pee"), which started us up again. It always took a number of bouts of laughter, escalating and subsiding, before we could calm down, and then we all breathed greedily, as if we had come up for air from an oxygen-deprived environment.

Bonanza may not have been in my top five favorites, but it was only 9:00 at night—too early to go to bed—the show easily watchable, with its thunderous, trademark song, which sounded like a team of galloping horses, and its down-home themes of family and the land.

83

Curious, the felt absence of women in this family consisting of a patriarch and his three strapping sons. It was a brilliant subplot when you think of it, viewers always hoping for any one of four possible romantic storylines. Stalwart Ben, the head of the clan, sober in judgment and handy with a gun if it meant defending the homestead. That the actor was in fact a Jew from Ottawa, the son of Russian Jewish immigrants, gave me quite a chuckle when I was older—a Jew portraying the quintessential American Western Hero, like Irving Berlin, who wrote "White Christmas." Then there was Adam, the inconspicuous and forgettable eldest son. Next was huge Hoss, the family muscle, short on brains, but with a heart as big as Montana. Another chuckle as rumors of the actor's alleged homosexuality spread sometime around the outing of the Village People. And finally, the youngest, best-looking son, Little Joe, played by Michael Landon. It was no accident that he was also a teenage heartthrob, gracing covers of magazines. His hair was much longer than the rest of his TV brothers, his jeans and plaid shirt personifying the rugged, hippie look that was so much in style and worked nicely with his cowboy persona.

At 10:00 was *The Andy Williams Show*, which my parents liked. It was a bit of a yawner. Crooner Andy Williams was a very bland Sinatra. The show was steeped in some generalized, American, traditional family ideal, with stars like Donnie and Marie Osmond, and Christmas specials with spectacularly decorated trees and heaps of presents. Andy Williams became far more exciting and infamous when he married the very pretty and slight, but hopelessly wayward, Claudine Longet, who seemed unfit to hurt a fly, yet was accused of gunning down her ski pro lover in cold blood.

At 11:00 the news came on, and once again my parents were shut off from the rest of the world and mesmerized by what they were watching, as if they were going to find out that war had broken out again. For me, it was a boring end to an interminable day. I reluctantly faced the hard night and eventually fell asleep to wake up to a long week, which would only improve by Friday.

Chapter 11

God, Part II

It became increasingly apparent that my religious indoctrination was a solo venture. My parents had dutifully presented the Judaic perspective to both my brother and me, even though they were strenuously against it all.

I had taken to Judaism well, as it provided a holistic environment, including Hebrew school and friends, Junior Services and a love interest, Saturday afternoon Hebrew cultural activities, and a Sunday afternoon youth group, recently started up at the synagogue. Finally I had something to do on Sunday to help offset the day's ennui. How my parents coped with my "faith," I can only wonder.

The first defector was my brother. Six years older than I, he was in the final year of Hebrew school and just shy of the privilege of being bar-mitzvahed. His class was taught by none other than the Rabbi who ran the school, a man thoroughly convinced of the sanctity and integrity of the Torah and its teachings, which he apportioned to his students. His was no easy task. We lived in a white, Anglo town, Jews by far in the minority, and as much as the protagonists in the Old Testament were intriguing figures, they had nothing on Elvis and The Beach Boys. Undeterred he persevered, gathering the "boys about to become men" into the fold, hoping to stir in them a deep sense of purpose and an understanding that upon them rested the hope of the future of the Jews.

It made sense…. Other ethnic groups also clung to their cultures, as strangers in a strange land. Reluctant to water themselves down into the majority, yet unable or unwilling to stay in their country of origin, immigrant parents were faced with a paradoxical existence at best. But for children, a different story. Their skins absorbed it all.

85

And so the inevitable happened. Though Rabbi Golden was happy climbing a sand hill, making questionable headway one step forward, two steps back, sometimes breaking even, sometimes getting ahead, his students lived in the "real" world.

One of those magical evenings... Though Hebrew school began in the late afternoon, by December the sun set early and quickly, too quickly for the blinds to be drawn, or worse, to interrupt the impassioned didacticism of Rabbi Golden. The outdoor safety lights came on. Suddenly, plump snow flakes were illuminated, blowing wistfully but steadily outside, in full view through the four large windows that bordered one side of the classroom. The first snowfall was always so enchanting, especially for children, especially in a town that worshipped the coming of the season.

It was my brother who spoke aloud what everyone was thinking, coming from a place deeper than Rabbi Golden could ever get to.

"Hey, Santa Claus is coming!"

The moment was stunning and seemed to hover as students were poised between two incompatible ideologies. Then there was a huge outpouring of laughter. Everyone watched Rabbi Golden for his reaction.

In the true spirit of being an educator (from the Latin meaning "to draw out"), Rabbi Golden could have taken my brother aside and said, "My boy, you have a gift. Your sense of timing, delivery, irony and wit. Like many of the tribe—Hackett, Dangerfield, Allen, Mason, and our own Wayne and Shuster. To make people laugh, now that's a blessing!" But it seemed that Rabbi Golden had no funny bone whatsoever. He turned bright red like Santa's snowsuit and quaked. "Get out!" he screamed. Thus ended my brother's Hebrew school career.

Perhaps both parties had overreacted. Rabbi Golden hadn't meant it literally, but my brother never returned to class.

There was still the matter of a bar mitzvah to consider. Private classes were held for those about to have the honor bestowed upon them. My brother attended these, so in that sense the cord wasn't completely severed.

My parents were having many discussions, in Polish, their secret language. The bar mitzvah was being planned. It would take place at the synagogue. The list of guests was confirmed. My brother was learning his part.

Bar mitzvah boys were treated like celebrities and featured in the Sabbath service, like a guest lecturer or keynote speaker. They were summoned to the "bema" (the altar), given the Torah to hold, and asked to read, or more accurately, to sing a selected passage. Some boys sang better than others; they stayed on pitch while others were tone deaf. Some boys sounded like song birds, because their voices hadn't changed, a sound so desirable it was forever captured by castrati singing Gregorian chants. Others, who had reached puberty, cracked and croaked like they were down with a cold.

The typical bar mitzvah boy was draped in a brand new "tallis" and sported a shiny, satin skullcap. He would wear a brand new suit, crisp white shirt accessorized with a tie, and patent leather dress shoes. He would lead the procession out of the sanctuary and then hold court at "kiddish." Relatives took their turn congratulating him, the men shaking the bar mitzvah boy's hand; the boy may have just recently learned to make sure his handshake was firm. The women insisted on kissing him, the smell of powder filled his nostrils, and, on his cheeks, oily red imprints evidenced several pairs of lips. The exuberant expressions of "mazel tov" (good luck) filled the room.

His peers would come up to him, uttering playful, ribbing remarks, and noting the "monkey suit" he was wearing for the occasion, so out of sync with the daily attire of boys. They exaggerated their handshakes as they mimicked the men, and then sincerely wished their friend well. Strangers who had attended the service because it was the Sabbath approached him with a "mazel tov." Everyone knew who he was and what milestone he had reached.

His parents availed themselves of a prized commodity in Jewish culture, called "nachas" (pride in a parental job well done). They too were dressed up, he in a smart suit, she coiffed and bedecked—more "mazel tovs." Any siblings of the bar mitzvah boy got some of the spotlight, under the "apples not falling far from tree" adage.

A few hours would intervene once "kiddish" was over, and before the evening part of the fete began.

From the standard to the flaunting, bar mitzvah celebrations boasted, at the very least, a dressy affair including a hall with tables, linen tablecloths, and centerpieces, a multi-course dinner, a large cake, an elaborate sweet table, a live band and dancing, and professional photographers. It called for a costume change for the women—the mother and any sisters. Guests could number as few as one hundred or as many as six. Over the years, each bar mitzvah celebration was outdone by the next, until one Toronto family pretty much outspent and outclassed every other Jewish family in the city. At this event, lavish displays included a gilded throne for the bar mitzvah boy to sit upon.

The agenda for the evening would begin with the grand entrance of the bar mitzvah boy and his family, and the introduction of the head table, at which generally sat the immediate family and grandparents. Then followed the blessing of the bread and wine, a short speech, the first course, musical interludes, the second course, the first dessert, and the bulk of the speeches, mostly laudatory, but peppered with some gentle teasing of the bar mitzvah boy.

Siblings would present slightly embarrassing anecdotes about what it was like to live with him. These were, at the very least, censored, but often ghostwritten, by the mother. Then the mother spoke—a deeply heartfelt testimony—and the father after her, taking a lighter approach, clearly making the best of what had been many exasperated discussions between him and his wife. His speech invariably began with a tribute to her and how tirelessly she had toiled to make this such a fabulous affair, which was code for how little he had done. Then, a public acknowledgement of how great she looked, asking for a round of applause, a useful decoy to mollify her and hopefully to dull the memory of her angry disappointment with him during the planning stages. Finally would come the bar mitzvah boy's speech, thanking his parents for everything they'd done for him and how he wouldn't be there if it wasn't for them...wink, wink. Music and dancing.

A highlight was the theatrical spectacle of lighting the candles. Somehow, this "religious tradition" came to be combined with the secular tradition of candles on the birthday cake. The hybrid was show-stopping: a great big cake, maybe in the shape of a Torah, topped by tall, thick candles. Those close to the family would be called upon, one by one, to come forward and light one candle until the number thirteen, plus one for good luck, was reached. These last two would be reserved for the celebrated bar mitzvah boy and family.

For the more religious Jews, there would be a short evening service attended by the mandatory "minyan" (ten men) required for prayer. Then more dancing, including the heart-pumping, Israeli dance, the "hora," which always got the crowd moving in concentric circles, the inner one often made up of the members of the head table.

It wasn't unusual for the boy's friends to have formed their own circle, which would quickly devolve into "Crack the Whip." Slowly, their suit jackets would rise, shoulder pads around their necks, sleeves riding up their arms. Their neckties askew, shirttails hanging out, it was as if the boys were being held upside down and shaken. It wouldn't be long before the last boy in the "whip" would be flung into an unwitting guest or two and treated to a stern, disapproving leer and a wagging finger.

Then, the dessert table. A bountiful buffet of tarts, squares, cakes, mountains of fruit, fruit molds, chocolates, non-dairy ice creams and sorbets, coffee and tea, atop a number of linen-covered, long, rectangular tables. More music and dancing.

During the course of the evening, the bar mitzvah boy would mingle, stopping at each table to say hello. As if on cue, he would be approached by one guest after another. Once again the relatives and friends shook the bar mitzvah boy's hand, but this time they each pressed into his palm an envelope. This would immediately be filed in one of his inside jacket pockets, until these were bursting, whereupon the boy would unload a handful of enve-lopes into his father's hands for safekeeping.

As the night drew to a close, guests began to plan their departure. Amid the expected goodbyes to people they knew, a profuse "thank you" to the family, and a final "mazel tov" to the bar mitzvah boy, female guests could be seen absconding with one of the centerpieces, a practice that spanned many cultures and so could be considered more specific to gender than to ethnicity.

Later that night, all the envelopes were torn open, the cards separated, and the money counted to see what the take had been. The final tally could be quite sizable.

In the ensuing months, the photographers had the family pore over hundreds of proofs to decide which ones would become the mementos forever preserved in a beautiful, leather-bound album, photos that were cropped and photofinished and in focus, capturing all of the important elements and feelings of the night.

As my parents considered planning this momentous occasion, two troubling points kept coming up again and again: bar mitzvahs cost money, and celebrating a bar mitzvah meant subscribing to Judaism....

I can only guess that the bar mitzvah standard, and what actually took place for my brother, followed the same logic as the conversation in *King Lear* between Regan and Goneril as they systematically reduced their father's entourage.

This was the result:

There were four couples invited over to my cousin's modest North York home for a celebratory drink and dessert.

I wore a pretty, blue party dress, which had a layer of chiffon over a satin lining, and a crinoline sewn into the hem. A blue flower with a few soft, green leaves, fashioned like a rose, and made out of fabric, was sewn into the wide sash and positioned to the right. The long ends at the back were tied into a big bow. The quality of the tying was most important, and well executed thanks to my mother. She ensured that the two bow loops were equally balanced, and not off kilter with one loop higher, so they didn't look like the blades of a propeller on a grounded airplane.

My hair was brushed into a ponytail. Then, hand over hand, my mother smoothed my hair, before placing the blue, plastic, hump-shaped fastener on top to house the ponytail. An elastic band, held in place by two tiny hooks on one side of the fastener, went underneath my hair to two tiny hooks on the other side. A wide, blue, plastic hairband with miniature teeth helped smooth any unfortunate bumps that brushing couldn't eliminate. White ankle socks with tiny, embroidered blue flowers, and black patent leather, Mary Jane shoes by Schaefer, *the* trusted name in children's shoes, completed my outfit.

The kitchen table stood, without chairs, in the breakfast nook, covered by a linen table cloth and then a plastic one. So much easier to clean up spills. There was one birthday cake for my brother, with blue icing piped around the square perimeter, and a smaller one for me, with pink icing. It made perfect sense to me. His birthday cake was bigger because he was older. Since our birthdays were one month apart, it was decided that we would celebrate them together.

The adults socialized in the living room, and the kids stayed in the basement for the most part, busying our selves with this and that. As kids, we quickly sized up the environment and made do, using our imaginations and trusting that some sort of play would emerge.

When the time came to sing "Happy Birthday," to light, blow out the candles, and cut the cake, my brother and I were ushered into the breakfast nook and handed knives to pose for a single, "candid" action photo. My brother held his knife firmly, his thumb locked into place on top of the knife, elbow out for balance. His cuts would be clean. My mother held her hand over mine, my fingers lightly curled around the handle.

Picture and event were over in a flash. The cake was cut and distributed. There was coffee and tea for the adults. Not one reference was made to Judaism.

With the money received from the four couples and my cousins, my brother got a brand new, electric Underwood typewriter, state of the art, worth about $165.00.

I'd had a really good time. Sharing a birthday with my older brother gave me a sense of importance by proxy. And any occasion that included birthday cake was a winner. At the age of seven, I wasn't that hard to please. But what about my brother?

The case against having a bar mitzvah was this:

My parents believed that bar mitzvahs were nothing more than a showcase for bragging rights, a competition in the never-ending game of keeping up with the Schwartzes. From a religious standpoint, it was ludicrous to spend inordinate amounts of money on a thirteen-year-old boy who, in secular terms, was barely out of Grade Eight, and closer to the bed-wetting stage than he was to "becoming a man." Other families had money to spare on such extravagance, but not my family. They were not going to be drawn into a situation that forced the comparison between them and others. Maybe they knew they couldn't keep up, and so changed the nature of their wound into activism. Thus, my brother became the vehicle for their brave iconoclasm, perhaps one of the very few boys in Toronto whose parents had the guts to stand up to a tradition that had been warped into something of a circus. Such hypocrisy! Judaism for materialists! Who needed that, was their thinking.

Maybe a certain, thirteen year old boy...

To my brother's ears, the case against having a bar mitzvah wasn't that convincing. He was a reluctant and unsung hero. He had many years ahead of him to develop a principled philosophy about life and the world. In the meantime, his needs and desires were of the ordinary kind for a boy of his age. All that attention... Everybody coming up to you and congratulating you, gifts translating into more money than a worker could make in a year. That heady feeling of being surrounded by hundreds of well-wishers, being honored repeatedly in the months leading up to the gala, being exalted at the gala and, for months afterwards, basking in the glow of the memory. He felt he had missed out on a rare opportunity to shine, for reasons that were out of his control to decide and beyond his comprehension to feel good about.

Chapter 12

Hoods Aren't Bilingual

My brother's penchant for being an upstart wasn't limited to Hebrew school. His pithy one-liners, although clever and funny, almost led to his being beaten to a pulp.

The teenagers hanging around where I lived were "hoods." That meant their potential for lawlessness was like the presumptive power of a revving motor. They were intriguing and very scary, worthy of notice, but you couldn't stare, because it was dangerous. Adding up all the glances I'd stolen resulted in a fairly comprehensive understanding of these boys' customs and culture. They were definitely tough. No one wanted to find out if they'd make good on their threats.

They carried pocket knives, mostly used for carving their initials on park benches in peacetime, but everyone knew that knives were also weapons. They wore jeans—long, with wide cuffs—pointy boots, tee shirts. Their backs were curved as if they were guarding their hearts; their stomachs, taut and concave. When it was hot they thought nothing of walking around shirtless with their smooth chests, their nipples tiny and hard like the spots of candy on the long paper strips you could get at the smoke shop where they bought smokes and I filled up my little brown bag with my favorites and whatever else I could get for ten cents. If I wasn't saving the candies for eating out of my desk at Hebrew school, then, after I was done, I'd cup my hand around the top of the bag, blow into it so that it filled with air, and pop it. It was loud, like a gunshot. Not bad for ten cents.

I watched the hoods as they scuffed their boots along the pavement, dismissing all the teachers who'd ever told them to pick up their feet, bringing their heels down at the end with a decisive clop, which wore them down on one side. I watched their rounded shoulders, which looked like sockets, their arms hanging forward, their biceps like the bellies of hairless cats, their hands clenched into fists, and caught a glimpse of a long fingernail for who knows what.

They walked with their hips first, the rest of their body arriving a millisecond later. Their faces were bony, and they squinted in a perpetual state of contempt; their Samson hair, with their pompadours and ducktails, shone from using Brylcreem; their combs were always handy. Their fathers looked like middle-aged Chet Bakers. Hoods conjugated "fuck" with linguistic alacrity, so the word's usage could be stretched to its grammatical limit in ever sentence they uttered.

After the spirea bloomed in the hedges of the neighboring houses, the hoods found refuge in the parkette on Atlas, which became their home until the first frost. They eschewed the afternoons filled with the high-pitched squeals of children, and preferred the evenings, which held the scent of nature, the damp cool of the sand box, the exhalations of smoke, and the wafts of waxy lipstick perfume coming from their girlfriends' mouths.

Their girlfriends were studies in and of themselves. Every inch of them showed attention to detail. From their teased crowns, to their side parts—which caused a curtain of hair to sweep across their foreheads and rest over one of their two, perfectly penciled tadpoles of eyebrows—to their eyelined lids with little ticks at the sides, their foundationed and powdered cheeks, their coral lipstick. Their kerchiefs, their pedal-pushers, their angora sweaters hugging their Playtex "Cross Your Heart" bras, which promised to "lift and separate" just like the ad said, though in some cases what was lifted and separated were balls of Kleenex. Their necklace chains, from which was suspended a single charm, were deliberate in length and meant to lead to a glimpse of cleavage. They chewed and cracked gum, either Wrigley's or Chicklets or Thrills, which kept them busy while their boyfriends talked or fidgeted.

Hoods were a different species than the rest of us regular folk, and for the most part kept to themselves and went about their own business. Like the mob, most of the violence was infighting, so if you didn't bother them, they didn't bother you. But if you somehow got them going, like messing with wasps, things could get pretty nasty.

My brother came home in a panic, breathless and terrified. "I'm dead," he prophesied.

"What are you talking about?" I followed him, worried sick.

He went into his room.

"Shut the door," he said quickly. "I don't want mommy and daddy to know."

"Know what?"

"Dammit, what am I going to do?" He rocked back and forth on the bed, fighting tears.

"About what?" I was getting really frightened.

"He's going to kill me."

"Who?"

"I don't know his name. He's a *hood*!"

With that one word, I now knew the enormity of his situation.

One of the exciting trends on the Ontario education front was the introduction of the French language in Grade Seven. Both my brother and I had a good ear for languages. His experience of French preceded mine by six years, but when I did get there I concurred with what he had felt at the time. He thoroughly enjoyed memorizing vocabulary lists and acing the quizzes. He wrapped his lips and tongue around the different pronunciations, particularly the rolling *r*s, and the nasal endings of "-en," "-on,""-an," and "-in."

He expanded with a feeling of worldliness. The students would try to actually speak in French to one another and see how long they lasted before they exhausted the supply of words they'd learned. When my brother came home he would say phrases to me in French, and I in turn would be impressed.

"*Comment ça va*?" He would say to me, with the inflection of a Frenchman.

And then he would tell me what to say back.

"*Ça va bien.*"

French sounded so dreamy. Even profanities like "*sacre bleu!*" and "*tabernac!*" sounded like cooing romance.

It had happened in the wink of an eye, as these incidents tend to do. The chances of an interaction between my brother and the hoods were slim to none. How one caught the attention of the other, and how that prompted one to address the other, wasn't clear, but the conversation went awry quickly, and backs were up. My brother was no match for the hood, which was why the hood felt it beneath him to even consider wasting his energy. This would have been a gift, if only my brother had recognized it, like seeing charity in the action of a fisherman who tosses a puny catch back into the water. But rather than being grateful to have escaped with his life and showing the hood the reverence he felt he deserved for his magnanimous gesture, my brother looked at the hood and delivered this parting line:

"Eh. *Fauteuil!*"

The hood froze.

"What did you just say?" the hood said, in threatening disbelief.

Since there was a street between them, my brother felt dizzyingly confident enough to add:

"You heard me."

"I dare you to say it again."

My brother paused.

The hood was flanked by his buddies. Three pairs of eyes glared at my brother. The one on the left grew impatient. "Ahh, he's scared. Come on, he's just a little shit. Let's get the fuck outta here."

And as they turned away, my brother placed his palms at either side of his mouth to maximize the reach of his voice and yelled, "*FAUTUEIL!*" Then he took off like a shot down the lane and disappeared.

"You little fucker! If I ever see your face around here... I'll be looking for you! You're DEAD! You hear me!"

So the story was recounted to me.

"Oh my god," I said, as my heart sank. "What are you going to do?"

"I don't know. I'm up shit's creek for sure."

"But you have to leave the house, go to school.... They're always hanging around."

"Tell me about it."

"I can't believe you swore at him. Why did you do that?

"But I didn't swear."

96

"You told a hood to *f*-off."

"No I didn't!"

"Okay, so you said it in French, but you still swore."

"I didn't, that's the thing."

"You said "*fa-*" something to him."

"*Fauteuil.*"

"Yeah, that."

"I know."

"Well that sounds a lot like *f*-off to me."

"But it isn't," he insisted.

"Then what does it mean?"

"Armchair."

It was one of those moments of clarity and irony that, after the initial shock, can only be followed by doubling over with laughter.

Talk about a rock and a hard place. There was no way my brother could approach the hood with this explanation and escape being throttled first. As if the hood would even believe him. In any case, hood values were more along the lines of "Kill first, ask questions later."

I just sat there shaking my head at the bizarre predicament he was in.

And then, because we were siblings, I joked, "I can't believe you called him an armchair and he wants to kill you."

"Shut up."

But I had to hand it to him. It was witty. A word that not in a million years would sound as benign as it was. A sound sure to inflame and incite, whose meaning couldn't have been more uninspiring and innocuous. My brother was pure mischief, albeit a dead man.

I was always impressed with well-organized teachers, teachers who had preplanned their lessons by placing tabs in their texts so they could open to the right page without fumbling in the moment and risking looking foolish. And when they read an excerpt to us we were convinced somehow that, because it was written, it must be so.

The afternoon in question, I was a far cry from the trembling kid huddled under the covers waiting out the night. Bolstered by some belief in reason and proof, I held myself together as I walked towards their habitat, the stake they had claimed, the group of them sitting on a bench at the mouth of the park.

"Excuse me," I began.

The looks I received ranged from amusement, to mild irritation at having to bother with me. The hood to whom my brother had misspoken seemed to come out of a reverie, like the snake in D.H. Lawrence's poem. In other words, even though his venom was fatal, he wasn't in the mood for killing.

"What do you want, kid?" the hood said, clearly implying I should make it short.

"That boy, the one who said some bad things to you…"

The hood stood up a little straighter and leaned his body in my direction, his eyes narrowing. "Yeah, what about him?"

"He's my brother."

The hood raised his eyebrows momentarily and sneered, as if to impart that this new development wasn't going to make much of a difference.

"Yeah? So what."

"He didn't mean what he said."

Now they were all chuckling.

"Yeah? Well he should've thought of that before he opened his big fuckin' mouth." His cronies laughed.

I persevered. "I mean, what he said is not what you think."

Now they were confused.

"What are you talking about, kid? Why don't you just run along and tell your brother he's in very big trouble." His pals nodded.

"But he didn't swear at you."

The hood was losing his patience.

"Oh he didn't, did he?" he mocked.

"Look." I brought it forward. The tab was secured under f in the glossary of my brother's French textbook.

I continued, "He said, '*fauteuil*' to you, right?" I saw the hood bristle. "But it's not a swear word. It's French." The look of sur-

98

prise on the hood's face indicated that I had clearly found a loophole.

He appeared guarded, but interested.

"Here." I showed him the book.

"See?" I pointed to the word *fauteuil*. "It's pronounced 'futtoy.' I know it sounds bad, but it just means armchair." There was a pause.

"That's all that my brother said to you."

The hood was weighing the information.

"Please don't beat him up."

The hood looked at me for a long time, it seemed. I don't know what he saw. A little girl in summer shorts and a matching top, ankle socks and running shoes, hair in a ponytail. Eyes shining with a kind of hope. I wasn't very threatening. But I also wasn't afraid for myself. I felt immune from his violence, safeguarded under the unspoken commandment, common at the time, that you never fought dirty, never picked on bespectacled peers, on the unarmed if you had a weapon, or those weaker than yourself—younger boys, and girls for sure. The tension was thick, and time was moving painfully slowly.

"Okay."

I ran off, elated, couldn't wait to tell my brother that I had saved his life. The execution was stayed, the pardon granted, the bounty lifted.

He was free.

99

Chapter 13

God, Part III

It was just me now. My parents had pretty much scuttled their religious pretenses, and my brother was well on the blissful path to atheism.

My devotion was far from deep. It was simply easy to follow the rules and hear the folklore that encouraged me to comply.

The scariest and most rigid of the traditions was Yom Kippur, the Day of Atonement. Beginning the evening before with the poignant service Kol Nidre, the tone of solemnity and humility in the face of the Almighty was set. The horrifying prospect of God deciding, on this day, who should live and who should die in the coming year was explained to those like myself, still of quite a tender age. I remember being stopped in my tracks when I heard this, a detonating shudder like an electrical charge running through my body. Immediately, I asked what I needed to do to get on His good side. The rules seemed straightforward enough. A twenty-four hour fast, no food or water. I wondered if I could brush my teeth in the morning. A drop of water could plausibly be ingested during the process. Would that one drop condemn me? And if I didn't brush my teeth, what then? Would God have an aversion to that? Or was he fine with an entire congregation of worshippers emitting fetid prayers.

I was told that whatever you did the rest of the year, you had to make sure that on this day you were super good. It seemed illogical to me. Couldn't God see through that? Anyone who took that kind of a chance, I thought, was playing with fire and, I guess, brimstone. Well, it would be better to be good all year round, I was told.

For the most part, it was comforting to be instructed on what to do and when to do it. But more and more, things didn't make sense to me. For example, on the High Holidays you had to be dressed up in your "Sunday" clothes, and then put on running shoes or slippers. You weren't allowed to wear your leather dress shoes. I was given two different reasons from two different people when I asked why. The first person said that leather was hard to fashion and constituted work, something in keeping with the "no work on Sabbath" idea, and the second person said that one should tread softly on this day. Neither answer resonated with me. Instead, my inclination was to laugh at all of us because we looked rather silly, dressed up and then deliberately mis-shod. Hard to take the whole thing seriously. Was God testing us? Did we misunderstand him? Does He have a sense of humor? Is He throwing His weight around? Some of my questions weren't proper to ask.

I followed the rule and chose to wear running shoes, having drawn the line at slippers. Still, I had a strong feeling that the footwear ruined the look of my outfit. In that moment, it was obvious that I had been more influenced by female fashion than by religious fervor, and I hadn't even reached puberty.

The Jewish New Year—Rosh Hashanah—and Yom Kippur usually took place in late September and early October. Because Jews used the lunar calendar, and the Western world used the Gregorian calendar, the dates would change from year to year. If you lived in Toronto, Canada, the Jewish High Holidays could be either surrealistically balmy, with the whispering breezes of Indian summer, or damp, cold, and autumnal.

This Yom Kippur was hot. The break between services found the entire congregation on the street, chatting and milling about. Those who were determined to sport their new fall clothes, wools and worsteds, knew best what atonement meant as they sweated with regret.

I could easily see up the street from where I stood on the pavement, and noticed that my parents had come outside. I waved to them and we walked towards one another. They were dressed "to go out," so they didn't look out of place with the rest of the crowd as we stood talking within its perimeter. It felt good to be with them. For a moment, I was like other members of the synagogue who came as a family. But it wasn't long-lived. After we spoke, they left me to my grumbling stomach and fervent prayers to God,

102

asking to be spared, while they walked another block east along St. Clair to shop at a bustling Polish deli.

The little bells vibrated and chimed as the door opened. There was produce everywhere. On the right, bags of buns and bread, shelves of plum jam, and cherries floating in cherry juice like bubbles in a lava lamp. A refrigerated display case on the left ran the length of the store. In the first section were cured meats, then cheeses, and finally prepared foods like perogies and salads. Bleached-blonde ladies in aprons stood behind the counter, their voluptuous figures a slightly enlarged version of their youth. Mascara, lipstick, and powder on their faces didn't hide tiny wrinkles. Gold chains, from which crucifixes hung, stayed put, lightly adhering to the perspiration on their wearers' chests as the ladies took orders, then bent down to reach and pull out heavy mounds of meat.

My parents gave their order in Polish. They stocked up on krakowska, a large, salami-like meat, which had a number of little areas all held together by fat and bologna. One section was particularly succulent. Kolbassa was the other order. They asked for a sizable piece, cut from what seemed to be an endless length of pipe covered in a paper fabric skin the same color as the meat, the inside laced with tiny specks of pepper. Both items were made from pork.

The Jewish bakery on the same strip as the deli was closed for the holidays, but my parents had already thought of that and had ample bread at home.

I came back to the apartment following the High Holiday services, with hours to go before sundown when I could finally break my fast, having done the prescribed homage to God as he faced the task of deciding my fate. My parents had already eaten at their usual time, 5:30, ruled by nothing remotely spiritual.

My mother broiled the lamb chop I would have for my dinner. She lit the tiny pilot light uneventfully. There was one time when she had been worried because my father had been late coming home, and she'd turned on the gas, but not lit the pilot light. When she did remember to light it, she'd unfortunately forgotten about the gas. Our unsuspecting heads were bowed towards the open oven, and there was a small explosion, which singed our eyebrows and lashes and our hair at the hairline. It was the first time I'd ever smelled smoldering hair. An indelible memory, even without the reference to gas, Jews, and burning.

I could hear the fat on one side of the chop sizzling away, and began to smell the lamb. My mouth filled with saliva.

When the meat was broiled, my mother transferred it to a plate. She then spooned out some farfel—a side dish of tiny, pasta-like kernels made of flour and egg—scraped some of the caramel-ized bits of meat from the aluminum foil, and added them to the farfel. It tasted divine.

I ate alone at the kitchen table. At some point, it occurred to me that the playing field seemed rather uneven. My brother was out, his priority clearly teenage pursuits, and my parents were blithely going about their routine, their satiety an automatic solution to pangs of hunger, which occurred every few hours of every day including today. Meanwhile, I was lobbying the Big Guy to extend my lease on life for another year, a deity at whose admonishing insistence I was compelled to forgo food and water for twenty-four hours.

Why were they not afraid?

I posed the question to my parents….

"I don't believe in God!" my father ranted. "Where was he when the Nazis came, where was he when six million Jews died! Orthodox, not orthodox, they all went to the gas chambers!"

My mother, on the other hand, took a more diplomatic approach. "Well, I would fast, but I can't because I have an ulcer." Apparently, there was some fine print related to the fasting rule, an escape clause exempting certain people, namely the sick and the elderly. I felt that she qualified as the former; she had complained of stomach trouble often enough.

But when she was more inclined to talk about it, she, like my father, based her disillusionment with God on the fact that her father, whom she considered extraordinarily religious, kind-hearted, and humane, perished right along with everyone else. All his piety, devotion, supplication, countless "mitzvahs" (good deeds), which were manifestations of doing God's work on earth, didn't amount to anything.

104

Noah had an exemplary character, which was why he was chosen to repopulate the earth. What issue could God have had with her father, what bone to pick, that prevented Him from salvaging him from the human wreckage? The only feasible answer was that there were no magic tricks, just the exceptional capacity of humans to inflict suffering upon one another, unchecked, and unabatedly.

Then her pity would turn to scorn. She seemed to scoff at her father, poor, foolish man, helping others and being taken advantage of, naively believing in the good of humanity. What was his reaction when, instead of water coming out of the shower heads as promised, the sealed chamber filled with gas? She would go on about this, in essence blaming him, as if somehow, had he been less gullible, he might have seen the writing on the wall long enough to have packed his belongings, gathered his family together, and escaped before the borders were closed.

At other times she would tell a more Dickensian tale.

My grandfather owned a grocery store. He had the reputation in the town for being an honest, devout, good man. Life was simple enough. People came in to buy food and then paid for their purchases. In turn, my grandfather was able to care for his own family—a wife and four children.

Perhaps it was difficult to extrapolate what the results would be of the events that took place in September of 1939.

My mother remembers standing "all day" watching the German army roll into town, the spectacle of it. An endless parade. Wide and deep rows of soldiers, like toy soldiers coming to life, so robotic in their movements. Dressed impeccably in their uniforms, sun reflecting off shiny surfaces, illuminating helmets and rifles and buckles and jackboots. A mass moving as one. You can't help but be more amazed than terrified. However, it isn't Macy's annual Thanksgiving parade, which heralds the benign likes of Santa Claus, although the similarities are chilling. After the tens of thousands of soldiers, come the tanks and the placards depicting Hitler's stern countenance, repeated images that make your head spin like the ones Andy Warhol would popularize two decades later, of Marilyn Monroe, Jacqueline Kennedy, and Campbell's Soup. Today will change everything.

At the grocery store, the implications of occupation emerge. Jews are restricted from various activities, fired from their jobs, and placed under a strict curfew. A shocking number have been shot dead in the streets, just for emphasis.

Jews try to go about their daily business. Like ants after their hill has been destroyed by the whim of a kid kicking the mound with a running shoe, the ants pick up where they left off, adjusting to the new surroundings.

But now customers can no longer afford to pay for the food they buy from my grandfather. He accepts credit, cushioning the blow with acts of charity. My mother, who helps him in the store, is the one who balances the books and begins to notice that the people who don't pay are highly unlikely to pay in the future. She alerts my grandfather to this. He is unmoved. She doesn't understand him, thinks he's exercising poor judgment. He cannot convince her that asking for the money back, or stopping their credit, is an awful thing to do.

"Even if it means that our own family starves?" She takes his argument to the logical extreme. "That you would put your family at risk because customers can't pay for the goods you sell them? Do you really think that they wouldn't ask for the money back if they were in your shoes?"

"I can't answer for them."

"What if they're playing us for fools?"

He laughs at her tangential utterance. "That's not for us to know, or be concerned with. Each man has to answer to God and his own conscience. I can only do what I feel is right."

"But we have no money."

"God will provide."

That last point is completely lost on my mother, who sees the slow devolution of human nature all around, and as the desperation increases, like caged mice they turn against one another.

My grandfather is not a mouse, it seems. He doesn't waver in his actions, though his family is clearly suffering from the effects of his choices.

Then something very strange happens....

One day, an envelope appears at the family house. How it is delivered, and from whom, is a mystery. In it is money, enough money for the family to live on. Somewhere in the town is someone who has become my grandfather's savior. Someone who seems to know my grandfather's plight. Someone who is aware that my grandfather is trying to help his fellow people in these times of need, but is becoming increasingly unable to provide for his own family. Who is this "someone"? The family can only guess, but will never know, nor have the chance, ever, to express their deep gratitude. "God will provide" doesn't seem so far-fetched a belief. The money arrives faithfully and anonymously every single week, without fail, until life in the town takes an even uglier turn, from occupation to deportation.

It sounded to me like the show I'd watch on TV, *The Millionaire*, where a benefactor would give one million dollars to an unsuspecting recipient and watch what happened. Or Pip in *Great Expectations*. In my grandfather's case, his good fortune greased the wheels of perpetuating his charity towards others. Small comfort for my mother. Even her telling this story to me didn't for a second mitigate her deep wounds; it just reinforced the callous, arbitrary, and, most poignantly, Godless randomness of the way the world functioned, or dysfunctioned.

Years later, after the crematoria had cooled in Europe, the bits of skeletal remains that hadn't burned to ash had been swept away, and the bulldozers had tilled the soil with the bodies that filled the open graves, uproarious laughter emanated from a hotel in upstate New York.

It was roughly a two-hour drive from the Bronx, Brooklyn, Queens, Manhattan, Long Island, and the suburbs of New Jersey. Many of the Jews who made this journey had arrived in the U.S. before the turn of the century and through to the beginning of the First World War. Originally, they had come across the Atlantic as parents with little ones, or as young, single men looking for opportunity, or as young, married men scoping the situation before bringing over a wife and any children. Of the families that came, some of the siblings were born on North American soil; their children's children were for sure. These were called the "gaileh" (the yellows), the first generation, as opposed to the "greeneh" (the greenies), who were born overseas. Those who came from Europe after World War II were greenies.

Pogroms, and the hardships of immigration with its inherent poverty, were the stories of the gailehs' parents, and the trials of the Great Depression were the events that the gaileh themselves had gone through, which would stay with them forever. The horrible tales of relatives who were being murdered in Eastern Europe were sickening echoes, but these were second-hand experiences.

The gaileh had several decades more than the greeneh to establish themselves in the New Land. They went to school, had good jobs, were married, had children, bought homes. But they knew all about anti-Semitism on U.S. ground and tried to protect themselves as best they could with anglicized names, education, self-employment, and safe refuges. The Catskill Mountains provided the latter.

The Catskills loomed and beckoned. Nestled in amongst the verdant and fragrant pines were hotels that catered to their guests' every whim. "All-inclusive": your hands never had to reach for your "pocketbook," the American term for purse or wallet. Grossingers, the Nevele, the Concord, somehow became a Jewish Las Vegas. Jews vacationed there, ate, and were entertained. In the evenings, the women would dip into their safety deposit boxes and bring out their bracelets, earrings, necklaces, rings, brooches, hairpins, watches. Dressed in shimmering sequins and rich brocades, bodices supporting ample bosoms, clutching their bejeweled evening bags, which housed lipstick, a compact, Kleenex, and a room key, they paraded in the lobby, arms through their husbands' arms, until it was time to sit for dinner. The third "all you can eat" meal of the day was served. A buffet so splendid, sumptuous, and plentiful, as to leave nothing to the imagination.

After eating too much, the guests once more assembled casually in the lobby and waited until show time. Then the doors opened to the nightclub, and guests wended their way around tables and chairs to find seating that gave them the best view of the stage.

The voice-over introduced the comedian who would be the evening's act. His resumé was impressive: an ordained rabbi, coming from a family whose father and brothers were all rabbis. Choosing to be a comedian over being a rabbi was probably not the funniest moment in his life. The irreverent Jackie Mason, with his side-splitting, hair-raising brand of comedy, wowed the audience, who laughed until tears came, laughing at the unlaughable.

He enumerated the countless times Jews had struggled. "If it wasn't in Egypt, then it was Spain, the pogroms of Russia, the Holocaust. Why? Because Jews were the 'Chosen People,' which is supposed to be a good thing." And, quoting Sholem Aleichem, the Aesop of Yiddish tales, "If this is what it means to be the Chosen People," he looked up as if to speak to God, raised his arms, and shook his hands, "then why don't you choose someone else for a change!?"

My mother heard Jackie Mason's punch line in one of his comedic stints on TV, laughed, and agreed. But her sense of humor was a little different from the gaileh. When they laughed, it didn't shake their faith, their insides didn't rumble and ache because they were twisting with disheartened rage. The gaileh were moving on; some of the greeneh, like my parents, never could. The Holocaust was something that all Jews didn't feel equally, more a consequence of being human than of ethnic solidarity.

When I considered my parents' perspective on the existence of God, it seemed to me they had a good case, though I did have a brief resurgence of faith.

There was a possibility that God may have answered Darlene's feverish bedside prayers.

She might have used the words "Now I lay me down to sleep," but maybe God was moved by her sad predicament, or was attuned to another wish she imparted—that her father would stop beating her mother, that the shouting and screaming would end.

Maybe, in impassioned moments, bruised inside and out, her mother wished her father dead. Maybe God wasn't that adept at distinguishing the literal from the figurative, because, soon after the family moved into their first house, Sal was diagnosed with liver cancer. He died a few months later at the age of twenty-seven. Needless to say, the violence stopped. Did God work in mysterious ways, or what?

That too wore thin with counterpoints of how strange it was that He seemed to love a good riddle and had this penchant for being cryptic. Why didn't He just come out and say and do whatever He pleased. After all, He was God. Then there was the argument of free will, etc. But over time, in my mind, the pro-God side could not keep up.

Other circumstances conspired to erode my "belief." My religious friends moved to Jewish neighborhoods in North York, exchanging their old homes for brand new construction. My family wasn't going anywhere. Thus, distance diminished my sponsors' influence upon me. I completed my Hebrew education, in that I went as far as what was offered at the synagogue—three years. The fact that I was female meant that there was no big loss as far as the tradition went. In other words, I wasn't the target market. Even the feminine version of "bar"—the "bat" mitzvah—hadn't become the trend yet.

Most symbolic was that the synagogue, with its floor-to-ceiling, Chagallesque, stained-glass windows highlighting moments of the Old Testament, the sanctified structure that had housed the zeal of so many supplicants, turned out to be just another piece of real estate. It became the center for another culture and another religion: the Hungarian House. Then, forty years later, it was sold to condo developers.

So after a long, circuitous, lonely amble on the path of "The Jewish Way," I simply stopped walking.

Chapter 14

Watch and Learn

If the Jewish Way was a path, then the Secular Way was a vast field, and I was developing in a manner other than spiritual. I had reached a certain threshold. I could do things for myself, like get washed, make something to eat, put on a sweater when cold, wear a hat in the heat. I knew some history, geography, I could read and write, function arithmetically.

I knew something of the world at large, to whom I should be talking to and not. All the caveats that my parents drummed into my head had finally stuck. I was aware that there was more than only good in the world. For instance, despite the authority teachers wielded, injustices took place at recess that went unaddressed at the least, and unpunished at the worst.

I'd already gone through a rite of passage that every human must endure: the pangs of disappointment. At the age of four, I had the presence of mind to verbalize the following sentiment to my parents: "You hurt my feelings." Not much was done about it. Instead, my words hung in the air like a sign bearing a surname held at the airport, waiting to be recognized, but with no one coming forward. Another letdown was discovering that the sealed fireplace in the living room would make it impossible for Santa to come visit, and oh, by the way, Santa didn't apply to Jews.

Instead there was Hanukkah, a Jewish holiday, which offered, in my view, a ridiculously meager alternative. You could play with the "dreidel" (top), spinning it endlessly for little gain, perhaps even getting a few dollars in Hanukkah "gelt" (money), compared to being the recipient of many Christmas presents because people were mandated to buy them for you based on a list you'd sent to "Santa"; sing a Hanukkah song or two, no match for the melodious Christmas carols, which permeated airwaves and school hallways, or were sung by warmly-clad neighbors with good voices going door to door; listen to the Hanukkah story about a miracle of oil lasting eight days, compared to the Christmas tale of a virgin giving birth to the Son of God; you could eat "latkas" (potato pancakes) for Hanukkah, compared to a Christmas dinner of stuffed turkey, mincemeat pies, eggnog, and shortbread cookies; you could light the "menorah" (Hanukkah candle holder) one candle at a time until you reached eight, compared to being enchanted by the plethora of twinkling Christmas lights on the tree inside, as well as those outlining the perimeters of roofs, porches, and foliage. No contest.

We didn't even have a menorah. I suspect it was an ambivalent means by which my parents paid their respects and simultaneously rejected Judaism. My mother did buy special Ha-nukkah candles, a colorful assortment, which came in the distinctive blue box with its illustration of a lit menorah. The most fun I had was deciding which color to choose. Lighting a match and applying the flame to the candle's end to melt the wax made for a good contact, which adhered nicely to the top of the Campbell's Soup cans my mother decided would stand in for our menorah.

I had a vague notion that the future held more disappointments—the sad realization that things were not as advertised, and worse, that the fine print of disclaimers would ambush you and leave you with only yourself to blame.

I was allowed to go out on my own with friends, to Dufferin in the west, and to Bathurst in the east. Towards Bathurst were Woolworth's and Kresge's, two mainstays of the five-and-dime department store, competing for the retail market. Linens, towels, and clothing for the whole family, kitchen gadgets, sundries, and, of course, the lunch counter. Coffee was served in thick, almost indestructible china cups on matching saucers, as an accompaniment to muffins, pie, and sandwiches like toasted westerns. I had my very first grilled cheese sandwich there—salty and butter-soaked white Wonder Bread, melted Kraft cheese singles oozing and hot with every bite.

For more recreational activities, there was a movie theater at each end of my tether, the St. Clair, to the west, and the Vaughan, to the east, both roughly equidistant from where I lived. At the former I saw *Ben Hur*, and at the latter, *Sex and the Single Girl*.

I will never forget either movie.

Ben Hur—the dust being kicked up by chariots, and horses careening around the arena, the wheels of two chariots locking, metal shavings flying, the eardrum-popping sounds of iron grinding iron, the sand, the sweat, the blood, the poor lepers, and the unwanted Jews. Stalwart Charlton Heston starring as Ben Hur was as much of a stretch as Natalie Wood portraying the likes of Helen Gurly Brown, but film was a larger-than-life medium.

In *Sex and the Single Girl*, I was entranced with Wood's white, figure-hugging, knee-length dress with high heels to match, and the martinis shaken and poured as lubricant for Mel Ferrer's seduction tactic. Enter Tony Curtis, aka Bernard Schwartz, who looked every bit of tall, dark, and handsome.

What more education did I need?

But I still could not go out for long stretches of time or distance unaccompanied by adults. This meant that my parents' plans were mine too. My least favorite was the picnic. The outing happened once every summer. Food preparation took place the day before, an enormous effort my mother executed as she bustled about cooking this and that.

Chicken was barbecued on the rotisserie, a gigantic kitchen gadget that commanded the room, permanently mounted on a utilitarian, white enamel trolley. Stainless steel, and bigger than a bread box, with its own plastic cover and the formidable name of Black Angus, the rotisserie reeked of power. It was bought "in the States," that phrase meaning a place where you could get things of quality unavailable anywhere else.

When Black Angus was turned on, it had its own sustained cadence, which sounded like a cicada snoring. Any other electrical draw was eliminated to make way for it; essentials, like the few lights that had to remain on, suffered under the strain and showed their debility in a fluctuating dimness just shy of blowing a fuse. Meanwhile, potatoes jostled about in boiling water, the first step in the laborious process of refining them into skinless cubes, which then slithered around in mayonnaise along with chopped egg and diced Strub's kosher dill pickles.

Every kind of food wrap, from aluminum foil to plastic to waxed paper, was pressed into service, and then, one by one, items were packed into the soft-sided tote to be conveyed on the long trek. Liquids posed the greatest challenge, as lids often didn't live up to their promise of preventing spillage. We lived in the exasperated age between Bakelite and Tupperware. Having little money for luxuries like specific single-use items didn't help. My mother had to be resourceful.

One of the advancements of the times was instant coffee, which had the unfortunate consequence of forcing household percolators into retirement until fresh coffee made a decisive comeback, decades later. In the meantime, Maxwell House's "Good to the last drop" slogan promoted modernity and led the way in brand preference. Housewives looked for the telltale logo on the glass container—a cup on its side with one drop left—and readily reached for the product because lightening their workload was clearly more of a priority than coffee flavor.

Once the brown, powdery contents were consumed, my mother recognized that another use lurked in the forlorn container. My mother washed it out, eradicating its coffee smell, and then peeled off its identifying label. It seemed likely to work in theory, but in practice, when it was filled with liquid, it leaked. My mother tried different ways to secure the seal—aluminum foil to fatten the contact, or wedging the container in between other foods to restrict its movement. Her aftermarket ideas helped, but didn't solve the problem.

When all was said and done, there was always too much to carry. I came with my own baggage: swimsuit, a change of clothes, towel, hairbrush, flip-flops, bathing cap.

The first leg of the trip was traveling along St. Clair to Bathurst. Waiting for the streetcar, I was impatient and uncomfortable standing on the narrow, concrete landing strip, a sitting duck for the sun, cars whizzing by making me dizzy. Once on the streetcar, there were the twin indignities of the hot breath of outside air coursing in through the open windows, and my clammy, exposed skin sticking to the Naugahyde seats.

But the worst was the admonishment of the tiny, brass plaque reading "KEEP ARM IN," a shocking thought, as every child had either heard tell of some poor kid losing one, or had conjured up horrifying images of forearms being broken right off, flinging about—airborne bowling pins. It could happen if you were tempted to touch the oncoming streetcar as it rushed by, or because you were daydreaming, your arm dangling out feeling the breeze, not expecting the other streetcar to take up so much space. There was no warning before the two streetcars blew past one another in opposite directions, and the thunderous drum rolls of steel wheels on tracks meant it was too late.

From St. Clair to Bloor was the bus. That first step seemed so high, and if you didn't drop your money into the box, snatch the proffered transfer, and find a seat quickly, you were catapulted from one side to the other, bumping into people, or steadying yourself if you could grab one of the poles, if one was free. If, if, if. Prior to the Bloor/Danforth subway line, at Bloor you caught the streetcar all the way to High Park—more terror about keeping your arms in, which meant holding them both stiffly by your side, as if they would otherwise disobey. The large, permanent sign that read "High Park" meant only that the tedious trip to get there was over, but more tedium awaited.

Bags and blankets now had to be hauled, and a picnic spot found. Going deeper and deeper into the park was a given. Someplace near the wading pool with some privacy would be nice. Finding it would be a challenge, but eventually we would settle. The blanket was spread. In plentiful supply now during peace time, it was the same brand used on army cots to achieve those coveted hospital corners. Gray, itchy wool on itchy grass. I would stand as long as I could, then give in. Within minutes, tiny ants clamored up on the blanket and began to explore the expanse, negotiating the curve of a leg, or scurrying across a hand that propped up a semi-reclined body. More itch.

Since an authority in bathing trunks with a whistle and a clipboard had already scared me into thinking that I would choke on my own vomit and die if I ate before swimming, I chose to put on my swimsuit and go into the water before having lunch. I was a little leery about the complex process of changing from shorts and tops into a bathing suit behind the precarious curtain of a towel, which my mother held for me.

She seemed all too cavalier about the task of guarding my private parts from view, continuing to speak to the others—another couple and their daughter—without any letup, the towel at one moment going slack, to which I reacted with a loud "Mom!" through clenched teeth. Her trivializing comment—"Oh don't be silly, you have nothing"—was triply insulting, calling attention to my size, dismissing me, and talking out loud about "them."

True, I may have been flat-chested, but who would have given me the message that there was something to hide in the first place? Next time I wear my swimsuit under my clothes. Curious...swimsuit fashions for young girls. Mine had the semblance of a bodice with ruching for the breasts that I didn't have. To accentuate the places where bulges were absent, the fabric was a deep red. White, contrasting fabric puffed out to add contour to my undeveloped hips and came in at the top of my leg, held there by sewn-in elastic. Was this a form of training, or precursory styling, or some subversive idea that little girls' bodies were actually women's bodies in miniature?

I watched the little boys running around flagrantly bare-chested, their breasts looking exactly like mine, and I wondered why I had to endure a yoke halter around my neck, tied in a knot and then a bow, just in case some quirk of physics loosened the straps and the entire front fell forward revealing my imaginary bosom. Instead, the coarse cotton chafed my skin with every movement, the whole effect echoing in a ghostly, pale outline after a day in the sun.

I waded into the lukewarm pool, shocked that the water wasn't colder, looking around at babies' sopping, diapered bottoms, not quite able to link the two concepts with lateral thinking. Their shrill squeals made my ears hurt, and the crazed, careless splashes of the boys caused me to squint. Swimming was impossible. I made my way toward the round, concrete center of the pool at its greatest depth of three feet, smelling the dank mixture of leaching rust from steel bolts and brackets, soaked cement, and chlorinated pool water, which vanquished whatever bacterial secretion it came into contact with.

Leaving the pool meant wet feet wedging into dry flip-flops and then attracting loose bits of dirt and dead grass along the way—another visceral annoyance. While the towel felt good, it could not effectively prevent the persistent drips coming from between my legs, the last place to dry, drips that would trickle down to my feet, attracting more dirt, more grass.

My mother dispensed lunch on teetering plates weighted and weakened by potato salad on one side and folding helplessly in the middle, chicken pieces falling over each other. Beverages were poured into waxy Dixie cups. Once passed to me, the cup was in a constant state of "about to topple," to the point where it totally occupied one hand. I knew enough to be wary that, despite the appearance of flat blanket surfaces, the ground beneath would be uneven. With a drink in one hand and an ailing plate in the other, eating now became as elusive as the grape from Tantalus's reach.

Soliciting assistance, in the form of another hand, eventually made it possible for me to eat, but some extra taste was there that didn't quite match with the ingredients: infusions of plastics and chemicals, a symbiosis that had occurred during the time that ensued between earlier packing and later unpacking.

With two prescribed activities out of the way, it was now that I felt the pressure to make friends with the other couple's daughter, our kinship being presumed on the basis that we were the same sex and would therefore surely become best friends. Her name was Genya (the G as in "good," the e short). I could call her Jean, an anglicized approximation, but she was definitely not a Jean, maybe more of a Tatania. She and her parents preferred speaking in Polish and would defer to English for my benefit. My parents spoke Polish when they didn't want me to understand what they were talking about, so it always felt adult and exclusive to me.

Since Genya was older by a few years, it was tacitly agreed upon by both of us that she must be well beyond me in the ways of the world. And she was. Haughty, coquettish, superior, disdainful, devious. Though instinctively I didn't like her, I was fascinated at how she toyed with everyone and showed off. I noticed that she flirted with unquestionable certainty that this would yield her excellent results. And it did. Her mother convinced herself that her daughter was just extroverted, as if this were the only way she could make peace with Genya's suggestiveness. As for Genya, she looked upon me as a student in need of a mentor and was more than willing to show me the ropes

When the camera was brought out, Genya played to it, a concept completely foreign to me. In my environment, the camera was used sparingly, and I had only considered it as a means of freezing moments in time, moments that were actually happening, not manufactured.

But Genya staged photo ops, directed and starred in the shoot. Corralling her mother and leading her to the large maple, then pulling me over as well, Genya positioned us either side of her mother. She instructed her mother to put an arm around each of our shoulders, while Genya and I held hands, our arms extended in a waltz for three. Then she flung back her head, mouth agape, and broke role just long enough to order her father to take the picture. Mesmerized, I watched her instead of looking at the camera, forgetting completely that I too was in the shot.

The next one was of Genya and me. We sat on the blanket, legs straight and crossed at the ankles, arms outstretched, hands folded on our knees. Genya planned it out. I did the best I could at being told what to do. It was a strange posture for me; up till now, I had only been photographed either standing or seated. This seemed awfully grown-up. Our legs may have looked languorous in their length, but posing that way felt awkward to me.

Though the final instruction was perverse, I followed it anyway. I had always smiled, "*cheese*-ing" eagerly, while shutter buttons captured images. Sometimes I could hold the smile, and other times I would try to stop laughing, but I smiled each time. Genya insisted otherwise, and I felt I couldn't go against her. She looked at me sternly and said we weren't to smile; in fact, we were to frown, *on purpose*. I didn't know how to do that, so I watched her.

Her eyelids lowered halfway like a window blind blocking the sun, her mouth slightly pursed, chin a little raised, head tilted, she looked blasé. My turn. I used muscles in my forehead I'd never known about, muscles that conspired and then converged in the area between my eyebrows. I could barely see out from under the awning of skin I created. Then I concentrated on the corners of my mouth, forcing them down in an angry pout. Snap, the photo was taken, misleading all of eternity.

In a day so predictably tiresome, I learned something entirely new, which was at once invaluable and dangerous. Genya had taught me artifice.

Chapter 15

28" Glider

Money was always tight; that was a fact. But the accounts were perfectly balanced between the extremes of overspending and the available means, and though there was a narrow margin, the household was run efficiently and painlessly. The rent from the tenant paid off the mortgage, and my father's salary covered the rest. The first priority: quality food on the table. It was my mother who did the "books," a more satisfying power than she experienced with her own father, who wouldn't hear of solutions to their financial woes. Now she was the boss.

Every Friday, my father came home from work, and after supper, when the table was cleared, he handed my mother a small brown paper envelope. She sat at one end, and he at the other, watching. She opened the envelope and removed a neatly folded bundle of cash, his weekly earnings. On the front of the envelope were itemized notations and the sum.

He worked in the classic factory—the sweat shop—paid by the piece as a skilled laborer. Marx had written about him sympathetically, and so had Dickens. Then unions came in to rescue workers like him and protect them from the whims of their employers. His own boss was a gaileh, the son of an immigrant who came to Canada before the war. The disparity in social position between my father and his boss was great, though both were Jewish. The boss had been handed the business from his father, who had built it up from nothing. As gailehs were prone to do, the boss availed himself of all the opportunities Canada had to offer, the most significant being education. The boss's father and my father were peers—both immigrants and similar in age—but they may as well have been different species, one, a tree, the other, a car.

My father was a good worker, always arriving on time, doing his task as a cog in the wheel of a men's coats assembly line, completing sleeves for days on end, or collars, or back panels, before sending them off to the next tailor. He never complained, or tried to get away with anything, and remained employed for years and years. During union negotiations, he went along with the group and got lost in their numbers so as not to stand out. Once agreements were reached, he went back to being a dutiful employee and got lost in those numbers.

My mother scrutinized carefully the bookkeeper's math, making her own records on a sheet of paper. She always paused and then wavered, with pen in hand, before launching herself into writing, like an athlete poised and swaying before the big leap forward. Then she wrote quickly, the serifed font of European penmanship, stylized 1s and crossed 7s to stem any confusion between the two numbers, their forms so different from North American handwriting.

When she was satisfied that the totals were correct, she took the money and was given carte blanche to do with it whatever was needed. My parents were trendsetters in their circle of friends. The other men in their group put their wives on strict allowances, with the unfortunate effect that wives at times squirreled away some of the money to be used for items the men would never have agreed to, which was why their husbands would remain none the wiser. My parents had implicit trust in one another, and neither one ever betrayed it.

Another unfortunate reality of the "shmata" business (literally meaning rag, but in this context, clothing) was that fashion had its seasons, and with coats, the seasons were fall, winter, and spring. Production would stop for a few weeks several times a year. The implications were serious: no coats, no money.

My mother planned for these periods of drought, not an easy task. There were no credit cards to tide them over, no relatives to lend a helping financial hand. Just number projections. Yet there was never a letup in the services my brother and I received, no noticeable want for anything that we were used to when there was money coming in.

For me, these interruptions in my father's work were celebratory. All through elementary school it was the same. At 12:00

noon the lunch bell rang, and students poured out of open doors, like rivers flooding their banks come spring. My father always arrived a few minutes early so that I'd never be waiting. We'd walk home together, have lunch, and then he'd walk me back to school. That was our routine. It was wonderful to have his company. His unobtrusive, watchful presence exuded safety.

With his indefatigable patience, he had already proved to be a good playmate as a never-ender to my skipping rope. Now he would be my athletic coach. He was the one who taught me the skill invaluable for any Canadian kid: how to skate. Though I suspect he'd never skated in his life, either he knew instinctively the principles involved and could communicate them to me, or I was a natural—a more remote possibility.

Handy Atlas parkette had its very own rink, otherwise known as the basketball court once the ice thawed. On the day in question, my father and I walked over to the rink. I sported my brand new figure skates with their white skate guards, slung over one of my shoulders by their laces tied up in a bow, just like the big kids. Proper-fitting footwear was not to be compromised. Hand-me-downs were out of the question. My parents never scrimped on these things. Somehow, there would be money for items deemed worthy. New skates saved my feet and my reputation, kids not being the most forgiving when it came to suspecting poverty.

I sat on the bench while my father helped with my skates, his fingers stronger than mine, risking the cold to get the best grip. He pulled each lace until he felt resistance, and asked me if it was too tight. When I said no, he continued. The first section complete, there was one more decisive tie before crisscrossing and looping the laces around the series of hooks, which were lined up in twos up my shin. My feet were protected by two layers of socks. There were no special hockey socks for girls, no feminine version of the ubiquitous gray wool knit, its broad, white band at the top, with one red stripe running through it.

Skating was much more difficult than it looked. I stood shakily, every slight movement slippery, a foreign sensation given that our bodies rely on our feet to stop us from toppling over. I was the same as every kid starting out, arms hanging forward for bal-

123

ance, looking like a miniature ape, back tilted at seventy-five degrees, sliding despite every effort not to. One false move, a few Russian dance kicks in the air, arms circling in reverse, and backwards you fell, hard, on the ice. Propelling oneself and gaining speed, as the antidote to the fear of falling, seemed to defy all logic, like convincing yourself to dive headfirst into water for the first time.

My father helped right me again and again as needed, encouraging me to put one skate in front of the other, push off, and trust the momentum. Eventually it worked. All I had to learn was how to stop, but for now, the accomplishment of gliding around the rink held much more glamour, so snow banks or my father's arms to break my speed would have to do.

That took care of winter sports.

Spring meant bicycles. Training wheels were lost on me; I couldn't "feel" what the body needed to do to create balance, because the two baby wheels did that for you. I had to learn without those aids. Legs on either side of the bike, placing the bike wheel just so for equal weight distribution, one foot on one pedal, the other foot poised on toes—that was the starting position. I could feel the total support coming from the palm of my father's hand on the back of the seat. My other foot lifted and went to the pedal. Then, a gentle push. Short-lived, but after several tries, success.

The pivotal moment came at Hillcrest Park. Somehow I had acquired the use of someone's bike for the occasion, a 24" wheel, a little small for me, but perfect for a beginner because the ground to be reached in case of a fall would be that much closer. The concrete surround of the wading pool provided a stable surface, the circle not too tight to make turning an issue in the already steep learning curve.

I didn't remember having to beg and beg, or painstakingly amass enough allowance to pay for it, or do chores in order to earn it. In non-Jewish homes, and on TV shows like *Leave It to Beaver*, that was the standard practice of teaching your children fiscal responsibility. For me, the omission of this important parental lesson didn't on any level give rise to the mistaken notion that "money grew on trees," though the image was lovely. I was as aware as I could have been that my father eked out a living, and that my mother prudently disbursed his salary. What they did impart was that quality was worth spending money on. Frugality, when it came to good, nutritious food, proper clothing, certain household items, etc., was disgraceful.

There were things my family could do without, a third blouse or jacket for instance, and even a car. I knew that in Grade One we all wore the same clothes through the week, and it was nothing that any of us felt was shameful or dirty, or signified being less privileged. But, like skates, certain possessions seemed to make the "must have" list. And so one day I was informed that I would be getting a bike.

On a Thursday after my father got home from work, when the stores were open until 9:00, he and I got on the streetcar, then the subway to the Queen Street station, and followed the signs to Eaton's.

Sporting Goods was on the lower level—a vast array of merchandise, the air heavy with the pungent, rubbery smell of bicycle tires and tennis balls.

There they were, lined up diagonally, all the front wheels turned to the same side, standing like ballerinas at fourth position in the classroom. CCM was *the* name in bikes and hockey equipment. I already had envisaged what my bike would look like: bright red frame, 26" wheels, whitewall tires. There was one exactly like it at the store. We talked it over with the sales clerk. The trend that lay ahead was the speed bike. A forerunner of the ten- was the three-speed. I considered it, and knew this was the way of the future. I also felt instinctively that I would use my feet, rather than my hands, to stop forward movement, and the slight delay to think first rather than act felt dangerous to me. So I declined.

As a point of comparison to the red, he pulled out another bike. Electric blue frame, 28" wheels, white fenders, black wheels. Girls' bikes had a dropped bar, unlike the boys'. As kids, we all speculated why, and somehow came up with a bizarre idea that girls could "hurt themselves" on the horizontal bar. Bolder tellers of this "fact" would go so far as to say it would "make girls lose their virginity," or those who knew the anatomical term would say, "It would break their hymens." Later bike models were more gender-bending in their designs, as girls became less interested in the girl/boy bike distinction or, more importantly, had debunked the "fact." I, however, felt that whatever protected me from injury was perfectly fine, and at the age of nine I wasn't inclined to activism.

What appealed to me about the bike was its color, an unusual hue more akin to boys' colors; maybe gender-bending had already begun. The other factor was more subtle. The dropped bar had a gentle curve in it that wasn't simply and practically parallel to the frame, as with the red one. The serifed font, which said *Glider* on the bar, evoked in language what the design had captured in the curve. Either I had an aesthetic sense early on, or I was the target market for a well-thought-out ad campaign. Either way, I was enchanted.

But the blue bike was also more expensive than the red one. It cost sixty dollars. I remember my father and me exchanging glances, holding each other's gaze as thoughts were transmitted back and forth. I was of the mindset to get whichever one my parents felt they could afford, and my father would have given me the one I wanted most. It was a touching moment. In deciding between the blue and the red, we agreed that buying the larger one made sense since I was still growing, and that the extra cost was jus-tified by the difference in their sizes. The blue *Glider* was mine.

The bike would be delivered COD by the elegant Eaton's truck. COD, "cash on delivery," was a system that reflected a variety of social and economic norms, specific to the time, which fell by the wayside as "the climate" changed. One attitude that existed was trust. Eaton's was confident that when your parcel arrived you would be at home, ready and able to pay in cash. That meant that Eaton's drivers carried around quite a lot of money by the end of the day. You could also pay by check, uncertified. Stay-at-home moms, solvent customers, and delivery schedules that were prearranged and prompt ensured successful transactions.

Hindsight would have pegged the drivers as easy targets for assault and robbery; customers would have soured the deal if they emerged without the cash, or bounced their checks. Outsourcing delivery jobs left customers with tedious, all-day waits and no way

126

to ask the driver when to expect the parcel. After two-income families became the standard, lost wages became collateral damage of taking a day off work to wait for a parcel to arrive, adding fury to tedium. But we were safe from all that for another decade anyway.

My bike arrived faithfully, and safely COD, all shiny and stylish. I loved looking at it, how every part of it had been thought through. The white plastic handle grips, the vinyl seat upholstered in white in the front where it narrowed and in blue at its widest. The white fenders, black tires, blue frame. There were accessories to adorn it. I didn't go in for streamers much. Something about them felt gauche. But a bell, that was a must, inconspicuous yet announcing. A basket would have come in handy, but would have ruined the lines, so I left that one for a time when function might trump form.

My seat was adjusted to the lowest position, with all that room to grow. I could stand comfortably, one foot on either side of the bike, the dropped bar creating lots of space, and push off from there, one foot on the pedal. When I got fancy, I would imitate the boys, clearing the horizontal bar with a graceful move that lifted the leg straight up from the side of the body and extended it out and up, then over to rest on the pedal on the other side, like getting on a horse.

I was mobile, a thrill that would never leave me as I graduated from bikes to cars. The 28" wheels provided a lofty view; I found myself stretching my upper body even a little higher to make the most of it. My traveling range was Davenport to the south, Avenue Road to the east, Dufferin to the west, and Eglinton to the north. The most frequent trip was down Arlington to Tyrell, and then either left or right amid the gracious homes and verdure that surrounded Hillcrest Park.

Kids with bikes weren't hard to come by. I thought of us as a bicycle gang, though the connotation of gang was purely benign and could easily have referred to a group of co-eds in bobby socks and poodle skirts, off to the soda parlor.

Hillcrest Park was a worthy destination. It was the neighborhood recreational facility, which offered the standard amenities of a wading pool, grounds for picnicking and strolling, and a play area for children. And then there was the tennis court, which distinguished this park from other parks—a testament to the surrounding real estate with its large lots, big homes, in a word, money. The original idea for having a community tennis court may have been to make public a hitherto "private club" activity. Billboard ads, with Barbie- and Ken-like figures in tennis duds walking down the street for a rally, would have captured the ethos.

In the summer, children of the well-to-do in the area would be exposed early to cute white outfits, Tretorns—the name in tennis shoes—and an endless supply of plastic cylinders containing freshly buoyant, fuzzy, neon green balls, three to a package. In winter, the children would find themselves on a beginner slope, wearing ski paraphernalia, which they would quickly outgrow, only to be re-equipped seasonally without a second thought.

But Hillcrest Park was just beginning to "decline." This could not have been foretold. Many variables contributed to who would reside there, based, perhaps, on which immigrant group was disembarking in Halifax. Thus, the park's demographic changed. The wealthy who had originally settled there had moved, or were on the move.

A fellow student, and friend for a short time in Grade Six, was a perfect example. Her family was constrained by the quaint neighborhood. They were already showing a preference for modern design. The father sporting around in his silver Jaguar XKE convertible; a contemporary sculpture of a huge, white, concrete die on the front lawn, sitting on one of its points, three diagonal dots visible on each facet, indicating their street number, so incongruous with their traditional, red brick home. It wasn't a surprise when they bought a very sizable lot in Etobicoke, hired an architect, bade farewell to the staid designs of the early 1900s, and built instead a '60s mod home with wall-to-wall broadloom, an en suite bath and private balcony for each bedroom, a laundry chute, intercom, and whatever other conveniences money could buy.

Those of us who still lived in the area inherited the park. Tennis would be a steep social climb regardless, so whether the court's surface was asphalt or concrete, it wouldn't have mattered to me. Even to my untrained eye, it was obvious that the tennis courts

128

were being neglected. Dips in the surface created tiny pools in the rain; cracks and missing bits were numerous. It would be hard to justify the allocation of municipal funds for repairs, and private money had forwarding addresses. So the courts, nets sagging and catching leaves, stood as a reminder of a previous, more pristine time. Ignoring the state of the courts, some brave novices bought cheap rackets and a package of balls, struggled first to hit the ball over the net, then to try to keep the ball inside the lines, and finally faltered while chasing a wonky serve, only to return one even wonkier.

For us members of the bicycle gang, the park had everything we needed. There were paved paths designated for pedestrian use, which made pedaling easy, and when we rode on them we felt the thrill of being rebels. The playground was worth at least fifteen minutes. At the swings, we improvised by flipping over the leather baby seats, flattening them, getting on, pumping with our legs to a dizzy height until we could hear the grinding noise inside the steel pipes, feel the jolting chains, then bring our shoulders forward and let go before jumping off.

Then to the teeter-totter, where it became clear in an instant who weighed more. The lighter one was on guard. At any moment, the heavier one could bear down with enough force to send the other one up off the seat, and then back on with a smash—another alleged way for girls to get "injured." Or, after co-operatively teeter-tottering and creating a feeling of trust, either one could just slip off the seat, unbeknownst to the one still on, who would then crash to the ground.

The roundabout was another fun stop. It was meant to give little ones a ride. Older siblings or parents walked briskly beside, hanging on to one of the rounded steel bars that radiated from the center, then letting go and watching the roundabout go round and round, the young riders laughing delightedly until it slowed to a halt. We came up with a different game, but the roundabout had to be unoccupied. Running headlong beside it, pushing against the bar with all our might until we reached maximum speed, we would then jump on for a woozy ride….

129

That was what was supposed to happen. There was a simple explanation for why many an ankle got twisted in the attempt. It was called physics. Years of turning and turning and turning had created a narrow, deep groove around the perimeter of the roundabout. The space between the groove and the edge of the roundabout was slight. One false move and then…intense pain. It was still a risk many of us were willing to take.

Off to the slide. The large slide, of course. We ensured that the slide was as slippery as possible and then went down head first. Next, a little, upper body workout on the monkey bars. Finally, a silly moment, careening about every which way on the cartoonish duckies and chickens, straining the heavy, spiral coils that connected the plastic body to the steel base, our feet on the tiny rests, our legs wide open and bent because we were too big.

The edge of the park led to a wooded and steep slope, at the bottom of which was busy Davenport Road. Early in our schooling, we had learned that the top of this slope was the former shore of Lake Iroquois. The fact fascinated me, as I imagined wading into the lake and then continuing down as the water got deeper and deeper. All of the surrounding area would have been submerged.

If nature called, there was a little "house" to go to. A utility building really, comprising a clubhouse for the tennis courts, a place to store arts and crafts supplies for activities run by Parks and Rec, and washrooms. There seemed to be an austere style that Toronto architects were going for in public buildings such as these, and in water treatment facilities. I found them beautiful.

The structure had wide stone steps and a shady, cool porch. Once you were inside, any sound echoed, bouncing off the concrete floors, which were covered in glossy paint for ease of cleaning. The women's washroom, which was in the basement—cavernous and prison-like—had a small, opaque window near the ceiling, not big enough to dissipate the smell, mostly foul, but with a waft of industrial-strength cleanser. The door had a solid latch. My worry that the latch's pin wouldn't fit into its other half was unnecessary. Other latches in previous experiences weren't so reassuring. Either they were broken, or the doors or frames had shifted, contracted, expanded. Taking the risk of exposing oneself literally, and adding in the potential for interruption and certain embarrassment, was not a pleasant prospect. At least in this bathroom I could relax.

There was one toilet, an elongated, heavy, black, wooden seat with an opening in the front, a cold, sweating, porcelain base, a pipe at the back going up the wall, with a lever attached for flushing. Young behinds took up about a third of the sitting space. It felt like I could fall in. On the wall beside me was a small, stainless steel, paper dispenser, on which was etched humbly the company name "Onlywon." Their name may have said it all. These dispensers were in every possible public washroom space. Scratchy crepe, thin, and surprisingly non-absorbent, the tissue was obsessively folded, one sheet neatly enclosed in the next and so on, through to the last. You pulled from the bottom of the dispenser, drawing out the tissue between two steel edges curled back like a scroll to create a slit.

As I became more adventurous, I biked to the definitely upscale Winston Churchill Park, at the southeast corner of Spadina and St. Clair. It was situated on a big chunk of land, had an active tennis club, steep tobogganing hills, and the infamous ravine that terrified me when I was younger.

The ravine, it was rumored, was rife with hobos, nefarious in their intent, unlike Red Skelton's much-loved, country bumpkin TV character, Clem Kadiddlehopper. A hobo, as the legend went, was a twisted mix of poverty and sexual deviance. Hobos could lure you into the ravine and molest you, their immorality surpassed only by their destitution. I never did actually see one, but I would shiver noticeably going by, even if I was on the north side of St. Clair, with two sets of streetcar tracks and four lanes of traffic between. In time, the ravine would be purged of its ills, and a path cleared for well-heeled joggers and cyclists and those out for a stroll.

When I was on my bike, I had no obvious address. Having that kind of mobility freed me from the sequestered living space that was at once a source of anonymity and shame. Coming home was a little like Cinderella after the ball, the carriage turning into vermin again. The tiny vestibule at the foot of the looming stairs wasn't long enough for the bike to fit. The door to the apartment wouldn't open wide enough either. These annoyances took away some of the splendor of the activity.

I opened the door, wedged the front wheel in, and lifted the bike so that it rested precariously on the third stair. This meant that I could get the other end inside, with just enough room to close the door behind me. Then I backed the bike down and off the stairs. Still, the front wheel wasn't aligned with the rest of the bike. At best, it was turned away from the wall, taking up valuable access to the first stair. At worst, it would collapse unexpectedly with a tremendous bang and a clang when I was nowhere near it and scare me out of my wits.

Every spring meant the dawn of biking season, and at the end of every fall, the bike was brought in and stored. And so went the routine, until one summer, when I was just shy of my mid-teens, and my brother asked if he could borrow the bike to use instead of his car in the area around his apartment.

I had already begun to question whether he was a liability to me, though I was still in awe of him. Maybe it was because I had been hurt many times when my veneration for him wasn't reciprocated. Maybe I felt that he hadn't shown me enough gratitude for saving his life from the hood. Maybe it was the time that he came to me asking for a handout. I found it quite unsettling that I, a sibling six years his junior with limited ways to make money, as I was not legally employable, was in a position to bail him out. I reluctantly agreed to lend him the bike, and also remember catching a whiff that my brother regarded my hesitation as selfish. I second-guessed myself. I was innocent of the charge, yet somehow felt implicated, and caught by the devil's advocate.

Not long after that, my brother informed me the bike had been stolen. To redress my loss, he had procured a gold, 26", white-walled Raleigh with a plastic, wicker, rainbow-colored basket. But it felt more like duplicity than compensation. I did ride it though, would have to, since the reality was my own bike was gone.

Even in a random universe, there were days when something struck you oddly. How it became determined that, on a particular afternoon forty years hence, you'd go to an area of the city you didn't frequent. Why it would be that, for a short spell, you'd decide to be a passenger rather than the driver. That chance would have it, the only parking spot available, though at first you tried the side you were on, was on the opposite side of Roncesvalles Avenue. That upon opening the passenger door, the one piece of information at eye level from a seated position was the word *Glider*. There it was. Could it be the one that I had owned? Still, it was the exact same model out of the Eaton's inventory. The many times it might have changed hands, to become the present owner's vintage bicycle, was a question that couldn't be answered. There it stood before me, locked to a meter pole, a little worse for wear, but with an indomitable spirit emanating from its serifed font, still gliding after all these years.

Chapter 16

Siblings...

My admiration for, and frustration with, my brother began at an early age. Photos supplied information that was missing in memory. In one of them, the bewildered look on my two-year-old face said it all. In another, I was proud as a peacock, perched on my father's shoulder, close to the tree my brother climbed—the little sister copycat, as if I'd achieved what my brother had. The same day, a third photo was taken of the two of us; I'd been wrestled to the ground, looking perplexed and irritated, legs akimbo (underwear showing), my head bent into my chest, restricting my breathing, my brother holding me from behind, beaming, unaware of the effect of his grip.

What I remember as the pattern of interaction between us was this: I was ever hopeful for my brother's attention and generally devastated by his lack of regard for me, which I attributed to not having that much to offer him. I guess we were agreed on my "usefulness." But that didn't stop me from trying.

I was aware of him at all times, looking for him through the bars of my crib in my parents' bedroom on the top floor of the three-room flat we rented on McCaul Street before we moved to St. Clair. He slept on the fold-out couch in the tandem living room, where my mother would sit every afternoon at 1:30 in addictive anticipation of the next episode of *As the World Turns*.

I remember the fun ride my brother and I shared in the back of the mover's truck on the way to our new place. Prior to when seat belts and car seats were mandated because they saved children's lives, there we were together, like equals, giggling at being catapulted from one side of the truck to the other, cushioned by clothing and other belongings and enjoying our incapacitation, as mere pawns of left and right turns and bumps on the road.

I loved him dearly, even when I witnessed him making me a delicious beverage of milk, Nestlé's Quik Chocolate Powder, and a heaping tablespoon of Ajax Cleanser. I was reasonably assured that, had I been prepared to take the elixir, he would have prevented me from actually drinking. But it never got to that point. I had some prior knowledge that Ajax was poisonous if ingested, so I wittingly declined the offer.

I loved him, even though he tricked me repeatedly, relying on my ignorance of whatever was the latest antic he'd learned from his schoolmates in the art of taking advantage of the lesser species.

"Come on." He proposed a deal: "Hit me as hard as you can."

I hesitated.

"Come on."

He seemed to be insisting. I didn't get it, though. Why would he be inviting the prospect of physical pain?

"But it'll hurt you." I said.

"It's okay…really. Come on, as hard as you can."

I thought about it. I did want to hurt him, at least a little. After all, he deserved it. From the "Indian sunburns," which left my forearms smarting, to any number of Three Stooges stunts, like the one where Moe is holding Curly at arm's length, the palm of Moe's hand anchored on Curly's forehead, Moe's forearm locked, Curly boxing and swiping futilely at Moe, who is just out of reach. Or Moe's famous "Pick two fingers"…only to find you're poked in the eyes. And then, when you get wise to the prank and try to return the favor, up goes his hand to his nose, creating the perfect barrier to retaliation.

Revenge swelled inside me; I saw opportunity. I looked at my brother for signs of dissembling. There was nothing behind his back. Both hands were visible. We sat kitty-corner to one another at the kitchen table. Nothing was underneath. His one hand was placed before me, palm down, fingers outstretched, waiting for "it."

"You're going to move your hand at the last minute!" I called his bluff.

"Nope, no I'm not."

"I don't believe you," I challenged.

"I'm not, I won't move it, I promise."

He sounded earnest, but I wasn't entirely convinced.

He continued. "Look. I won't move my hand, I swear. You can hold my arm down with all your weight if you want. I'M…NOT…GOING…TO…MOVE…MY…HAND."

"Swear to God and hope to DIE?" I was banking on the notion that even an atheist might have trouble saying this.

"Yes."

"Say it."

"I said, yes."

"That's not enough."

"Okay…I swear to God and hope to die!"

I looked him over for signs of crossed fingers or legs. He was clean.

I was keenly aware of vestiges of misgiving within me, but like fog dissipating, the outlook seemed fair.

"Okay. What do want me to do?"

"Hit me as hard as you can."

"All right, you asked for it."

His palm was on the table, a sitting duck for what was about to happen. I made a fist.

"You sure?" I gave him one last chance.

"Yes."

I brought my fist down on his palm, in an act that was unfamiliar to me, and then quickly looked at him with an expression of regret.

"Come on," he said. "You can do better than that."

"Didn't it hurt?" I was surprised.

"No. Try again. Harder this time."

"You're joking."

"No. It didn't hurt at all."

Maybe there was restraint in my "blow." He didn't seem to be in any real discomfort. I suppose I could muster more strength and try to deliver a harder punch.

I upped the ante. "Well?"

"It still didn't hurt."

"What's wrong with you?" I looked at him as if he were an alien.

"Nothing. You're not hitting me hard enough."

His supportive feedback helped, and I was able, with his reiterated assurances, to get to the point where I felt unencumbered by his feelings.

Now I was determined to have an impact. His pain would be my glory. I whacked him with all my might.

The moment passed....

I searched his face for evidence of extreme bodily harm. Nothing.

I shook my head in disbelief. "You're not hurt."

"No. Not at all."

"How can that be?"

"Well, it just doesn't hurt."

I had to agree. He wouldn't have been able to hide that from me; I would have detected the slightest wince.

"Hmm..." I pondered.

"Okay, now it's you turn," he said cheerily. I blithely placed my hand on the kitchen table.

My nociceptors worked exceptionally well. They faithfully relayed the message, by means of electrical impulses, along my peripheral nerve to my spinal cord. There they entered my dorsal horn and released chemicals—neurotransmitters—which then activated a gaggle of nerve cells that convened to process the information before sending the message to my thalamus, the sorting and switching station in my brain. The message was delivered to three brain regions for optimal comprehension: my somatosensory cortex, which was able to understand my physical state; my limbic system, which was able to understand my emotional state; and my frontal cortex, which instructed me on how to think about it. Finally, the message was vocalized in a pre-linguistic expression which, spelled phonetically, was:

"OOOOOOOOOOOOOOOOOOOOOOOOOOOOOOOWWW WWWWWWWWWWWWWW!!!"

I glared at him with the look of deep betrayal a child feels when first harmed by a formerly loving source.

"YOU SAID IT DIDN'T HURT!!!!!!!"

"But it didn't," he maintained, through stifled chuckles, trying to assuage my anger, and yet still feeling the thrill of successfully duping me.

"YOU ARE SUCH A LIAR!!!"

"Look. I'll prove it to you."

It was then that he showed me the trick.

When he placed his hand on the table, he made sure that his palm was slightly raised. That provided a buffer, a space to cushion the blow, he explained as he demonstrated the difference to me. All this information was supposed to make me feel better and send me on my way to perpetrate this act upon future, unsuspecting victims. Clearly, he had learned this first-hand, so to speak, from another elder, and so the lesson got passed on in the underground training facility that benchmarked these rites of passage among the young. It was a mixed blessing for me.

After an adjustment period, during which I licked my wounds, I came around soon enough and renewed my devotion to him. I knew everything about him, what he did, whom he knew. I could name everyone in every class photo of his. I knew his teachers' names, what he was studying, when his tests were, where he was going when he went out, and with whom. I knew which girl he liked and why. I concurred with him, from looking at his class photos, as to who were the "dogs" and who were the "lookers." I knew when his ink cartridges for his fountain pen needed to be replaced, when his colored pencils needed sharpening. I marveled at his slide rule.

Whenever I could, I either copied, or competed, to inglorious results. It was during the phase when one compulsively practiced one's signature that I felt I'd never catch up to him. The uniform slant of his cursive writing, though illegible, looked impressive. All the more, compared to my still awkward printing. Any surface that existed had his signature on it. That included whatever was mine, like my school photo. On the left side, there were spaces to list one's classmates. His name was in a number of those spots. I returned the favor, though I couldn't manage to stay within the confines of the lines and spaces. Instead of feeling good that I had defaced his property, I was upset at the substandard state of my small motor skills. My intrusiveness had little effect on him anyway, as he was on to the next thing, which was inventing a middle name to add pedigree and extend his signature's length. This enabled him to initialize his first two names and be like J.P. Morgan, E.P. Taylor, J.F. Kennedy, or to pare it all down to monogram size on fantasy towels, sheets, robes, and ascots. My brother chose Bartholomew, and thus became JBG.

My enchantment with him peaked when he was in high school. I followed him about, hung out in his room for as long as possible before he noticed me, got annoyed, and kicked me out.

His was a proper bedroom, albeit most of the furniture had been acquired randomly for the tenants to use during their short stint living with us. He had a desk, which my parents had purchased from Eaton's for him, with drawers that housed all of his school supplies, pens, pencils, rulers, erasers—one for pencil, one for ink—a small stapler, typewriter paper, stencils for school project titles, Magic Markers, which made you woozy when the tops were removed, and so on.

A bookcase he'd built, which was fortified by the books on the shelves rather than by the nails he'd hammered, stood beside the desk. There was a wooden, utilitarian chair my parents had as an extra. He'd stripped off the paint and restained the chair to match the desk, the final woodworking undertaking that confirmed carpentry would not become a hobby of his. The rough patches from impatient sanding and bumpy shellac told the tale. An old dresser with a mirror, which went with the double bed, completed the room.

A map of the world was taped to the wall above the desk. He knew where all the faraway places were, like Zanzibar and Tahiti, knew all the nations' capitals. A music stand was permanently set up, so that my brother could pore over the trumpet part in the score of one Broadway musical after another. Lerner and Loewe, Rodgers and his counterparts—Hart, Kern, and Hammerstein.

Though many of the songs had worked their way into my consciousness because they were popularized on the radio and on

140

TV, the thick, heavy scores provided repeated access to the melodies and the lyrics. My brother rehearsed the songs until he perfected them, and I learned the words because I would go into his room when he wasn't there and practice. While I did love the music, my primary motivation was to be doing what he was doing.

Playing an instrument in high school differentiated the academic students from the others. An educational edict that was prevalent at the time streamed students either towards Grade Thirteen and on to university, or to finish Grade Twelve to pursue something technical, mechanical, or commercial. There were no hybrids, no sense that the two streams could be combined in any way. So, if you took music, you weren't permitted to take typing, a skill that would find many "academics" less adept than their "commercial" counterparts, once the computer age told hold. Maybe the meek did inherit the earth on that front.

It was no mystery, among the teaching staff, that those who took music were "better" than the others, and allowances were constantly made to accommodate the needs of the music program. Even the system of alphabetizing the classes, though perhaps a coincidence, was strikingly similar to a form of evaluation. 9/10/11/12/13 A and B were the music students, and the rest up to K referred to everyone else. Someone in 11F might easily have felt at a disadvantage.

If you were in music, you played in the orchestra or the band, and some played in both. Though being in music was a status symbol in itself, the band was perceived as being more hip than the orchestra, and clearly band music was more modern than classical.

The trumpet had its own cachet. The parts written for it featured it prominently, rather than simply using it to accompany the melody. Also, within the trumpet section, there were preferential parts for first trumpet, as opposed to second and third. Out in the real world, Herb Alpert and the Tijuana Brass topped the charts. Someone who was in the band and playing first trumpet had a lot going for him. At the time, a female playing first trumpet was rare.

My brother played the trumpet well. I knew, because I tried it myself. He showed me how to hold it, one hand around the base of the valves, the other atop the valves, pinky and thumb securing your hand to allow the other three fingers the freedom to manipulate the various combinations of valve depression that would produce sounds. You had to lick the mouthpiece, make sure all moving parts were well lubricated, and you were ready to play.

I brought the instrument to my lips and caught the faint, funky scent of saliva coating the inside of the tubes. There was a special lever at the bottom to release saliva when enough had built up inside, and you could hear the crackling sounds from liquid molecules being propelled by breath. Periodically, I watched my brother trip the lever and force a blast of air that would empty the tubes, droplets of saliva disappearing into the red velvet lining of the tiny compartment in the trumpet case, which housed the second mouthpiece

Poised and ready, I pursed my mouth, or embouchure, the technical term, and exhaled my breath in a burst. The sound was primal at best, more akin to farting than to music. I pushed down on the proper valve with its mother of pearl top, which felt tepid compared to the cool metal and brass of the rest of the body, and tried to play a note or two. Not so easy. When I lowered the trumpet away from my face, a telltale, red pressure spot on my upper lip was left over from the endeavor. Suddenly, I remembered that Satchmo's was permanent. I looked at my brother, a wave of concern coming over me, but in a few minutes the mark had gone.

I handed over the trumpet, and he did all the preliminary, trumpetty gestures that indicated he knew what he was doing. Like DJs, with their earphones worn one ear on and one ear off, jerking their body to the beat, the trumpeters had their own ritual. They would lick their lips boldly a number of times and limber up by fluttering their three fingers on the valves to prepare for performing.

And then he'd play. From *Carousel*, the exuberant "June Is Bustin' Out All Over," the heartfelt and musing "If I Loved You," and the haunting, heroic anthem "You'll Never Walk Alone." From *Oklahoma*, "Oh What a Beautiful Mornin'," "A Surrey with the Fringe on Top," "I Can't Say No" (a song that became the joke about the high school slut), "People Will Say We're in Love," and the musical's eponymous number—the pride of the state—"Oklahoma." It was the same with *Brigadoon, South Pacific, The King and I, Flower*

Drum Song, The Sound of Music, Show Boat, My Fair Lady, and *West Side Story.*

But "Trumpeter's Lullaby" was the ultimate virtuoso performance, because of the technically demanding triple-tonguing sequences that dominated the piece. It was very hard work, first to use your tongue to create the staccato effect of the triplets, and then to bring it all up to speed. He did very well.

Many of his friends were also in the band, so socializing outside of band practice would be the natural result. I knew them all by name, had met them as the little sister, watched them barrel in to collect my brother—boisterous and booming boys—and then file out, leaving me in a black hole of silence once the walls had stopped reverberating from their presence. I'd have to wait until the next day for the story that ensued that night. But before he left, I'd watch him get ready.

TK pants, Right Guard deodorant, button-down collar shirt, crew neck sweater with the shirt collar just showing, a splash of Canoe cologne—a product geared towards teenagers as opposed to the "men" who used Old Spice—Brylcreem for his hair—"A Little Dab'll Do Ya," just as the ad said—hair parted to the side and flipped back in the front, *à la* JFK—that hairstyle to be superseded by the Beatle haircut—socks, suede desert boots, and one of the many varieties of outerwear, like car coats and reversible trench coats that my father, as a tailor in a menswear factory, was able to procure for him. I was the lucky beneficiary on only two occasions, when the designs were unisex. Once it was my blue ski jacket, and then, years later, my double-breasted, navy pea jacket with anchor-embossed brass buttons. My brother, however, got to sport all the new styles as they emerged.

When he went out with girls, his preparation was more deliberate, as he hoped for the close shave the Gillette blades promised. One of his friends would always have a car, and they would double date. The girls had beautiful names, like Lisa and Charlotte and Cindy, and lived in big houses. The relationships were short-lived; my brother had a habit of breaking them off. His trademark refrain, with original lyrics to the rhythm of "Na na na na, boo boo," sung at the end of the evening, meant he had done it again.

I thought him grand.

Chapter 17

…Sons…

I was too young to understand how my brother's relationship with my father began to fall apart, but I was aware of the tension between them and that their exchanges were often strained. I sensed that there was nothing in the way of mentorship, such as teaching my brother how to throw a ball, or bestowing fatherly advice—those precious moments of being taken aside that invariably began with a thoughtful "Son…," the preamble to a metaphysical utterance that sons would remember their entire lives—or planning experiential father and son outings in the wild with a tent, or encouraging my brother to develop the endless patience required to wait for a fish to take the bait.

The disparity felt even more pronounced when juxtaposed against sizable doses of father imagery on TV. In *Father Knows Best*, the title said it all. *Leave It to Beaver* depicted a sage, enlightened ruler who welcomed the input from his closest advisor, his wife, but ultimately knew better. Fatherhood got even more challenging, and fathers more endearing, in TV shows riddled with the ghosts of dead wives, like *The Andy Griffith Show*, *Make Room for Daddy*, *Family Affair*, and *The Courtship of Eddie's Father*. More dead wives in *My Three Sons*—the corporate version of *Bonanza*—and in movies like *To Kill a Mockingbird*, where the persona of Atticus Finch captured our hearts. Nothing on TV even remotely resembled my father.

His own father died of consumption at the age of twenty-seven, when my father was only three. As the middle child of three sons, not quite the *My Three Sons* of TV, my father left school after the equivalent of Grade Six, willingly sacrificing his future education in order to help out his mother financially. The eldest brother was able to fend for himself, and the youngest was sent to an orphanage. Things improved somewhat when his mother was able to marry a man much older than she, a turn of events for which she was supposed to have been enormously grateful, as a woman whose prospects were almost nil at best.

Maybe some of this accounted for why my father wasn't much of a father figure to my brother. Maybe it was because my father wasn't that interested in sports or wasn't that outdoorsy. He was unshakable in his routine, which began at the same time each morning with a cup of coffee and some bread. He prepared his own lunch, left at the same time to catch the same streetcar to arrive at the factory in order to punch in at the same time, punched out at the same time, and came home predictably at 5:30 p.m. for the dinner my mother had cooked for us. Maybe the frenetic pace of boyhood jarred with the repetitive order of his day-to-day existence. Maybe it was none of those things.

My relationship with my father was entirely different from my brother's. Nor could one posit that my father favored me. Nothing like that accounted for the chill between them. It was as if they always fought over the same piece of turf. My father seemed to think my brother was overconfident, didn't work hard enough, took too many risks, adopted the "buy now pay later" attitude so glaringly anathema to my father, who wasn't going to be unprepared again, not after what he'd been through during the war. My brother felt provoked and so countered with derisive comments about how he'd already outperformed my father in every category.

When my father got frustrated he would prophesy, "You're going to be a bum and live on the streets!" or characterize, "You're a good-for-nothing!" Which my brother rebutted with "I've done better than you. You're just a tailor in a factory."

That was the gist of it. My father made no secret of how he opposed my brother's approach to things, though possibly what lay beneath was his fear that my brother wouldn't succeed. My brother resented my father's acerbic brand of reverse psychology, though what really may have galled was knowing how little faith my father had in him.

Three times a year, with every report card, the wound would be reopened. Or whenever my brother needed money. The topic of school was complicated. The topic of money had a lot to do with the mores of dating at the time, and the fact that it was still a

146

rule that boys would pay. A part-time job for a top student wasn't the norm. School came first. In my father's mind, the deal was: excel in school, and then be given some money as a reward. My brother's understanding was: get reasonably good grades without working too hard. Having money was another matter entirely. It had nothing to do with school, but everything to do with being a teenager trying to fit in. Their differences would not be reconciled.

School was regarded by many immigrant parents, especially Jews, as the gateway to freedom from the "oppressors," the latter being everyone in a position of power, real or imagined. So, if you went to university and came out with a professional degree, then no one could push you around and, more poignantly, fire you. My father was hypervigilant over my brother, knowing what a re-sponsibility it was to provide for a family and how that role was generally assigned to a male.

Signs that my brother was doing what he wanted when he wanted, instead of studying, were terribly distressing to my father and elicited his contempt. What was my brother doing with the opportunities that were there for the taking? Nothing. The drive to excel didn't seem all that evident in my brother's behavior, unlike in his Jewish peers, who consistently came first in their class and were destined to go to medical school. Scholarships could carry my brother forward and pay his way, if only he would apply himself. He was throwing his life away. Did my brother think of that? Clearly not, my father felt.

High school in the sixties was a stressful time. The departmental exams were province-wide finals, which all students wrote at the end of Grade Thirteen. The results were ranked and then published in all the Toronto newspapers—*The Globe and Mail*, *The Telegram*, and *The Star*. It was a great honor to be named either first, second, or third in your class, in your school, in the province. Unbelievable marks, well above 90% in all subjects, were reported. And there was also talk of students having nervous breakdowns. The standards were far more exacting compared to many years later; at the time, two spelling errors in English Composition could ruin your final mark. If you weren't up for all that competition, there was still the accessible award of graduating with honors, and the prize of the Ontario Scholarship for those who earned 80% and over. That scholarship pretty much covered first-year tuition. My brother ended up with a 75% average. What was done was done.

Eruptions notwithstanding, my brother handled the conflicts with my father by inventing a more desirable reality. Partly to goad me, and partly to cheer himself up, he would express the following:

"I'm adopted. You're mommy and daddy's kid."

I looked at him quizzically. Something about the conviction with which he delivered this news felt plausible.

"What do you mean?"

"Well, look at us."

We both looked into the mirror attached to his dresser.

"See?"

"What?"

"Look at your nose."

"Yeah. So?"

"Well, now look at mine."

"Okay." I was still confused.

"Your nose is like Dad's, but mine doesn't look like anyone's." Evidently, my brother got something out of his Grade Ten biology class.

I compared the shapes, and he did have a point.

"And when you, Mom, and Dad are in the sun, you all tan, but I burn."

Right again.

I had heard a lot about the life they'd led previous to my arrival, when it was just the three of them. I didn't really buy my brother's story that he wasn't theirs, but I felt inclined to believe him for his sake. He had found a way to escape the pressure-cooker world we were immersed in, the small flat with nowhere to go when people became angry.

"So, who are your real parents?"

"The Rockefellers!"

Leave it to my brother to think big.

Asking why the Rockefellers gave him up for adoption never really got anywhere, and so it became the unconfirmed tale of

148

my brother's origin, alluded to whenever things got rough. My parents even got in on the action, when my brother came to them for money.

"Go ask Rockefeller!" my mother would bellow.

That was what happened when it seemed everyone had a sense of humor. Other times weren't so funny. Then, fantasy would elude my brother because of the irrefutable sting of my father's words or, more often, his hands, his belt. How my father could presume that hitting my brother would somehow inspire scholastic dedication was mind-boggling. It turned out the way it generally did; those who had authority in the household could only get away with inflicting physical pain until the one who was beaten grew up. Then, delirious fury was newly intercepted by the threat of rebuke.

And so my father's hand, which was often raised and would follow through, now froze, though the intent was still clear. My father lunged at my brother; my mother, realizing she had unleashed a wildness in my father, began to scream his name while grabbing his arms in a failing effort to hold him back. He fumed and raged while my brother taunted, "Yeah go ahead and hit me!" knowing this act would be colossal stupidity on my father's part, yet aching for the excuse to belt my father in self-defense. Somehow, my mother got through to my father, and his arms went slack. In turn, my brother, quietly seething, slipped on a hockey glove and put his fist through his bedroom wall, to the sound of plaster particulate crumbling around the lath.

My brother could have used his bare hand, but his self-protection outweighed his self-loathing. Why injure himself over it?

In retrospect, my father's rages were quite predictable. But, at the time, they felt alarmingly surprising and unrelated to the man who was also my athletic coach, playmate, and chaperone. Even then, it seemed to me that it boiled down to a belief that my mother was in some sort of mortal danger and that it was his singular mission to defend her. He became instantly mobilized and reacted like a trigger, and then she reneged on whatever it was that had upset her and infuriated him. But it was too late. That behavior…compared to the gentle, quiet, patient, devoted, family man.

There was an obdurate inflexibility in both my parents; something had been forever rewired so as to bypass trust in, or respect for, another's way of doing things. Even agreeing to disagree was untenable for them. Instead, disdain, scorn, disgust, disapproval delivered with biting insult in words or actions conveyed the message. In my mother, it was the injustice and hurt she caused, though she posed no real risk of bodily harm with her slaps. But, in my father, it was disturbing.

As a witness to my brother's face-off with my father, my mind moved to my own survival, and whatever my father hoped would stir my brother's academic commitment ended up motivating me instead. But that still felt somewhat hollow, as part of me felt my brother's pain.

I saw it every time my father and brother spoke, even if it was about the weather. I saw it when they joked and shook hands: the glare in my brother's eyes. The shiny, reflective surface indicating that entry was permanently barred. No way in, no effect felt.

Chapter 18

...and Sports Jackets

My parents' lofty ideals, though laudable, had an eerie quality of fanaticism, which rankled. Loyalty, honesty, integrity, and trust were wonderful values to uphold, but the suspicion and cynicism with which they interpreted and deemed nefarious everyone else's motives was exasperating. No information was processed by my parents without a derogatory comment. "Oy, Peril. Bist tsee git!" ("You're too good!"), my mother would often say to me, as if this were a lamentable trait, and I would be destined to be everyone's fool. To them, any delivery of exciting news meant the messenger was being hopelessly naïve. An act of generosity was nothing other than a means of control. Trusting a good friend with a secret heralded certain betrayal.

It was so easy to inflame them. Innocuous things to me were catastrophic to them and seemed to hurt them, and, in turn, their explosive reactions hurt me, though my brother appeared immune. I tried hard to make sense of their points of view, thinking that maybe they were looking out for me, their "life experience" trumping my ignorance. But the disproportion of reaction to event, and then the added insult of finger-pointing, eroded much of my empathy towards them, while, for my brother, empathy had become an unrecognizable echo. So it was little wonder that, when it came to the matter of the sports jacket, the affront to my parents was tantamount to a crime against humanity.

My brother was doing well projecting his pedigreed persona, making real his dreams, moving beyond the invented middle name, the classy signature, and the sixth sense that his worldliness didn't match up with the two hapless immigrants who had raised him.

He had befriended a wealthy crowd, his good looks, wit, and charm gaining him easy entry. Not quite the homicidal, tragic

151

figure of Montgomery Clift in *A Place in the Sun*, but similar, in that class still spoke volumes. Despite that, he was enthusiastically included as one half of the other couple on double dates, invited to splendid cottages on Lake Simcoe, met parents in the sparkling, marble vestibules of gracious, Forest Hill and Rosedale homes before taking a seat at their mahogany dining-room tables to enjoy a sumptuous meal served on Rosenthal dishes and drink expensive wine from Waterford crystal.

It all began that summer after he had worked as a camp counselor in the Adirondacks. How my brother got there was a story of upward social mobility—my brother's unflagging spirit to lift himself up out of the quagmire of provincial, unimaginative Toronto and its ilk. His climb started with the commonplace practice among Jews of sending their children to summer camp, first as campers, and then, when they reached an employable age, to become camp counselors looking after the very campers they used to be.

Numerous camps flourished from the '60s well into the '80s and seemed to appeal to certain demographics, social classes, hobbies, and interests. Camps Winnebago, Ogama, and New Moon catered to the North York and Bathurst Manor suburban crowd. Camps Wahonowin, White Pine, and Manitouwabing pitched their programs to the educated, wealthy, and sophisticated who resided in upper and lower Forest Hill. Camp Shalom offered a religious slant, which appealed to the more orthodox Jews.

The original concept came from the Jewish Camp Council, which ran Camp Northland for boys and Camp B'nai Brith for girls. There was even a family version called "Moms and Babes" for children too young to stay overnight without their parents. The idea was to give Jewish kids a taste of the great outdoors and to offer "haves and have-nots" alike the experience. In a socialist spirit, the JCC geared camp fees to income.

While there were "haves" among the clientele at Camps Northland and B'nai Brith, my brother must have felt at his core that getting anywhere meant knowing the right people. And so he turned his attention to those summer establishments that made no secret of their substantial fees. Kids whose parents who could afford

152

to send their children there met other privileged kids, and so these camps became a fertile ground where the well-bred could intermingle.

Enter my brother. Camp Tamaran was a perfect case in point. It was a private camp for boys, nestled in three hundred and fifty acres of pristine Muskoka, a region of Ontario known for its forests, bedrock, lakes, and money. The camp's catchment area burst through the U.S. and Mexican borders, welcoming boys year after year for the rugged, yet old-boy experience that would be formulaic for their development as future members of exclusive golf and yacht clubs and as the subjects of articles in *Fortune* magazine.

The activities offered at Tamaran were not for the faint-hearted. Any remote signs of wimpy whinniness would be strenuously discouraged and eradicated by the end of the summer. Archery, horseback riding, riflery, waterskiing, kayaking, canoeing, hiking, fishing, biking were each transformed into a highly competitive sport. In this respect, Tamaran life resembled boot camp more than pastoral, recreational bliss.

Boys would be boys...and, because there were only boys, strange things were bound to happen. Like the water skiing run gone terribly wrong. Rural legend possibly, but the tale told was of a camper—an avid and talented water skier out for an evening's jaunt.

The typical beginner's water ski excursion would commence with the skier bobbing awkwardly while trying to keep his ski tips up out of the water, his knees bent, arms extended holding the pole, which was tied to the ski rope, which was attached to the boat. There was always a driver and a spotter. When the exhilarating words "Hit it!" were communicated from skier to spotter to driver, the driver would gun it, and if all went well, the speed of the boat would pull the skier up onto his skis, and the ride would be underway. If at any point the skier fell, the spotter would see where, the boat would circle the skier to bring the rope within reach, and the entire process would repeat.

An intermediate skier would be adept at skiing in and out of the wake and would be learning the skill of dropping one ski and placing the free foot in the half stirrup behind the foothold to proceed on a single ski. This was called slaloming.

An advanced skier would begin and end the run on one ski only, first immersed in the water, and then improving in technique to the point where he could be sitting on the dock with only one ski on and be pulled from there. At all levels, the protocol for the end of the run was the boat driving past the dock and steering clear of it, while the skier let go of the rope, glided towards the dock, sank into the water, removed the ski, and swam the rest of the way.

Quick minds immediately got to work to make a competition out of the skier's getting as close to the dock as possible, the objective being to glide a short distance and reach the dock before sinking into the water. If the run began with the skier being pulled from the dock, and the skier could glide back to the dock, the entire run could be accomplished without the skier ever getting wet above the ankles. Achieving this goal required the cooperation of the driver of the boat, who would be gauging a decreasing distance to the dock, the spotter, who would report what took place, and the skier, who could navigate the glide once he had let go of the rope.

The gauntlet was thrown. The first run gave the competitors an idea of what was involved. With each successive run, more distance was shaved off the last. Word spread of the feat being attempted, and a crowd grew to watch. Authority figures seemed to be conveniently absent but, if the news travelled, they could appear at any point and stop the proceedings. Each attempt, therefore, had to be bolder than the one before. The penultimate run held within it the taste of glory. One more time would clinch it.

The crowd got their money's worth and more. The boat drove towards the dock and, in a fancy manner, veered hard left. The skier was on a speedy trajectory. He reached the dock all right, and if his skis had been shorter then he surely would have been rushed by the crowd and carried off as a hero, the accolades lasting all summer and for many years later chronicled in the oral archives of camp lore. He was, in fact, carried off and taken by ambulance to the nearest hospital. His skis…they hit the dock, deflected to a vertical position, and shoved his privates—testicles and all—up into his body.

154

Then there was the story about the star athlete expected to outdo his peers and win the coveted first prize in a camp-wide, all-day triathlon. After the miles of running, swimming, and cycling, pushing hard to perform beyond his last record, he suddenly collapsed and died of a heart attack.

The competitive spirit was always there, even well after dark. Inspired by the unlikely combination of archery and the cinnamon, ginger goodness of Voortmans cookies (the name in camp treats), a group of boys invented a game, which didn't require any accessories in the way of special clothing or apparatus, and which could be played indoors, safe from mosquitoes and bad weather. The hole in the center of the cookie served as the target. The game could be played alone, or in a group of any number.

There had to be enough space around the cookie to make it a challenge. Participants were evaluated on speed, precision, aim, and the ability to continue to take many a turn. The group gathered around, ensuring fairness by having everyone standing equidistant from the cookie. The contestant who could ejaculate the quickest, hit the target, and immediately go again was the victor. Whether or not the end of the contest included forcing the loser to eat the cookie was a matter for speculation.

Maybe these incidents were just folklore, part of the camp experience that contributed to the sense of community, which developed and consolidated over the course of a summer. But the camaraderie was strong and typical of all the summer camps in Ontario.

As a camp counselor at Camp Tamaran, my brother socialized with many sons of important fathers. He befriended both staff and campers alike and found to his delight that there was life beyond Ontario. Muskoka was to Ontario what the Adirondacks were to New York State. But if you compared them directly to one another, it was the difference between a rhinestone and a diamond. And so, at the end of that summer, he set his sights on the greener pastures south of the Canadian border.

Applications for the next summer were processed in the spring prior, and when my brother was offered the position of camp counselor, his world opened up. The camp was on Lake George. To my ears it sounded prestigious; I imagined a sizable lake with stately evergreens and clear, clean water.

He came home from the experience entranced and in love—a summer romance with a Jewish girl from New York, who had naturally straight blonde hair, which would have baffled the Nazis. Her anglicized name had all the ethnicity drained out of it, and she could easily have had Anglo-Saxon ancestry. I was happy for him, but mostly thrilled with the camp tee shirt he got me. The deep, navy color, a true, marine blue, evocative of yachts and yachtsmen. The refined cotton that only got better with wear.

He also brought back with him a beautiful tweed sports jacket, which he had purchased in New York. A rich weave with flecks of red, brown, gray, and black. The fashion was to wear a sports jacket with a changing roster of solid-colored dress pants that would pick up one of the jacket's color subtleties. The look was considered more casual than wearing a suit and was very popular with the younger crowd. Ties were also an option. A couple of other changes updated the garment. The back now had two slits making a flap, instead of the one slit in the middle, and two buttons on the front instead of three, the last always left unbuttoned. One of the trendsetters was Steve McQueen in *Bullitt*, with his easy gait and irreverent style. Lapels were yet to expand, along with pant legs, in the following decade.

My parents and I pored over the jacket. My mother teased about "champagne taste and a beer budget," but the compliment was there. My father looked at the workmanship and approved the details of the pockets, the lining, the stitching. My mother was pleased that my brother had purchased something of quality, which would see him through a variety of social situations. He modeled the jacket for us. It fit perfectly and looked fantastic on him.

While in New York, my brother had been able to visit with a branch of my mother's family, though many limbs of that tree had been severed. My maternal grandfather had four brothers and two sisters, and all but two had immigrated before the war, little knowing that this decision would save their lives. The branch that was prematurely lost included my grandfather, my grandmother, two aunts, their husbands and children, and my uncle. My mother was the sole survivor in her immediate family.

The relatives who had moved to America didn't strike it rich, but they were able to make a go of it, have jobs, raise families. I had met one of the four brothers and his wife—my mother's uncle and aunt. They seemed ancient to me, stooped and gray, though kind and loving. They lived in the Bronx, a brown, sooty place in general with many apartment buildings. The one they lived in had tiny windows and a small, brass elevator with wonky mirrors, like at the fair, but these visual aids addressed a more insidious ill: they allowed the prospective elevator patron to see into every corner in case someone was lurking, waiting to mug you. Mugging was a real threat. It had happened to my uncle in broad daylight while he was walking down the street close to his home. People were on their guard everywhere in big American cities.

Another brother had already died on American soil, but his wife somehow took to the family as if it were her own. My mother's aunt by marriage, she was a diminutive thing with a face that jiggled and a voice that quivered from early Parkinson's. She had very fair skin and ubiquitous freckles, fine, curly hair, small, dull, blue eyes, and a singular mind-set. She was considered somewhat of an elder in the family and was respected for that, a justifiable veneration in her opinion, though to me it felt unfounded, maybe because much of her favor was lavished upon my brother.

She had a daughter, Fay, all grown up now, married to Marv. They had a daughter, Cheryl, close to my brother's age. Fay and Marv were younger than my parents and were the first generation born in North America, thus quintessentially American. I liked the fact that English was their native language. In other words, no heavy Yiddish accent. Also, they were, in my view, just like the characters on TV. Pretty Fay with her shoulder-length, wavy-curly, blonde hair and short bangs, looking like Donna Reed; Marv, like the successful husbands in casual attire, gracing the perimeter of the pool, talking to Benjamin in *The Graduate* about his future. Finally, I could relate.

Everything about how Fay and Marv lived was fabulous. Their modern, suburban, split-level house was a case in point, with colorful, Formica kitchen countertops, electric can opener and kettle, double sink, garburator, dishwasher, breakfast nook, a fridge that made ice, thermal windows, a sunken living room, an en suite bathroom off the master bedroom, a wood-paneled den, a finished basement with a rec room, a tiki bar, bar glasses with star patterns, and gold lamé upholstered bar stools.

That's who my brother visited while in New York. It was a pleasure for Fay and Marv to show my brother the sights, direct him to where to shop, take him out to dinner, put him up at their house. And my brother was great company—a bright, witty, teenager, like the son they didn't have.

Shopping was always especially good in the States. Our southern neighbors outdid Canada product for product, and so it made perfect sense to buy clothes while in New York. Fay, offering a woman's eye, and Marv, who knew the best shops for men, were more than happy to help my brother pick out the sports jacket.

My brother told the story to us. The sports jacket was expensive, he explained tentatively, almost apologetically. My mother assured him that he was absolutely right to have bought it; it was truly beautiful, and quality would last. How much did it cost? Suspense was created in a guessing game. My mother estimated $300.00. She wasn't far off. At $285.00, it was worth it, considering how well-made it was.

Something lay in that sports jacket…a symbol of the future, perhaps. One could get away with any pair of dress pants, as long as the fit and cut were right. Dress shirts couldn't easily be discerned as being more or less expensive when worn under a jacket with only the collar showing, shoes were pretty standard, a haircut at the barber's still two bits. But the sports jacket would stand out and be counted. The motivating factor for my parents was that their children should have far better than they ever did. The sports jacket gave off a pervasive aura of class and elegance. If you didn't come from money, a jacket could at least be bought, and when worn, capture the same attention as those of refined lineage. Assuming the wearer could pull it off, and there was no question about that.

It was difficult for my brother to ask, but he managed to get it out, and my parents willingly reimbursed him in support of his idea, after the fact. It was a decision they felt they could back. In that moment, my parents' and my brother's values coincided. They wanted my brother to succeed, and although my parents and brother had differed in terms of the means by which he would get there, they all agreed that one had to look the part.

Harmony prevailed for the time being.

Chapter 19

Summer Camp

Camp was a lifesaver for me. Very different for my brother. Camp took him to the next best thing. But for me, it was perfect in itself because of what it offered: the great escape and a huge relief from life in the flat. For three weeks a year in July, I would have the distinct pleasure of sharing the same address with my cabin mates. No weird expressions on people's faces as they tried to imagine where someone could possibly live on a main street like St. Clair, no embarrassment for my parents' less-than-civil behavior and out-of-place look, no night terrors, alone, in my bedroom, which never shielded me from my worst fears.

Fourteen of us slept on identical cots reminiscent of the dormitory environment in *Madeline* books, where parental absence seemed so wondrous to me. The only threat to sweet slumber lay in my imagined worry, during spectacular summer thunderstorms, that the tall evergreens surrounding our cabin would act as lightning rods, a bolt surely finding its way to the wooden structure that housed us, setting it ablaze while everyone else slept. Thankfully, good weather was the norm.

The other nocturnal disturbance was more of a nuisance: the dive-bombing sound of a mosquito buzzing in my ear, myself a sitting duck, flailing unsuccessfully in the dark, moving the air around, fending off the mosquito momentarily before it launched its instinctive attack, motivated by a relentless attraction to my succulent blood. Sometimes I would sleep with my blankets over my head and around my ears, trading overheating and near suffocation for the security of knowing I was out of the mosquito's reach. It was a good strategy, unless I happened to sweep the mosquito under the covers, a consequence I would discover when I heard its start-and-stall buzzing sound and felt the disheartening realization that I was sleeping with the enemy.

Our days would begin early; reluctant, warm bodies sheltered from the damp cold would risk exposing an arm to catch a pair of pants, socks, until we could successfully exchange our pajamas for what we would wear at breakfast. We operated as a unit, headed by our counselors, and made our way through the woods to the huge clearing, down the hill to the mess hall. If we had closed our eyes we would still have known exactly where to go, following the sweet aroma of vats of hot chocolate, which were poured into tall, stainless steel pitchers and placed on the long, wooden tables, ready for our eager consumption.

We waited outside in cabin groups, from the youngest to the oldest, girls on one side, boys on the other. I eyed the other cabins of girls, comparing the number of pretty girls they had to ours, sizing them up against us. I also looked over the crop of boys, beginning with the cabin that was our counterpart and moving up even to the older ones—the C.I.T.s (Counselors in Training) and the counselors—hoping to spot someone cute. There were always a few who were intriguing.

We sang camp songs, our voices ringing out, lyrics indelibly written in our minds.

"I go to Camp BB so pity me
There ain't a damn boy in this nuttery
And every night at nine they lock the doors
I don't know what the hell I ever came here for
And when we're on the bus and homeward bound
I'm gonna turn this camp right upside down
I'm gonna smoke and drink and neck and peck
So what the heck
The hell with Camp BB eee-eee!"

Our musical repertoire was very eclectic and included haunting Indian laments with melodies based on fifths like drumbeats, many popular folk songs like "Five Hundred Miles," some gospel hits, "When the Saints Come Marching In," which for a Jewish camp was quite ironic, and the rousing "Ninety-Nine Bottles of Beer on the Wall." The songs united us and gave us spirit.

When the doors to the mess hall were finally opened, we rushed in like mad coyotes, the collective sounds of eight hundred

162

children amplified by wood-beamed ceilings and hard floors. And we were never quiet, except during the announcements of the day, delivered by the camp's figurehead, the program director—the top of the heap in the hierarchy, which descended in order of authority to the head counselor, the unit heads (six cabins to a unit, seven units per boys' camp and girls' camp), and the counselors (two counselors to a cabin).

It seemed preeminently important to me that my counselors were beautiful, and some of them were quite exceptional in that regard. As I was continuously fascinated by what it would be like to be a teenager or a grown woman, I searched for worthy models who could express, in their beings, what lay in store for me.

Lara fit the bill. She had a face you could fall into, like the dizzying feeling induced by walking on a ledge and gravity enticing you over. Her eyes were large and a yellow, tiger green with the depth of colored art glass. Her hair was brown, but as the summer progressed, developed bronze and gold highlights from the sun. Her teeth were impossibly white, and more so against a darkening tan. Having her around all day minding us gave me lots of time to look at her, talking to her a joy. To imagine what she did after the lights were switched off for bedtime and she left the cabin to meet up with the other counselors to socialize, or see that special someone who would become the proverbial summer romance, was stirring.

And as the tans got deeper, the sexual energy rose like mist. That's what camp really was—in a word, sexy. After the damp of morning disappeared under the strength of the July sun, articles of clothing started to be shed. Balls of socks, shoes tipped this way and that from being thrown, jeans looking like the air had been sucked out of them. Sweatshirts were removed and then draped around the waist, fabric arms tied in front. Cut-off denims, flip-flops, a bikini top would get you through the day and into early evening, when sweatshirts were restored to their role as tops.

On the hot, hot, dry days, swimming was rapturous—cooling down our bodies, wetting our bathing suits, stimulating our muscles and tendons and nerve endings. When, finally, the cold of the water won out over the heat of our bodies, we hoisted ourselves back on to the docks, placed our towels on the wooden planks, lay down, angling our fronts to the sun, the soothing tickle of droplets drying on our skin, the sound of tiny waves lapping against the rusty barrels that supported the dock, like the faint tinkling of a steel drum band. The goal was to let the sun dry my bathing suit. It was the most efficient use of time and the easiest solution, given that bringing a change of clothes would have been viewed as pathetically uncool.

After a day like that, my skin always felt a little new to me; was more obvious in its sensations, warm and then cool later on; looked a little richer, especially against whites. Back to the cabin to get ready for dinner and the evening's activity, which was co-ed, maybe a sing-along around the campfire, hoping for a glimpse of whomever captured my fancy as I peered across the flickering flames and tried to gauge whether the spark of the firelight lit up the eyes of my interest and whether the trajectory of his vision was intended for me.

The high point would come when everyone broke to walk back to the cabins. Would a shadow approach me, a voice utter a sound, and a connection be made? I yearned.

More often than not, it didn't happen, and so I walked with cabin mates, joking and laughing, in part to compensate for the deep disappointment of not having an admirer, our quips full of bravado as we pretended "they" didn't matter.

The raucousness around bedtime was a further surge, an accumulation of burgeoning sexual desire with no outlet and no understanding, a vicarious sensation of counselors about to get their needs met by making out with other counselors, a frustration and envy at being too young and not having power as campers to make a break from cabin prison. We released some of it in pillow fights, or by wrestling with a fellow cabin mate. We sublimated by being overly affectionate with our peers, hugging and holding each other, tickling, maybe even kissing in jest, so we could touch and be touched somehow, some way.

A few of the campers had already paired off as best friends, so their physical closeness and exclusivity was even more coveted by the rest of us free agents. One such pair was essentially a gorgeous butch/femme couple, unbeknownst to them perhaps, as they were barely out of their single-digit ages. Always together and looking stylish, relating in a certain dynamic whereby the one was clearly the tomboy, the protector, and the other to be shown off for her feminine beauty.

Adrienne was tall, trim, flat-chested. She'd often wear cotton, button-down collar oxford shirts, and slim-legged TKs, which she had in various shades. Her hair was simply cut, shoulder-length, light brown, and relatively straight. Her blue eyes, incisive and alert. She had this endearing speech impediment, a lisp, which in future would be eradicated by a speech therapist providing one of the services offered under the auspices of the public school system. In the meantime, her squishy-sounding *S*s labored, got muffled and blurred, as her tongue trapped the air trying to escape through the backs of her teeth, which were clenched.

Janet was also tall and lean, though in truth both of them couldn't have been more than five feet. She actually had a figure already, small breasts to speak of, hips, and a waist. Long, voluminous, golden curls *à la* Jane Mansfield, and dark brown eyes, an unusual combination for a natural blonde. She dressed more girly—pinks and yellows, frills and puffs—compared to Adrienne's tailored, classic blacks and khakis. The pair were lovely to look at, made the rest of us feel like philistines around royalty.

At some point in the night, when we had expended all that energy and tension, one by one we fell asleep, didn't even notice when the counselors came back from their own romantic adventures, yearnings, frustrations.

Beyond the minutiae of camp routine, there was a palpable learning curve underway. While more opportunities for sexual experience would present themselves as I got older, there were two milestones that were definitely within my age purview to achieve, and both happened that summer.

The first took place in a natural alcove eroded by time and water and wind. There would have been a term, which would have appeared on a Grade Ten geography test a few years hence, for that landform, one I couldn't have known in the setting of this precious moment.

A group of us stood there, sheltered from the main road, which was continuously traversed by authority figures and possible tattletales. We huddled under the cantilevered piece of earth, which still had tufts of grass growing upon it and, if man-made, would have been an example of artful engineering. Careful not to fall into the lake, the proximity of which was a rhythmic reminder—laps of waves rolling in to expropriate the tiny bit of beach that we stood on—we watched as the earth beneath our running shoes turned the dark shade of wet, and weak sand surrendered into runnels, destabilizing us briefly so that we had to regain our footing, the potential for "a soaker," high.

I didn't even know why I was a part of what was about to take place. No plan had been ideated. No one was in charge. No one was chosen. The incident seemed thoroughly impromptu, yet had a fated element that couldn't be denied. Excitement and secrecy and the anticipation of doing something prohibited made for an exhilarating combination.

There it was, the agenda: the distribution, among the group, of neatly manufactured, rolled sticks of thin, white paper containing drug- and poison-laced tobacco, with a filter tip that could withstand the moisture of lips, cushiony soft for ease of drawing in smoke that would enter lungs as part of the breathing process and then be exhaled, with the smoke as proof of the activity.

Popular brands of the time were Rothmans, Player's, Craven "A," Craven Menthol, Cameo, du Maurier. Each appealed to a certain demographic. Rothmans had a masculine, corporate conservatism about it—white and navy, thin, cursive script—evocative of ascots and banks. Craven "A" and Menthol were for the younger version of those who would ultimately make the brand change to Rothmans. Cameo, which only came in menthol—considered a girly thing—was marketed to women of a certain social standing and elegance. Du Maurier's French name offered the alternative of worldliness to staid. And Player's seemed to be strictly blue-collar. The iconic old salt on the Navy Cut package said it all. Player's Plain was the modern convenience answer to rolling your own, and Player's Filter was taking it a step further.

166

Later brands captured the ethos of the times. Benson & Hedges' "I'd rather fight than switch" ad marketed the cigarette's charcoal filter by morphing it into the black eye on the gentleman exiting the elevator, thus capitalizing on the popularity of the suave, spy genre of James Bond movies and TV shows like *I Spy* and *The Man from U.N.C.L.E.* Virginia Slims piggybacked onto the growing feminist movement. The brand's success lay in the irony that women were now dying of lung cancer in equal numbers to men, a dubious distinction. And when cigarettes were found to curtail appetite, mortality rates for women far surpassed those for men.

Our ad hoc group had no brand loyalty whatsoever. As an expression of our inability to have agency over our lives, we had to pilfer the cigarettes from an unsuspecting source—a counselor who had left her pack unattended. There were enough sticks to go around, some of them a little bruised from the secret journey they had taken.

Lighting a match was another learning curve. There were cautious ways, like holding the flap of the match packet against the lighting strip and sandwiching the match between them so as to avoid lighting the rest of the matches. This seldom worked and was for amateurs. The number of discarded matches from failed attempts was par for the course. But with twenty or so matches to a packet, the odds were in our favor that some of them would ignite. When one did light, eager, novice cigarette smokers would invariably snuff out the flame, the cigarette end acting as an extinguisher rather than as a conduit. Some motor control helped work that out. Then it was a matter of how many cigarettes could be lit with one match. Usually one, before the match holder would have to consider the likelihood of finger burn. If match lighting continued to be an issue, one could always get a light from another cigarette. Only veteran smokers would have invested in a lighter.

Finally, we were all lit up. Now came the smoking part. We had a body of images to draw on: actors smoked in movies, parents smoked, ads depicted the culture of smoking. But nothing prepared us for what it actually felt like. The first puff was sloppy, a quick draw in and out producing a cloud of smoke, which didn't dissipate fast enough and instead stung the eyes.

167

An experienced group member informed the others that unless one inhaled, one was not considered to be smoking. How did one do that? Puff and then breathe in was the instruction. Seemed simple enough. The memory of that first inhalation would never be thoroughly erased, like a tattoo. The smoke entered my lungs and was immediately recognized by my pristine organs as the perpetrator of an egregious act. I coughed and coughed, my body convulsing from the effort. Apparently, that was a good sign. It meant that I had, in fact, inhaled. Then came the head rush. That woozy, almost nauseous feeling, the sense that my ears were slowly coming together and squeezing my brain, that numb achiness in my lymph nodes at the back of my throat, the momentary lapse of vision—these were all to be understood as expressions of success rather than as problems. Once the inhalations became easier, technique took the forefront.

The different ways to hold the cigarette: there was a "masculine" and a "feminine" way. The masculine way was to curl your forefinger around the cigarette and let the body of the stick rest upon your fisted hand. The feminine way was to secure the cigarette between the first two fingers held straight, puff, fan your fingers away, and bring them back for your next puff.

Then came the different ways to exhale smoke. Pursing your lips up, down, or to the right and left, directed the smoke whichever way you chose. Another way was inhaling and letting the smoke come out your nostrils, like a bull—a show of being tough. Inhaling and letting the smoke come out as you spoke made you seem like you were far from your novice smoking years. And making Os by sudden mouth movements, lips taut and open, forming a mold for the desired O shape, was the first step towards the ultimate accomplishment of having the Os pass through each other in succession until the smoke supply was depleted.

So there I was, happily smoking my first cigarette, feeling grown up and cool, courtesy of a rolled-up, beautifully designed object, just as intended by a brilliant advertising campaign that conditioned the whole western world, enticing us by its representation of the lifestyle we should want. Young ones like me, the target market, were impressed by the promise of sophistication that could be ours. If that failed, there was the prevailing psychological explanation of oral fixation, and if that too failed, there was the guarantee, in the highly addictive properties of nicotine, that this experience would not be an isolated event. There was no way to escape the allures.

The other milestone... It started with "damn," a stronger version of "darn," which seemed silly and childish. This minor expletive came easily enough into my speech, in much the same way as a mild chili for flavor. "Damn" offered a little punch in the form of a non-descriptive adjective, or standing on its own as an expression of pause. The same was true of "heck," as a precursor to "hell," which then led to the synthesized term "helluva" with its unique spelling.

"Shoot" preceded "shit." "Shoot" offered a compromise to those not entirely comfortable with "shit," but who were a little more risqué than "gee gosh golly." I was able to traverse this stepping stone quite effortlessly and felt emboldened by graduating to "shit."

"Bitch" got off on the technicality of being the word for a female dog, and so much could be made of saying the word with impunity, if one wished.

"Bastard," like "bitch," had another meaning, in this case the word for an illegitimate child, so no great backlash there.

"Bitch" and "bastard," however, opened the door to other, gender-specific words that were decidedly off-color, pertaining to the male and female genitalia. The lesser of the two was "prick." Even so, it was a pretty bad thing to be called. It meant that the guy's values were highly questionable, if not non-existent. That he was generally despicable in his relationships with people, untrustworthy, and egotistical. But for the more sheepish name-callers, "prick," as in pricking your finger, provided a safe haven.

The female version of "prick" was "cunt," a word that had no substitute and, when said, sent a shiver through everyone. It wasn't until many years later that the sting of it was mitigated by the code phrase "C U Next Tuesday." "Cunt" sounded like an enclosed area, like a little rat's nest, bushy and dirty, and what it connoted was the worst possible aspects of being female: base,

169

slutty, and trashy. The word was reserved for very special occasions indeed; those who said it did so sparingly. To use it often called into question the speaker's character.

Still weighty enough, but far more versatile, the true litmus test for those who swore and those who didn't, was "fuck."

Once again, it was owing to a group experience that I followed suit. I had to hear it several times among the members to sense that my involvement was being solicited and that not saying the word would set me apart.

And then I said "fuck" for the first time. I felt a little ill afterwards. Something had changed in me. It seemed that I had now joined the ranks of those with no class, who had dirty mouths that would be washed out with soap, or who sounded like sailors inured to loose talk because of years of male company marked by the lack of any need for manners and the prevalence of urine-stained toilet bowls, seats perpetually up.

My mother told me that she cried when she learned about the word "fuck." As an immigrant, she was eager to learn English, always asking for definitions to expand her vocabulary and fastidious about correct spellings lest her ignorance be uncovered. She enrolled immediately in night school when my parents and brother came to Toronto. Even when she became pregnant, she faithfully attended every class. Despite her thick Jewish accent, she became completely fluent in both written and spoken English. She must have asked about the word, as she would about any new word. "What did that mean?" she likely asked someone innocently. Did the person simply say it meant having sex? So was it her prudishness? Or was it explained to her that fucking was the basic, instinctive, loveless act of a penis moving back and forth in a vagina or an anus? So was it her disgust? All I knew was that she cried.

After my first utterance of "fuck," it got easier, like any virtue or vice. And soon I could make my way around the word and incorporate its usage where appropriate. "Oh fuck!"—to express dismay. "Fuck you!"—the more effective version of "Take a hike!" Some usage issue came about in the late sixties around the difference between "fuckin'" and "fucking," as in "You fuckin' idiot," or "You fucking idiot." As with other participles, dropping the *g* had far-reaching implications. It seemed to mean that the speaker was not "educated," or perhaps was rural rather than urban. In the mouths of students reading Kafka and Marx, "fucking" was the norm. On the street among hoods, it was decidedly "fuckin'."

Three weeks at camp went by all too fast. Promises to see camp friends would peter out come September. On the bus ride home, I felt that I was forever altered. My eyes had the focus only possible through life experience, compared to the wide and blurry vision of kittens and puppies. When I stood now, one foot was at a right angle to the other, as if I were ineffably bored, hand on a hip, hip turned out. I got the fashion message at camp to wear denim shorts rolled up, a windbreaker, and PF Flyers. Maybe I had even grown an inch. I swore I'd hang on to all my maturity.

There was a funny sensation in my stomach when we got to Barrie. Toronto would be an hour away. Was I happy or sad? It was hard to tell. We got off Highway 400 and on to the 401. Soon, we had slowed down to the speed limit on city streets, and the bus looked enormous against its surroundings. By torquing the huge steering wheel hand over hand over hand, deft turns were made. It seemed like an impossible task to get an oversized object into a small space, but the driver succeeded, turned into the narrow laneway behind the Jewish Camp Council building at the corner of Spadina and Bloor, and then we disembarked. My father was always there to greet me. It was good to see him. We waited for my duffel bag, and he carried it for me.

My mother was happy to have me home, but I was in culture shock. Everything seemed small—the ceiling heights, the rooms. The sounds were trapped and dampened. I couldn't have grown that much over the summer. And I hadn't. Within a day or so, I had shrunk back into my former existence.

Chapter 20

Muselmann

Parodying Eminem, Jew Jube—the fictitious, Hasidic hip-hop star—said it all. Dancing to the beats, with his long, curly "peyos" (sideburns) and his massive bling—gold chain, links the size to haul a boat, Star of David as large as the face of a clock in an institutional setting, weighing down the necklace—he rapped:

"I ain't no candy (w)rapper. It wasn't summer when my grandparents went to camp."

True enough. For my father, the trip to "camp" started in the dead of winter, January 15, 1945. Sadly for him, this occurred one day before my mother was liberated from the slave labor camp she worked in. She was saved by the Russians, to whom she would feel indebted for the rest of her life. Like Gene Pitney's lament in the song "Twenty-Four Hours from Tulsa," in which a man's world was forever altered, and Dinah Washington's rendition of "What a Difference a Day Makes," that one day prolonged my father's agony for another four months.

Word is received that the allied front is closing in. In an audacious and last-ditch effort to elude the forces and forestall the freedom of their prisoners, the Nazis round up the Jews to where the prisoners will be safe from liberation. Their destination: Buchenwald. Being worked to death is not an idiom; it is the mission statement at the camp.

My father is there for three months, and in that time his normal weight of one hundred and sixty pounds drops to eighty-five. He is now officially a **muselmann.** *Not the Muscleman of the Mr. Universe, Arnold Schwarzenegger variety—of oiled biceps and abs and lats, flexing and protruding—but the name for the dearth of muscle tissue, the body's feeding frenzy in its instinctive response to*

173

preserve life by breaking down fat and muscle in the absence of food.

It is the **muselmann** *we see in photos of heaps of emaciated bodies, like some sick, Halloween display. It is the* **muselmann** *who looks out with his shaven head and hollow eyes devoid of energy or will, unable to care to recognize either his captors or liberators. The* **muselmann,** *the same image from body to body, face to face, like an endless assembly of copies cheapened by repetition, each man indistinguishable from the next man, or woman for that matter, save emptied breasts and non-existent penis, summarily reduced by starvation, exhaustion, and listless hopelessness.*

Then, on April 7, 1945, the prisoners are rounded up again in advance of the advancing allies. This time they are on foot for the first leg of the trip, en route to Theresienstadt. These peregrinations are well documented in Elie Wiesel's slim, heartrending novella, **Night.** *There's no mistaking at Theresienstadt what the mandate is, and it's not a work ethic. At Theresienstadt one activity only is its claim to fame: putting inmates to death. If it is more than a month my father has to withstand the toll his body is taking, he will surely die anyway.*

Even so, my father tells two mind-gnawing vignettes of near-catastrophe at allied hands. In the first, he and nine other men are running through the forest. Planes are flying overhead, allied planes. It isn't clear whether the men are hoping to get the attention of the planes, which are clearly not Luftwaffe, or whether the men are on the run because of the planes, or whether the planes are aware of the tiny figures below darting in and out underneath the large tree crowns and becoming exposed in clearings.

It isn't clear why the pilots can't distinguish innocent civilians from Nazi soldiers; it isn't clear what the orders are that the pilots are carrying out. But what happens is this: shots are being fired from the planes...at them! They are running for their lives and they can barely run. The planes are meticulous in their attack, peppering the forest with gunfire in a decisive sweep. From the perspective on the ground, there is an omnipotent force above, ubiquitous, bent on killing. From the plane's altitude, there are specks moving that need to be stopped. The mission is a success.

Out of ten targets, eight are hit. The planes leave the area, sated. Two bedraggled and bewildered and distraught figures emerge; one of them is my father. This is what it means to be liberated.

In the second story, the Soviets have freed the prisoners. The inmates can hardly believe the fortuitous change in their circumstances. Can they actually trust that this is for real, and not another psyche-eviscerating ploy to further victimize them? Maybe there's some twisted prank, collusion between the allies and the Gestapo? Maybe the allies are Gestapo dressed as allies? What more could the Nazis do to them that they haven't done already? Yet, what they've already done seems inconceivable, born out of an unconscionable thought process, developing an ad campaign called "The Final Solution," which really caught on.

The Red Cross arrives. Care packages are unloaded and rise like building blocks around them. It's Christmas in **The Twilight Zone**. The volunteers feel like the instrument of God the savior and are heartened by it. The inmates are like abandoned, suffering animals sniffing around bounty, unsure of whether it's a trick or a miracle.

"Don't bite the hand that feeds you" turns out to be a potentially fatal maxim. To be wary of the Trojan horse comes closer to good advice, even though these gift-givers' intentions are benign.

Far away, relief in the form of food and clothing is being boxed and readied for shipment to those in dire need. To find out who determines what goes into the boxes will require tracing back the steps to some official meeting. Are there doctors who have been consulted? Is everyone aware of the uniquely precarious physiological state of the inmates? One of the ironclad features of the "Final Solution" is that the dead don't talk, and it's hard to believe the stories of the very few who do manage to escape. So who really knows what's going on when news can't travel?

Now the inmates are swarming around the boxes, their desperation trumping their suspicions. At least it's true that the allies are for real. The skeletal figures are ravenous wolves: wild, crazed eyes, trembling fingers clawing at the food and stuffing matter into their frantic mouths, tongues dripping with saliva.

For a brief spell, the gorging compensates for the deep chasm of deprivation, and then the body rebels. Feeble frames, unstable electrolytes, weak hearts, the **muselmanner** *are doubled over, racked with violent abdominal pain and cramps, vomiting, severe diarrhea, dehydration, which only death can and does relieve. This is what it means to be liberated.*

My father is watching closely. His instincts are almost too overwhelming to ignore, because his hunger has become a state of mind. Somehow, somewhere inside of him, he knows that he has the stomach of an infant, a newborn baby who can't digest certain foods and must eat slowly, infrequently, and in tiny amounts. He tells it this way, with biting irony: "They gave us butter...," to illustrate the rich fat content in the food, and to emphasize the profound ignorance of the allies, who thought they were carrying out some hugely benevolent task, "...and I refused to eat it because I knew it would make me sick." He means it would have killed him. Like dying from the cure, not from the disease.

No point in shooting the messengers. Young boys enlist from all over, and the ones from Smalltown, U.S.A., happy not to have died in an air strike, give out food to the hungry, just like good Christians should, and walk among the waifs, covering their mouths from the stench, while giving a wide berth to the hills of dead bodies, thinking, "This sure ain't Kansas." Can't fault them.

My father nurses himself from the precipice of death to relative, corporeal safety. His other wounds will never heal; how can they, when even those who are solicited to help, harm?

The truth had a way of coming out. Like a leak in a roof, the force of the water gradually prevailed, wetting and weakening each bit of plaster barricade, until eventually the water managed to trickle through a ceiling.

It began with a casual exchange of pleasantries.

"How are you?"

"We're fine, and you?"

"Good."

"The kids?"

"Also fine."

Etcetera.

"Does he still wear the sports jacket?" Fay asked my mother.

"Yes he does."

"Well, we wondered, because we hadn't heard anything about it from you, so we thought maybe the gift wasn't right for some reason."

"Gift? What do you mean?"

"The sports jacket we got for him."

"Oh yes. Of course," my mother feigned.

"We weren't sure what to do, because you hadn't called, and so we thought maybe we bought something he didn't like, although he seemed so excited."

"No. It's beautiful, thank you. That was very generous. I should have phoned. I'm sorry."

"Well, I'm glad I brought it up."

"I'm glad you did too."

My mother was mortified and livid. Thoughts flooded her, and she felt dizzy. Telling my father was like lighting the effigy of a villain in the midst of a volatile mob.

My father rushed towards my brother and succeeded in getting in a few punches, my brother seemingly caught off guard, or permitting them in some penitent way. Then my mother interceded, and my father stood there, leaning aggressively towards my brother with the part of his body that was unrestrained, the other arm slack in my mother's grasp. His eyes were glazed with fury and hurt, his throat constricted from the outrage of the implications of my brother's misdeed.

"Is this what I survived the Nazis for!" His body shuddered and his voice rattled. "So that you could lie and steal from us! What kind of monster are you! Who would do such a thing! Do you know how hard I have to work to make that kind of money!"

My brother's mind was somewhere else, listening to the words of his own making, imagining a time when he could escape into the vast possibilities that lay outside the flat, the street, the city, the country. Places he knew existed on the map of the world that was taped to the wall of his room.

"Alleh maneh sonnem" ("All my enemies"), my father added in disgust, meaning that one doesn't only have one's enemies to fear.

It was a hard thing for my brother to refute. He didn't even try. In my own budding sense of principles, I couldn't understand it. Why not just say that the sports jacket was a gift? Why invent an elaborate ruse that was destined to be uncovered? How could any good come of it? I felt for my father—his deep sense of being betrayed, though I was disturbed by the way he expressed it. I felt for my mother—her shame and embarrassment at being perceived by Faye as someone who wouldn't have called to thank her for such an expensive gift. Talk about a cat's game. My mother could never alter the impression, because the truth would have made our family look even worse. I felt for my brother, whose escapist dreams of sophistication didn't come cheap. No matter which face I looked at—my brother, father, mother—all I saw were broken pieces.

In an imaginary episode of *Leave It to Beaver*, Wally had already been told by his mother to "wait ©'til your father gets home." It was a solemn edict; implicit was the dread of rebuke, as well as the hope of redemption.

Wally sat on one of the twin beds, head down, shoulders slumped. His ears were cocked for the sound of the front door's brass knob clicking as it turned, the sound drifting up the stairs and through the bedroom door. Wally's body straightened up.

Ward had arrived home after a day's work. He was customarily attired in a suit and tie. June greeted him by taking his coat and hat, and, in that exchange, Ward kissed June on the cheek.

Ward was perennially good-natured; clearly, either his work-place was not a hardship to him, or he was blessed with the ability not to take his work home. But June's cheery face was cloudy today.

Wally heard the first exchanges of salutation, and then suddenly the voices quietened. June spoke in a whisper, apprising Ward of the serious, familial situation that had ensued. Wally's body sagged further, resigned to awaiting his fate.

Footsteps were now heard on the stairs, and then a knock at the door.

"Wally?"

"Yeah, Dad."

The doorknob turned, and in walked Ward.

Wally's gaze lifted. In his eyes was the fear of what he'd see reflected back to him in his father's demeanor.

"Your mother told me some upsetting news just now."

"Yes, sir."

"Well, son, what do you have to say for yourself?"

"Gee, Dad, I don't know what I was thinking. It happened so fast. There was the sports jacket. It felt like you and Mom kinda thought, too, that I'd bought it. Guess it figured. With Fay and Marv and all, well it would have been a pretty expensive gift, and why would you think *that* first, like you would expect it or something, which is kinda thinking people should be buying you gifts all the time. Then there was the whole money thing. All the guys seem to have plenty of it, and girls kinda expect you to pay, especially some girls, like if you don't have it, they kinda think you're not good enough, or that you don't have much going for you, like they're already wondering about getting married or something. Then it was too late. And with Fay and Marv living in the States, and time passing, I just tried to forget the whole thing. I'm awfully sorry, Dad."

"Well, Wally. When I was your age the girls were much the same as they are now. But the special ones see who you intend to become, rather than who you are at this age."

"Yes, sir."

"And you can't be like your friends. You have to be yourself and trust that it's you they want to be with, and not how much money you have."

"Yes, sir."

"Now, Wally. What you did was wrong. You misrepresented the facts and took money that wasn't yours."

Wally's heart ached, and his eyes welled up with tears.

"Your mother and I are not very pleased with you right now."

"Yes, sir, I understand," Wally's voice labored.

"You're going to have to pay the money back."

Wally perked up.

"Yes, sir! You can take my allowance, and I'll do as many chores as you and Mom want. I can work after school at the soda shop, Dad, and I've got the paper route."

"Remember, you have to keep those grades up."

"Yes, sir. I will." Wally could see into a better future, where his debt would be settled.

"Now, Wally, money can be repaid. But not telling the truth, that's a different matter."

"Yes, sir?" Wally worried again. "You can ground me 'til I'm fifty if you want to," Wally offered readily.

Ward suppressed a chuckle. "Well now, that won't be necessary."

Wally mistook his father's comment for a reprieve.

Ward quickly reframed. "What I meant was grounding you until you're fifty."

"Oh, yeah, Dad. I guess that would mean you and Mom would be kinda ancient."

Ward's eyes rolled a little. "Yes, Wally, your Mom and I would be 'kinda ancient.' Let's start with being grounded for two months, and then we'll see," Ward suggested.

Compared to the thirty-four-odd years it would take to turn fifty, this seemed terribly lenient to Wally.

"Gee, Dad. I didn't think I'd get off that easy."

"Well now, you haven't."

"Huh, Dad?"

"You see, Wally, when you decided to change the story from getting a gift to buying the jacket yourself, somewhere inside you thought you couldn't come to us, to tell us how hard it is to be a teenager and not have the money to be with your friends and go out on dates. Are you following me?"

"Gee, Dad. You're sounding awfully deep, but I think I get it so far."

"That's good, son. Maybe there's something about coming to your mother and me that seems hard to do."

"Well, now that you mention it, you and Mom are always going on about being responsible with money and not taking it for granted and stuff, and how little money you had when you were a kid, and how we should be grateful and all for what we have," Wally ventured.

"So if you were feeling low about money, you would probably figure we would come down on you pretty hard, is that it?" Ward assisted.

"Well yeah…gee Dad, this deep stuff is hurting my head."

"Okay, Wally. I'll try not to hurt your head too much."

"So does that mean we've finished our father-son talk?"

"Almost, son. I just wanted to say that sometimes it's difficult to tell people what's really bothering you, especially if you think they'll get angry at you. But it's important to be honest and have the courage to face the situation. I'd rather that you came to me and your mother with any problem, however impossible it seemed to you, than resort to being dishonest. And I will keep in mind that sometimes your mother and I can seem quite strict about things."

"Gee, Dad. Well, since you put it that way…"

"So you can tell us anything, Wally. We'll always be there." And with that, Ward placed a loving hand on Wally's shoulder.

"Thanks, Dad."

Unfortunately for my brother, Ward Cleaver was not his father. With the sports jacket debacle, the fissure between my father and brother became a rift, then gaped like a canyon. They were separated by powerful, immovable counterforces, which held them both in check. They viewed each other with heightened, irreversible suspicion, my father convinced of my brother's egregiousness, my brother feeling orphaned by a father who still lived.

———※———※———※———

Chapter 21

Civil Rights and Wrongs

Within a few years, my brother would successfully make his break and distance himself from the parental mindset that condemned him. In the meantime, he spent even less time at "home." I, on the other hand, was stuck under my parents' roof and also thrust into circumstances of…

…Martin Luther King, Jr., Malcolm X, Paul Robeson, Harry Belafonte, Leon Bibb, Sidney Poitier.

What did they have in common? They were all black men, and my mother was enthralled with them. It was Martin Luther King, Jr.'s impassioned, lyrical, exalting oratory that stirred her. Listening to him plead for the very basic elements necessary for human existence spoke deeply to her. His vision loosened in her a tiny fragment of hope, which broke off from a solidified mass of despair regarding the human condition. Could he make it happen? Would the future he imagined be possible?

Malcolm X, in contrast to King, was the badass rebel, the recalcitrant, swaggering tough guy, the Rolling Stone to the Beatle. His militant impatience, his assertive rage elicited my mother's defiance, long suppressed for fear of the "authorities," or "anti-Semites," who could be anybody other than Jews, and even Jews couldn't unilaterally be counted on or trusted.

Paul Robeson's tragic figure in *Show Boat* personified all the woes and burdens of his life. His otherworldly baritone voice sounded like the depths of the earth itself. When he sang "Ol' Man River," it was wounding. The climax, both melodically and emotionally, occurred with the lyric "I'm tired of living but scared of dying," a sentiment that evoked in my mother the untenable paradox she lived out during Nazi Occupation, a memory she relived in moments like these.

Harry Belafonte's gorgeous face and happy-go-lucky demeanor entertained and delighted her. How exquisitely ironic the upbeat melody of his banana boat song, belying the grueling work day of picking bananas, similar to picking cotton in "Ol' Man River."

Leon Bibb appeared with his guitar as one of the many musical acts on *The Ed Sullivan Show*. His compelling voice came through masterfully in the dramatic song "And They Call the Wind Maria," another heartbreaker.

Sidney Poitier was the elegant gentleman, starring in movies that exemplified his worthy stature: *Lilies of the Field, To Sir with Love, In the Heat of the Night,* and *Guess Who's Coming to Dinner*. He typified grace.

My mother thought these men were wonderful. They were physically attractive, highly principled, intelligent, cultured, and incredibly talented. Civil rights were on everyone's mind. For my mother this must have approached a kind of vindication for the fate of the Jews in Nazi Europe. These men were the esteemed generals in an army that fought tirelessly for tolerance and the acceptance of difference. Maybe the time had come. A window was open. The grim, unforgettable assassinations of JF Kennedy, Bobby Kennedy, Martin Luther King Jr., and Malcolm X hadn't shattered the glass yet.

I was moved by her consummate admiration for them. To me she seemed unburdened by her usual despondence and her disgust for the world and its inhabitants. She commented lavishly on their good looks. "Ah shaneh ying" ("A good-looking young man"), she declared, and her endorsement was not easy to come by. More often, she would snipe severely at those less fortunate physically, picking out their flaws. For women, the comment was "A zah meeskeit!" ("What an ugly one!") But towards these men, only compliments. I was also impressed by her openness regarding her attraction to them, a white woman towards a black man; it seemed that racial equality was implicit in her appreciation of their good looks.

I felt like I was permitted to expand into the possibility of something good, somehow, instead of being squashed by her usual

184

brand of cynicism as she predicted inevitable betrayal based on poor judgment in the sphere of human interaction.

Immigration of blacks had not yet really occurred before the early '60s. After 1962, the racial rules were relaxed. Those who did come to Canada were largely from the Caribbean. In a class of thirty, there was only one black girl, maybe a few in the entire school—my junior high, Grades Seven and Eight.

In my circle of friends there was one black boy. Even at our young age, it was clear that his pedigree was exemplary. Brendon Warrington MacDowell Trent was his full name. Each of these words resounded with substance, and none of them was misleading. He had inherited each significant surname that bespoke ancestry and heritage.

He was tall, lean, good-looking, with a warm, beautiful smile. He was a star athlete, an A student, and had impeccable manners and gentility. His older sister was in high school, distinguishing herself academically as well as musically, playing the flute in the band and in the orchestra. His family came to Canada before the wave of black immigration, which meant that his father's occupation must surely have been exceptional enough to have convinced the officials to put aside his color in favor of what he could offer to the country.

As kids, we were readily accepting of racial difference, easily inspired by the ideology of equality. Maybe we all identified with being oppressed, if not societally, then at the very least, as children bound to our familial authority figures.

Brendon was easily assimilated into the group, which included a few Jews and Italians in addition to those who were Anglo-Saxon. We were all in the same grade and matured in each other's presence.

A natural progression was to go to parties. A rite of passage to this more intimate form of socializing had already taken place after the graduation ceremony, with dinner out at Peppio's. This marked another rite of passage for me—the first time I had ever gone out to eat at a restaurant. I was elated. Peppio's was a premier Italian family restaurant at the corner of Dupont and Davenport, replete with red-checkered tablecloths, wine barrels, and the mesmerizing cocktail recipe placemat, which captured my interest and inspired fantasies of growing up and ordering Manhattans, Zombies, Daiquiris, Singapore Slings, Whiskey Sours, to name a few.

Being well below the drinking age, I came as close as I could, with a Shirley Temple looking every ounce the cocktail without the alcohol. Peppio's served it with a fully operational, tiny paper umbrella. Unbeknownst to me, this item was fashioned by the laborious work of a child's nimble fingers, in deplorable conditions on another continent. A world away, Western consumers like myself were oblivious, and instead, were delighted by how cute the umbrella was and that the tip of the wooden handle was speared through a slice of orange and a maraschino cherry. Chic.

Graduation indeed. It would be a while before I could move on to a more sophisticated dining establishment like the swanky Ports of Call. This restaurant featured several themed rooms, which were meant to make you feel like a world and time traveler. There were three bars: the Last Chance Saloon, the Singapore, the Ballon Rouge. And there were three dining rooms: Caesar's, Dickens', and the Bali Hai. For drinks, you had the choice of either American western, Asian, or French décor, and for fine dining, you could be in Ancient Rome, Victorian England, or sultry Polynesia.

It was the Bali Hai room that I dreamed about. The faraway, romantic, nautical feel of it. Not hard to imagine, as the room had a brook, a bridge, and a boat with tables for an intimate dinner. Chinese lanterns and candlelight, the ripple of moving water, leisurely dining with that special someone on an actual boat, all at your service on Yonge Street south of St. Clair.

And as for ordering an alcoholic beverage, that too seemed remote, as the drinking age in Ontario would be twenty-one until the early '70s. I waited to blossom, but in full swing were Le Coq d'Or, the Zanzibar Tavern, Friar's Tavern, the Hawk's Nest, the Nickelodeon, the Town Tavern, the Colonial. These establishments dotted Yonge Street between College and King, featuring live rock 'n' and roll or jazz and serving plenty of booze, which tested the rigor of the Ontario liquor laws and the ethics of the police on patrol. While these frenetic beats were battering, and alcohol-induced revelry was bleating well into the night, at The Riverboat in

Yorkville north of Bloor patrons drank coffee, smoked cigarettes, and listened to folk songs.

If you preferred instead to drink at home, then you'd be walking to the nearest, government-run liquor store. The LCBO—Liquor Control Board of Ontario—imparted a particular judgment upon the purchaser of its alluring product. There was nothing easy about buying alcohol, and that was by design. With alcohol-free zones, like the one in and around High Park, incentives were decidedly absent. A subtext of "Drinking is Evil" seemed to inform every aspect of the endeavor. If all this effort at deterring you didn't work, then you could find yourself at the LCBO, feeling guilty and ashamed.

The one closest to where I lived was on the northwest corner of St. Clair at Alberta, beside the Coles bookstore, and just down the street from Dominion, the most popular chain of supermarkets at the time, with its "Mainly Because of the Meat" jingle and slogan.

Upon entering the LCBO, sounds became hushed. There were a number of freestanding wooden counters with tiny cubby-holes for pads of paper forms, and even tinier, built-in cubes to house the short, light-brown pencils for the public's use. Once you filled out your form, you approached the main counter, which ran the width of the store, and one of the many LCBO employees would come out to serve you. These were often big, burly men who appeared a little rough, like the marines in *South Pacific*, blustering about women, in the song "There is Nothing Like a Dame." The employees were all English-speaking and white. Behind the counter and out of view was the alcohol inventory. After handing over the form, the man would disappear into the back and reappear in a few minutes with your order.

He handed you your purchase, looking at you with the full knowledge of what it was for—akin to buying condoms. Even those purchasing *Playboy* magazines had something of an excuse, because the articles were really good, but with alcohol, no way to escape scrutiny, or so it seemed. What contributed to the feeling of infamy was the veiling of the inventory from the buyer, as if the sheer selection would plunge you into an insatiable state, wildly wanton, drawn uncontrollably to this wine and that spirit. You needed to know specifically what you were ordering beforehand, and not know the other options. For a freer experience you had to go to the States, but in Ontario the disdainful eye of the Temperance movement still watched you. With your "brown paper bag" in hand, as telltale as the bottle itself, off you went to get plastered. Shame on you.

Liquor control indeed. No drinking on Sundays without food. Ladies' and Men's entrances in taverns kept the ruffians from the refined. Rules and regulations. No wonder I dreamed of the day I could order a cocktail.

Meanwhile, we were old enough to have parties and soon found ourselves being invited to a series of them hosted by one of the kids in the group.

I had been looking forward to the party, thinking about what I was going to wear, hoping that my hair would turn out and that I'd have a good time.

Getting ready was a painstaking process. Once again, my hair would pose the biggest problem. By now, portable household hair dryers were on the market, and, for approximately $14.00, I had been able to purchase a Lady Sunbeam. It came in a round, hard, plastic case etched with a shallow relief that mimicked white vinyl, and decorated with a thin, gilded decal that went around the perimeter. A plastic handle loop was provided for ease of transport. The case opened like a huge locket, revealing two separate compartments. The "top" was shallow, with enough space for the plastic cap, which was white with pencil-thin, gold swirls. The "bottom" housed the motor and heating element, cleverly positioned in the center, which allowed the hose and electrical cord to be coiled compactly after use. Nothing technical was remotely obvious. Everything was white, gold, and pretty. The hair dryer for household use was considered a major convenience for women, with its promise of professional results, though its invention must have given the salons an enormous jolt in lost business as women began to consider doing their own hair.

Not that it was a panacea. I had to sit there confined by the length of the electrical cord of a few feet, and even with an extension, my range was still curtailed. The noise from the motor and the sound of the rush of hot air coursing through the hose isolated me from conversation. The intense heat coming through the tiny holes in the cap made me swelter. Adjusting the temperature to something cooler would have lengthened the already protracted time it would take to dry long hair rolled around curlers, with some hair too remote from the air flow, and thus, the horror of frizziness always a disaster just waiting to happen. The results of the effort were more or less okay. I shouldered the disappointment of the difference between what was advertised and what actually came to pass.

Upon arrival at the party, it was clear that the living room had been transformed into a dance floor, and mismatched bridge chairs added to sedentary upholstered ones to accommodate the numbers. End tables sported bowls of chips and pretzels. On the kitchen counter stood tall glass bottles of Coke and 7 Up.

A mono record player, brought down from a bedroom, would play the latest 45s—an eclectic mix and fast and slow songs, fast being the obvious icebreaker.

We mingled. I felt a little shy, but nothing noticeable or debilitating. Socializing was honed in a singular direction: which boy I "liked," or not. The choices didn't vary that much. It was more about seeing someone "differently" than I had before. I was very clear on that point. If I was interested, I felt invigorated. When I wasn't interested, I felt nothing and, worse than nothing, a remote revulsion. Most of the time I just yearned and, at parties, danced.

Fast dances were easy enough to endure. I made little eye contact with my dance partner, except for peeking at how well he danced, and the findings often disheartened me. I was used to dancing with guys who couldn't; their frenetic, arrhythmic gestures were an embarrassment I had successfully dealt with through resignation and acceptance.

Slow dances were another thing entirely. Not much was demanded of either partner in this regard, and going in circles was a dance step that anyone could master. At some point in the evening, more slow dances would come on. The boys would ask the girls. Some songs were transcendent, like "Cherish" by The Association, a ballad of pleading and effusion for a love that knows no bounds, yet

189

is unknown to the other. Or very slow—"This is a Man's World" by James Brown, with its deep funk, and its pizzicato walking bass line setting the rhythm throughout. Or The Mamas and the Papas' "This is Dedicated to the One I Love," with its soaring melody and changing dynamics.

The dance convention had evolved a little since the '50s, which had evolved a little since the '40s. The hand that held the other's hand and extended out from the body in the '40s became cradled in the '50s and was then released in the '60s. Now we held each other with both arms, girls' hands on boys' shoulders, boys' arms around girls' waists. In the '40s, there were actual dances steps that varied from song rhythm to song rhythm. The foxtrot, the cha-cha, the two-step, the waltz were fairly standard for everyone to learn. In the '50s, one had to be versed in rock 'n' roll steps and the jive. Starting in the '60s, the concept of dancing separately from your partner became the norm, with the Twist, the Mashed Potatoes, the Hippy Hippy Shake, the Jerk, the Swim, the Hitch-hiker, etc. By the '70s, and beyond, dancing separately was the prevailing custom, with slow songs being dropped from the repertoire, and suggestive sexual gyrations incorporated to make up for the lack of contact.

But, for the time being, we danced our slow dances, "wearing out the carpet," going in predictable circles with no talent for the activity. Except for Brendon.

All the boys in the group were going through puberty. There wasn't a high-pitched voice among them. They were growing tall, getting muscular, the bones in their jaws were transitioning towards more definition. They wore cologne, freshly-ironed dress shirts, and "stove pipes"—a trend in dress pants for men, straight and wide-legged, not flared or bell-bottomed—and no blue jeans, plaids or paisleys, yet.

Brendon was old school at the age of twelve. He asked each girl to dance, as a gesture of gentlemanly politeness, not to leave anyone out. It wasn't customary for girls to ask boys unless it was announced as "girls' choice." Funny how we obeyed "the rules," even at a private party.

190

I always liked dancing with him. It was as if we both knew that it was just a dance. I never felt he had "designs" on me, that he was on the make. He was respectful, and yet could be physically close without it feeling invasive. My arms reached to his shoulders, my fingertips at his shoulder blades. His arms were comfortably resting at my waist, his hands one above the other at the middle of my back. He was tall, so my mouth didn't quite clear his shoulder, but I could see everyone as we danced.

Brendon didn't dance in circles; he danced in figure eights. It meant that we had to move as a unit, because the weaving sway was almost off-kilter, and so I had to rely on him to keep us steady, our backs and hips dipping into the motion. That momentum conveyed a subtle thrill to the experience, making it more rhythmic, more stimulating, more exciting. It was a secret all the girls knew about, which earned him the coveted accolade of being "a good dancer," especially according to one of us.

His deferential manner and good looks weren't lost on Gayle. How and when they converged, before it became public knowledge that they were an item, was difficult to pinpoint. But converge they did. In our estimation, they made a lovely couple.

Gayle was tall too, and sturdy. She had a big personality and could take care of herself. Like Brendon, athleticism came naturally to her, and she was comfortable with a baseball glove and cap, as if they were typical attire for her. She had large, blue-green eyes, with a fan of thick, dark eyelashes—a genetic trait that was evident in both her younger sister and brother—and luminous, white skin. She had curly, shoulder-length, brown hair with an exaggerated side part, which forced an unwilling tress to go beyond its limit and dangle down the front of her face, requiring her to take issue with it in repeated attempts to secure the lock behind her ear.

She had a broad smile, happily revealing crooked and crowded permanent teeth. It was a dead giveaway of social standing and values. Her family was working-class, white, Anglo-Saxon, like Lydia's. Spending money on an orthodontist would not only be prohibitive financially, but as far removed from what constituted necessity as could be. It would be some time before braces that straightened children's teeth became the norm across class, even a priority. And then, it wouldn't be uncommon to see adults, who had missed the boat during childhood, availing themselves of an appearance-altering opportunity that had eluded them because of their parents' unwillingness or inability to pay for the service. But Gayle continued to smile, undaunted.

When Brendon and Gayle danced, it was different. Their figure eights became tighter, and the steps much slower, as if they had halved the rhythm. Her face fit in the crook of his neck, and they moved seamlessly, their eyes closed. Their arms were totally extended, enveloping each other as far as their reach allowed.

Gayle hosted the next party. She lived a block away and, like me, above a store on St. Clair. Having this in common felt affirming, and going to her place was an eye-opener. I never imagined that a party could be held in such a space. All the parties to date had been in houses with dedicated living and dining rooms, in layouts that flowed, and backyards of grass and flowering shrubs. Yet here we all were. Her flat was not quite the same as mine. A little worse for wear maybe, with three young kids and two parents to house. It was a temporary stay, of course, until they bought something.

Her father was a firefighter—a "fireman" in the days before political correctness and affirmative action. Then, as now, it was considered a very good job. Her parents were much younger than mine. Her mother would have had her first child at around eighteen, compared to my mother, whose life path was intercepted by the war, and who bore her first child at the age of thirty-one.

We all milled about, space notwithstanding, negotiating obstacles to get to a bowl of chips and finding places to dance. It was a success.

It seemed to me I had completed my field research and addressed my deepest concern: that where I lived wasn't as much of an impediment to my social life as I had feared. Maybe I didn't need to be embarrassed to have people over. The number of invitees would easily fit, as it was a relatively small group. Borrowing a record player and 45s from someone would be simple, and providing snacks in the way of pop and chips, absolutely affordable.

I fantasized about being the next host. Almost everyone else had had a turn. Aside from it being a gesture of hospitality, hosting

192

a party filled a need that was harder to pinpoint. It wasn't enough anymore to go to school and then come home, to go over to someone's house for an afternoon or for a sleepover, to go to a movie. What got sublimated on the dance floor was as vital as air, though we never articulated it as such—touch, the proximity of another's body, the emergence of a new type of interest we didn't question, emanating from the same physiology that produced puberty, but also concomitant thought, feeling, allure. I could be the purveyor of "that." All I had to do was ask my parents.

I was excited about the prospect and about putting forward my best sales pitch. My mother would especially love the part about Brendon; he would accord perfectly with her fervor around anti-racism and civil rights, surely, considering what havoc hatred of Jews had wrought.

"Can I have a party here?" I asked my mother, knowing that if I'd asked my father he would just refer me to her anyway. "Gayle had one at her place and they live above a store too. Everyone had a good time. It's a small group, about ten of us. Please?"

I was prepared for my mother to begin with the security of "no" and then move towards "yes" as she got used to the idea and her fears dissipated.

"You wouldn't have to do anything. All we need are some snacks. I can borrow a record player. The living room would be perfect. People could sit or dance…."

My mother was looking skeptical and offered her typical, cynical commentary: "Ich duff doos a zoy vee a loch in kopf" ("I need this like a hole in the head"), but then seemed to ponder the idea. I felt encouraged.

"And one of the boys, his name is Brendon, is really nice. He's black and from a very good family. He's a top student too and so polite. You'd like him. He and Gayle are boyfriend and girlfriend. Isn't that wonderful? She's white and he's black and it doesn't matter."

"Die vist a schvartzeh!" ("You want a black one!") She was instantly enraged. "Villst huben schvartzeh kinder!" ("Do you want black children!"), she accused.

If I had been an historian, the idea that I could be married with children at such a young age wouldn't have sounded so ridiculous. After all, Lady Capulet indicated to Juliet, during perhaps their only mother-daughter talk regarding the marital viability of Paris, that she was already a mother at Juliet's age of fourteen. This would have put Lady Capulet on the birthing bed at roughly thirteen and married at around twelve, presuming that consummation had occurred after the wedding, in keeping with the sanctity of the family name.

If I had been thick-skinned, her attack would have deflected off me like those tiny balls with extra bounce, which hit the ground and then launched themselves way above, exceeding what was expected of their performance.

If it had been my brother, he wouldn't even have heard her, sealed off in the world he created to protect himself, where he was surrounded by witty conversation and fine wine.

But I was me, defenseless—a strange mixture of being appalled, humiliated, and helpless.

I attempted to use common sense. "What are you talking about? I'm not interested in him. He likes Gayle, and she likes him." My mother could not be convinced; she felt she was on to something, some undercurrent meant to obfuscate the facts. She was sure that she could see what was implicit, in ways that lay beyond the scope of even the most intuitive people. No way she was going to be fooled. She saw through the smoke and called out the reflections in the mirrors.

Then I was embarrassed, when I realized she had depicted Brendon and me sexually, something that hadn't really occurred to me consciously. She also projected this image of a mixed racial family, which she felt would have been viewed with nothing short of contempt by everyone. All this based on a party with a group of ten preteens who liked to dance and eat junk food. I was dumbfounded by her ability to put 2 and 2 together and get 4.1 repeated to infinity.

I could hear counterarguments in my head. I didn't like that I had immediately stopped defending Brendon, selling him out in a way, because I wasn't interested in him, colluding with my mother to dispel her worry—I wasn't going to go with a black boy. I couldn't express to her the distinction between liking him as a person and liking him as a boyfriend. I was ashamed. Then I felt guilty. I did like the way he danced. What if he stopped liking Gayle and started liking me? I wouldn't have been interested in him, but was that because I had now been influenced by my mother's attitude, which meant I wouldn't have wanted to be with Brendon because he was black? I shuddered at the thought. Either way was awful.

I took a few potshots at her, called her a hypocrite. How did she manage to adore the black icons of civil rights and in the same breath eschew the living example in Brendon? But it felt like I was on a kamikaze mission, a sacrificial gesture which, for a brief moment, made an impact, but ultimately didn't change a thing, except to make me feel worse.

There would be no party at my place, and the pain of the argument would register as a dull boulder that weighed me down and made it hard to move around in a world so at odds with the people closest to me.

Chapter 22

White Linoleum Tiles with Flecks...
That Move!!!

My parents tended to be reactive instead of proactive, except in one instance. Before renovation was trendy, my parents decided to upgrade parts of the apartment. There was a reason: it was about being able to keep the place "clean," a code word. Original wooden floors were everywhere, even in the bathroom. The hall floor, being the thoroughfare, was suffering under the strain of travel. Only the bedrooms and living room were in good shape. Even so, I sat many times, foot in one hand, tweezers in the other, investigating the angle of entry of the sliver in order to work out a technique that would draw out the tiny bit of wood with the least injury to my foot. Unfortunately, there were a number of botched jobs, as efforts to locate the sliver resulted in forcing it further into my skin. Blood and a bigger wound were consequences of the failed endeavor. As a preemptive gesture, I did try to avoid walking around in stocking feet, but regardless, slivers were very much a part of having wooden floors.

The hall, the kitchen, the bathroom, the flight of stairs, and the small vestibule behind the front door would now have linoleum tiles instead of hardwood. The tiles chosen were white with black and brown flecks. The change would brighten up the space considerably; dark brown (wood) was now white (tiles). My mother liked tiles because they could be washed down, unlike wooden floors. Still, she would have to contend with the wooden floors in the bedrooms and living room. Those floors did not have the protective urethane coating so prevalent in modern suburban homes. They needed to be waxed and then polished, a labor-intensive process with little recompense, as the floors never gleamed, compared to damp-mopping the smooth wooden surfaces of new construction, where the sheen never faded. And, once a year, my father and mother would undertake the thankless job of removing the buildup

197

from weekly waxing and polishing. The process included rags and turpentine and scrubbing on hands and knees, and, no doubt, inhaling toxic fumes. All because the place had to be "clean."

My mother's sense of being "clean" wasn't an obsession. It wasn't like her other routines, where she operated in a particular mode, or had things in a particular order. She was responding to a persistent threat, a force to be reckoned with, and she retaliated as best she could. They weren't easy to spot on the wooden floors. Dingy lighting didn't help. Frosted forty or sixty watt bulbs were the norm for fixtures during those times, and ceiling lighting wasn't yet considered a design concept. Nor was there a need to illuminate crucial procedures in the home, like there was in a hospital for those undergoing brain surgery. Rather, the light "on" provided basic ease of navigation, which the light "off" did not. Simple.

Brown on brown floors was camouflaging, and getaway routes abounded. They would scurry towards the first slit they could find, and there were many, quarter-round not sitting quite flush to floorboard or to plaster wall. Measuring about two inches long, looking as if they were portaging shallow hulls on their delicate but speedy legs, feelers out in front, their reproductive agility boosting their numbers, originating from anywhere and everywhere, able to survive on next to nothing: cockroaches.

Not cute like the ladybugs you'd allow to crawl up your arm, or the ladybug personas that made their way into the land of cartoons as characters in Disney movies, their images manufactured into stuffed toys for kids and beloved pets. There was no media spin on cockroaches. These didn't inspire the creative and marketing campaigns of ad agencies, except for Raid.

Raid's careful branding, the connotation of its name, and the packaging of the product—shiny cans of startling red and yellow, primary colors that screamed "alert"—added to its purported prowess. A depiction of the cockroach appeared on the can, so that the sprayer could identify the prey. As distinctive as its label was its smell. A noxious mixture of acrid sweetness with an undertone of toxicity, which made it difficult to breathe once the spurt was deployed, leaving you with the ambivalent sensation that it smelled poisonous enough to do the job...but what did you just inhale?

198

Raid's lasting "Kills Bugs Dead" slogan generally lived up to its promise, but death wasn't immediate. Pointing the spray in the right direction was key. *PSSST* coated the roach and rendered it slow-moving, but not dead. *PSSSSST*, oh, what the hell, *PPPPPPPPPPPPPPSSSSSSSSSSSSSSSSSTTTTTTTTTT…PPPPPPPPPPP PPPPSSSSSSSSSSSSSSSSSSSSSTTTTTTTTTTTTTTTTTTTTTTT…*. After about two minutes, the deed was done. Killing roaches this way was only marginally better than stepping on them. What was lost in immediacy was gained in not having to experience the crunch of their shells underfoot and having to scrape off their bits from shoe bottoms.

Surprise appearances were the forte of roaches. Perhaps it was their startle instinct, but it seemed they had a particularly disruptive talent for declaring their presence. The cool, rational idea that "it was more scared of you than you of it" couldn't be fathomed in the moment when I opened the bathroom medicine cabinet and a cockroach careened out into the sink and began its wobbly negotiation of the smooth, porcelain, sloping sides. All I could think was "YUCK!" and "EEW!" and feel my stomach turn. Then the shock passed, but the revulsion didn't. I now faced the prospect of killing it, filling my lungs with Raid, removing its dead carcass, and being left with the memory of the whole experience.

All this would be moot once the linoleum tiles were installed.

It was a bold financial decision, but one that made a lot of sense. The linoleum tiles fit snugly against one another and were glued with a strong adhesive that created a sealed bond. There was no question that tiles were superior to wooden floors in this regard. Caulking along the quarter-round would fill any gaps. The kitchen and bathroom were the trouble spots, each with its specific propensity for heat and moisture and the dreaded damp. Thus, the uninterrupted flow of tiles, which began in the kitchen and carried on into the bathroom, down the hall, and descended the steps to the vestibule, would ensure that there were no hiding spots.

When my parents were considering the purchase of a commercial property, the type of business in the store below was an important criterion. They were clear that they didn't want to live above a restaurant or a grocery store, expressly because of "vermin." They found a property where the business in question was a camera store. They were sold, so to speak. Discovering cockroaches was a bitter pill for sure, but linoleum tiles would be the remedy.

The tiles were installed and they definitely brightened up the place. The smooth surface was easy to care for, and every Thursday the tiles would be scrubbed before being polished. For scrubbing, there was nothing better than Spic and Span, a popular household product cleverly advertised alongside afternoon soap operas. Spic and Span evoked a transcendent level of cleanliness next to godliness and akin to exfoliation. Spic and Span's gritty texture meant business, its bright green color was hopeful, and its fabricated smell, somehow fresh. There were advancements in polishing too. Formerly, the wax had to be applied by hand in small circles, while the now liquid variety was simply poured on, distributed evenly, and left to dry.

For the sinks, toilets, and bathtubs there was Ajax—another gritty substance with a bitter smell, deemed to be the solution for surfaces that saw a lot of bacteria-encouraging matter. All-purpose Mr. Clean did double duty. Windex, with its onomatopoeic sound of squeaky clean windows, put the shine on anything made of glass. Pledge was used for the wood furniture, its ads depicting the ease of dusting, housewives rapturously spraying and wiping tables and hutches, devil may care, as they made their way around the house. And so the cleaning arsenal was rounded out.

I was looking forward to the prospect of finally being done with the nauseating feelings associated with either the anticipation of, or the confrontation with, cockroaches. I could relax instead and not be vigilant, poised, and prepped. It worked. Eventually, my mind and body got used to the idea that nothing was going to happen. No more trepidatious steps, making sure that the ball of my leading foot wasn't where my weight was, just in case I had to reconsider. No more bending forward to inspect the lay of the land before me until I could ascertain that the coast was clear. No more holding my breath for the tiger that lay behind the door of the medicine cabinet.

200

There was a marked shift in those years, with Timothy Leary singing the praises of LSD in his popular phrase—"Turn on, tune in, drop out." There was talk of Jefferson Airplane's penchant for mushrooms, implicit in "White Rabbit." Jim Morrison's obviously stoned performance of "Light My Fire," when he appeared with The Doors on *The Ed Sullivan Show*, demonstrated the state of mind of the times. The banning of The Byrds' "Eight Miles High" meant the authorities thought they had tapped into the song's innuendo. The Beatles went off to India to sit at the feet of gurus and Ravi Shankar. The marijuana trend was taking the Western world by storm. Had the thick cloud of drug-filled smoke released its moisture so that it trickled down to me?

Was there something intoxicating in the cool night air as I came home on my bike, or was it possible that exposure to the chemicals in the plethora of household cleaning products caused me to hallucinate? Otherwise, how could one explain it?

I came home at the usual time, opened the door reaching beyond the front wheel of my bike. Using the system I had honed, I put my weight under the handlebars, like an Olympian about to lift a plated barbell, and placed the front wheel forward and up a few steps to allow enough space for the back wheel to clear the door. Once in, I backed up the bike so that it would rest against the wall in the tiny vestibule. The effort was never smooth, and the fenders clanged in protest a number of times.

Was that just a fleck that moved?

I froze. I thought I had caught a glimpse of something amiss on the third step up from the vestibule floor. I stood there in silence, waiting for it to happen again. It didn't. I quietly moved closer and peered at where the fleck had moved. On any given tile there were five or six flecks. I looked at the step from left to right, at each tile and at each fleck. Posing as a fleck was a cockroach.

The psychic edifice within me, which had housed the hope of never encountering another cockroach, imploded. The tremors were felt far and wide coursing throughout my body, highlighting every memory where the reference existed, and reframing forever how to think about it now.

Not only was this profound blow to me lost on my parents, but it seemed that they handled it with limited credence, as if I'd told them I'd just seen Jesus' face in the residual oil pattern in the frying pan. To emphasize her lack of faith, my mother dismissed me with another favorite phrase of hers: "Huk mir nisht in chunyik!" The direct translation— "Don't bang my kettle"—softened the blow, but the message was "Don't bother me." For them, the tiles had solved the problem, and these chance sightings were the product of my imagination. It was a remarkable way of refusing to accept what had happened, or of mitigating failure, or of stacking up cockroach occupation against the Nazi version. No contest.

Every time thereafter, whenever I discovered another one, I would be attended to with this same, tacit disbelief, as if each instance were the exception to the rule. Also, I never heard about any of their encounters, so it seemed that I was the only one for whom the honor was reserved.

And the honor continued to be bestowed upon me. I insisted on telling my parents every time it happened, looking for vindication; they responded to me with the same cockroach amnesia, and thus we danced within the impasse until one morning years later.

In the meantime, that first moving fleck raised my alert level even higher than before the tile installation, despair adding a nice touch to the reopened wound. Ironically, though, cockroach detection became a little easier. One glance at the tiles, from the vestibule looking at the stairs, or at the top of the stairs looking down the hall, and a moving fleck was all it took. Reaching for the can of Raid became the mindless act of necessary evil, a day in the life of the executioner. The deep rumblings of revulsion in my stomach, a mix of Raid inhalation and killing, would subside until the next time. That was the sad practice.

I'd accepted that we had cockroaches. It was a shameful admission, never to be uttered, even though people openly disclosed that cockroaches were commonly spotted in decent hotels throughout Florida. In Toronto, having cockroaches meant you were coarse, somehow unclean—a reflection of your personal hygiene, it seemed. To despair I added mortification lest a cockroach be discovered if a friend was over. Thankfully, I was spared this. I had gotten used to cockroach custom, and as long as it didn't waver, my way of dealing with it would remain consistent.

But then things changed. Cockroach mores shifted. It happened that fateful morning when I woke up to find a cockroach nestled within a fold of my pajama top, just below my collarbone. Had there been a cockroach conference to talk strategy, during which it was decided that occupation wasn't enough, and it was now time to escalate to expropriation?

I must have sounded particularly convincing while I screamed. I had given an impassioned speech, ending with "That's it! We're moving!"

It was the next-to-last nail in the St. Clair coffin. The last nail was hammered in on the second and final occasion that the sirens rang out from the fire station, and the searing tones did not abate.

Another frigid night, with mounds of curbside snowbanks fixed, frozen over, and dirt-encrusted. December. The cold was like menthol in your nostrils; the damp dangerous, like going out with wet hair. It was late, and most people, with the exception of shift workers, were asleep.

The sirens wailed and were inconsolable. For me, it reaffirmed that quiet slumber was a foreign concept. I got up out of bed and went to the living room window to look out. The fire trucks had pulled up right in front! The glare of the intermittent red light circled inside the living room and in another context would have been a winning feature for the dance party I would never have. In this context, I was filled with dread. No sooner had I awakened my parents, than there was a sharp rap on the front door. My parents and I scrambled to find boots and socks, and coats to wear over our pajamas. More knocking!

For some reason, I felt a strong urge not to answer the door, didn't trust letting in "a stranger," despite the overwhelming evidence that the authority figures were legitimate and were attempting to save, not snuff out our lives. It was a strange reaction. Then logic prevailed. I went down the stairs and opened the door. A tall firefighter told us to get out as soon as possible, that the entire block was being evacuated. With several storefronts and apartments above, and the fact that all the buildings were attached, it was the prudent thing to do.

My parents and I emerged from the ambient temperature of the apartment, into the frosty night, and were quickly ushered into the back of a police cruiser.

Once in, the car door opened on my side, and I was handed a baby. The baby slept peacefully during all this confusion, though he had been transferred from arms to arms to an unfamiliar me. Even the fact that the baby was wrapped in a singed woolen blanket, the edges smelling of burn—edges close enough to his nose to be inhaled and wondered about—didn't make a difference. Not a stir. I looked at the baby's deep brown face, his tiny, curled eyelashes and puffy cheeks, his closed fists, and was thankful for his ignorance. Thus, the four of us sat waiting, while the fire two doors down in one of the apartments was being doused, and information was transmitted from firefighter, to police officer, to us as the affected parties.

Then the door to the driver's side opened, and in got a police officer. He turned to face the back of the car so he could see the three of us, said hello, then his eyes came back to me. He glanced at the baby, looked at me, and said, matter-of-factly, "Guess that's not yours," and then chuckled. He was sure. His confidence in this deduction reminded me of my mother's warning about interracial unions and the lack of acceptance I could expect. It was a sign of the times that this officer couldn't possibly imagine that, if I'd had a child with a black man, the baby might look exactly like the one asleep in my lap.

"No," I said, "he's not mine." But I was concerned about who he belonged to. Once it was certain that the fire was out and hadn't spread, and it came time for my parents and me to go back into the apartment, the baby was just taken from my arms. That was that. I tried to get information in the days that followed. The fire had been severe enough—the place was gutted, there was extensive damage, some people were sent to the hospital to be treated for smoke inhalation—but no one had died. I expected that the baby and mother somehow got reunited. A few days later was Christmas.

After eighteen years of our living on a short track of hallway with bedroom stops, and being at the mercy of tenants' whims, cockroaches, and fire, the property was listed.

On another tangent, I may have witnessed a significant period in cockroach evolution. When I first encountered them, they were large and shiny, blackish brown, and if one could visualize them without legs and antennae, they looked a lot like juicy, fat dates. Perhaps their bodies prevented them from infiltrating to the extent their species wanted to, and so they began to adapt, slim down, shorten, lose their lustre. Something similar was going on in Western industrial trends. Cars too were shrinking—shedding their fins, minimizing their interiors—to allow for more vehicles on the road and to be more fuel efficient. Downsizing in the private sector was increasing profits. The new and improved cockroach in Toronto was small, skinny, fast, and endemic.

Chapter 23

United We Stand

It wasn't only on the cockroach front that my parents were allied, quietly denying the infestation. "Do you see a cockroach? I don't see a cockroach." Their bond was impenetrable, even though on the surface they may have tussled a lot over little things. She was high-strung, and he was always getting into trouble, especially in the kitchen. He, in turn, was laissez-faire about it all and took her irritations in stride, mildly protesting. Innocuous couple banter.

There was no argument when it came to issues like politics and religion. She articulated her position with eloquent substantiation, albeit aggressively, and he seconded her opinions. He agreed with her, but lacked the skill to express it. On the domestic front, he deferred to her, but that was because he trusted her with money, and his trust was never misplaced. She ran the household well, looking after all the chores of cooking and cleaning, and being home to raise children. She valued the fact that he worked so hard to provide for the family—always punctual at work, good at his craft, and rarely absent. But none of this had anything to do with their bond.

Every day, from opening to closing, they stand in line. It is a solemn wait, for while they stand there, there is hope that someone in their family may have survived, though the odds are very grim. Once they've given their name, the truth will be revealed, and they will either rejoice in a way that will shake them to their core and bring them to their knees with gratitude, or they will be struck by a cruel blow and feel their loss all over again.

It is a rudimentary idea, but it works. Each person in line registers his or her family name, and the information is kept on file. Successive family members who sign in are reunited with their loved ones. Everyone knows to come here, the word spreads, though no Facebook exists in 1945.

My mother is one of the administrators, the person who greets you and takes your precious data. For you, she is the human link to the news you dread and yet seek. For her, you are another person with the same, not-quite-dead look in your eyes, the cloudy countenance, the sag in your cheeks, the pain in your heart, your spine barely able to hold up your body. Since you are here standing in line, it must mean you imagine something you can't risk admitting to, but it's there: the tiniest bit of hope you dare to possess so that the possible news that your entire family has perished won't annihilate you.

My mother has already been through it—one of the perks of the job, you might say. In addition to whatever files verify one's relatives' existence, or not, are the stories that circulate from one to the other, to the other, to yet another, in an attempt to create continuity and closure.

"Yes, I saw your father and brother," someone tells her. "They went together to the gas chamber." My mother ruminates over the fact that her younger brother had plans to marry and go to Australia, but didn't leave soon enough before the borders closed. Though her brother was young and nimble, his death, along with her father's, means that at the time of selection there was a glut on the market, making young men disposable; usually, able-bodied men were allocated to slave labor.

"Your sisters and their husbands and their children all went together. They refused to be separated, and so the guards let them be." Like the paw that mangles the characters' wishes in "The Monkey's Paw," the guards ensure that these family members end up "together" all right. No doubt, by "together," the family members didn't mean in a heap of dead bodies in one of the corners of the gas chamber. Technicalities, technicalities. My mother ponders the tenacity, naïveté, and blind courage of this fatal stance.

"Your mother was killed in her bed. She couldn't obey the order to leave the house, because she was sick, and so they shot her right there and then." The violent image of this act, this overkill, will haunt my mother forever. There it is: the whole family, gone.

Every day, my mother comes to work and hears the woes and anguish of those suffering idle hope and those about to suffer again great loss. But, as she is one of them, she knows how they feel, and it grounds her.

My father approaches the counter, and my mother starts with the customary greeting. They quickly realize that they are from the same town, and though their circles of friends and acquaintances never intersected, they "know of" one another. She knows of his mother's early plight of being a young, twenty-something woman, barely finished her biological growth when she is suddenly widowed, instantly impoverished with three young children she can't care for. He remembers her father—what a good man, a kind man, his respected reputation in the town. The disparate psychic molecules begin to cohere.

He's not the first man to be interested in her. She has fielded the advances of many a suitor and has listened to their ardent sales pitches against an unshakable bottom line of hers, which she can't put into words. It's guillotine-exact, nipping in the bud the unlikely, the incompatible, the ridiculous.

They make a date. They talk about what matters. Trauma leaves little room for chitchat. She has two non-negotiable conditions: "I don't cook. I don't want children." He is fine with both. After a two-month courtship, they are married.

It is a simple ceremony. There are no wedding planners. No band. No speeches. No white wedding gown. No bridesmaids, no groomsmen, no guests. It is somewhat like eloping to get married in Vegas, except that being just the two of them is a heartaching allusion to all the lost loved ones, and it's Poland in 1945.

There is only one photo. She sits at a table for two; he is partially standing and leans in beside her with his arm on her shoulder. There is a white tablecloth and a small floral arrangement. It looks like they've just had their coffee. He is in a suit. She wears a smart, fitted, knee-length brown dress. It isn't the convention to smile in photos. No one has yet invented the ad to say "Cheese!"

They have stipulated to the officiator that whatever he says must be devoid of references to God and the promise to make a

Jewish home—two things that seem unbelievably absurd to them. What is not said is this: This marriage is about the union of two people who know first-hand the horrors of the events from 1939-45, not empathically, not sympathetically, not detachedly, not secure in the fact that it didn't happen to one of them, but who accept unequivocally that they will continue to feel the sick, recurring shudder of the magnitude of violation and injustice, who won't tire of hearing it when it surfaces, as perforce it will, who won't, precisely because it wasn't that person's experience, offer insipid advice like "Move on, get over it, put the past behind you," and who, this time, most profoundly, will do everything in their power never again to lose another loved one. These are the actual marital vows.

No small wonder that things turned out they way they did for me, at what could have been the zenith of my high school career.

By now, the boys had traded in their stovepipes for beige, slim-legged pants, their open-collared shirts for buttoned-down, their white socks for dark. Their tubes of Brylcreem lay on their sides in medicine cabinets, still bearing the dents of previous use, abandoned and forming dry crusts at the tips.

The Beatles had brought in a new hairdo, which required nothing but air-drying and a bit of training to get those bangs to swoop in one direction and stay put just above the eyes. Still, without any hair products, bangs would be bangs, and so wherever the Beatles had made their mark in the world, boys could be found flicking their hair, many times a day, from one direction to the other so that their bangs would fall into place, or using their fingers to sweep those wayward hairs, which fell in front of their eyes, back above their brows.

Girls' skirts got shorter and less poufy, their bobby socks grew to knee-highs and changed from white to dark, their ponytails were taken down so that their hair fell about their shoulders and beyond.

By some curious conspiring of circumstances, everyone seemed to have traded in his or her ethnicity for what appeared to be some California dreamworld espoused in Beach Boys' hits. Maybe it was the peculiar catchment area of the high school I attended,

210

which encompassed a few exclusive Toronto neighborhoods extending from Christie to Deer Park Crescent, just east of Avenue Road, and from Davenport to Lonsdale. That would include the private enclave of Wychwood Park, with its gracious homes and a central, sprawling, ranch-style bungalow, which was the gem in the crown and determined the configuration of the surrounding lots. As well, all the lands around Casa Loma—the bizarre, ninety-eight room castle built between 1911 and 1914 in the Gothic Revival style of the 1740s, looming hugely and looking out of place among Tudor and Arts and Crafts abodes—and lower Forest Hill, which was a sizable area with mansion after mansion.

Maybe it also had to do with the specific state of the educational system in Toronto in the late '60s, when baby boomers were reaching their teens and needed to be schooled, and there was a lot of money available to house them. New programs, new curricula, new libraries, new books, state-of-the-art facilities. Parents who had formerly sent their children to private schools took notice and wondered what happened to privilege as the public system outperformed the private. And so a stream of ex-private school students came through the high school I attended.

The girls were pretty, lanky and fair, with long, blonde, straight hair, blue eyes, names like Cathy and Virginia and Cecily and Jane, and stately middle names inherited from maternal grandmothers who came from a tradition of high tea. The girls shopped at Harridges in the Colonnade on Bloor, or at Holt Renfrew across the street, and charged their purchases to their parents as per the understanding between them that money was no object. Their skirt and sweater outfits were unlimited in number and variety. Every day they wore something new. The boys were Cameron and Tim and John and Curtis. Their fathers were doctors, Bay Street lawyers or businessmen; they lived in huge, old houses; all their mothers were beautiful. The whole family skied in the winter and went to the cottage in the summer.

The rest of us made do as best we could, straightening our curly, wavy, frizzy hair with irons, or winding it around Campbell's Soup cans put to yet another use, since the largest rollers for sale were still too small and created more curls, the exact opposite of

211

what we were hoping for. We desperately resorted to depilatory products as puberty brought with it darker, shameful hairs on upper lips, arms, and backs, and created unibrows. Those with means sought plastic surgeons to correct "character noses," a lame euphemism for big and bumpy. Clairol's hair dye ads, preaching that "Blondes have more fun," plunged several ethnicities into depression, exalted those who were lucky enough to have the right color, and saved those few whose skin tone could get away with making a fortuitous transformation courtesy of a bottle of peroxide.

It was the momentous age of cheerleaders, "captains of the football teams," and prom queens, a lifestyle unilaterally transposed from our American neighbors, persistently teaching us, overtly and covertly, how to be teenagers, through an ever-replenished barrage of bikini and *Gidget* sequels and TV shows like *The Adventures of Ozzie and Harriet* and *Peyton Place.*

I was convinced it wasn't my "time," that was for sure—I had disqualified myself on the basis of a number of irrevocable factors. My hair was not naturally straight or blonde; my skin was more olive than fair; my eyes decidedly not blue; my height average where a few extra inches would have benefitted me greatly. I lived on a main street in a flat, instead of in a house.

My parents were hopelessly unrehabilitatable. Their thick Jewish accents were immutable, never to improve even slightly and, in my mother's case, most unfortunate, since she was fluent and literate in English, but would be judged as uneducated. Looks-wise they couldn't have been further from the standard. My mother was short and chubby. Her oral health had suffered terribly during the war, and she had been left with the effects of bad dental work: discoloration and thick, unattractive caps on the most visible teeth. My father was a little less embarrassing, tall for his ethnic group, but still shorter than his Anglo counterparts. Had he been a black rapper in the twenty-first century, his silver-capped canine would have been edgy and hip, but in the '60s he came off as foreign and was presumed to be from the central European underclass.

Their first names were completely alien in sound and spelling. My father's name wasn't James or William or Robert, my mother's neither Violet nor Joan nor Blanche. When asked, I tried to create anglicized versions for them, but knowing the truth galled me, and I was a very unhappy imposter. It didn't help anyway. Though my last name was "in English," it would take an unrelenting devotee to find me in the phonebook, perusing the columns and staying focused on the first initials and names, not giving up as the odds seemed to dwindle once all the *A*s through *G*s had been exhausted, and then the *H*s through *M*s. But faith was really shaken from the *N*s through *T*s, for what possibility could there be for *U*, *V*, *W*, *X*, or *Y*? And yet, there I was under *Z* followed by *y*—the first and second letters of my father's first name. Ours was the very last entry for my surname.

Beside his name, finally, would be my phone number: *LE* 7-4731. The *LE* stood for *Lennox*.

Lennox was one of the many lyrical Toronto Telephone Exchange names now lost forever. Each exchange represented a section of the city. Then, as now, the alphabet was divided among the numbers 2 to 9. With no area code preceding, the first two numbers stood for the exchange name. There was *Russell—RU* (78)—north of Eglinton to Wilson, in and around Bathurst Street; *Hudson—HU* (48)—east of Bathurst, taking in Lawrence Park and Upper Forest Hill; *Walnut—WA* (92)—most of the Annex; *Melrose—ME* (63)—north of Sheppard west of Bathurst; *Baldwin—BA* (22)—Willowdale: *Empire—EM* (36)—downtown west; *University—UN* (86)—downtown central; *Rogers—RO* (76)—west of Dufferin, north and south of St. Clair; *Cherry—CH* (24)—Weston/Etobicoke; and *Belmont—BE*(23)—around Islington Avenue. *Howard—HO* (46)—and *Oxford—OX* (69)—took care of most of the Danforth Road area. There were many others: *Wellington, Mayfair, Randolph, Mohawk, Clifford, Hickory, Garden....* And then there was *Lennox—LE* (53)—St. Clair west of Bathurst, and south of St. Clair.

Incoming calls expressly for me were infrequent at best. The phone was almost never for my father, more often for my mother or brother. If that wasn't enough, my phone number was very close to the one for the Baker Carpet Cleaning Company: *LE* 7- 4131. In fact, I think the phone rang more insistently from frenzied customers (who had ridden the trend of wall-to-wall broadloom and now found themselves with nasty stains and embedded dirt that only a professional could remedy) than it ever rang for me.

So when the call came, I was flabbergasted.

In the'60s, serendipitous calls like these were one-shot deals. Being at home to pick up the phone was the only way to connect. There was no call display to give you a heads up, no answering machine or voice mail to retrieve timely messages at your behest, no Pavlovian sound prompting you to check for texts and emails, no such thing as round-the-clock access to you in the form of a small, rectangular, communication device, which you would never be without unless by design.

"Hello?" I began customarily, not expecting it to be anyone in particular.

"Hi," she returned. I recognized the voice right away. It was my good friend from school. "What are you doing tonight?" she asked.

It was an odd question. At about 5:00 p.m., just hours away from Saturday night—the most significant night of the weekend—the likelihood of going anywhere at this late juncture was basically nil. With no prospects as a "Grade Niner," no connections, no sign of a boyfriend, what else could be done? She and I, and other friends waiting for our teenage lives to begin, spent many a Friday and Saturday night fantasizing about what we didn't have, sustained by stories of other, more fortunate girls who had managed to hit the big time. One of those was my friend's sister, who had been blessed with the sort of looks epitomized by the trend. And she was a cheerleader. Currently, she was steadily dating one of the two most sought-after boys in the school, both football heroes.

"Nothing," I answered, like it should go without saying. Then I wondered…"Why?"

"My sister and Colin want to double date with Steve tonight, and now that Steve doesn't have a girlfriend anymore, he wanted to ask you out."

What happened to me at this point was complex. On a visceral level, there was a surge of exhilaration; on a psychic level, an overwhelming feeling of great fortune. I was extremely grateful for

214

being noticed, when I had felt so undeserving. My friend had asked the most rhetorical question ever uttered: Did I want to go out with Steve? How many ways were there to say YES!!!

At six foot two, Steve McNally was a wonder of masculinity—tall, lean, muscular, a strong jawline, a face like Doug McClure—a secondary character, often appearing tanned and in a swimsuit, running with a surf board to the beach in movies made for teenagers. Steve was fair, his hair a darker shade of blonde, his eyes a greener shade of blue. He was a little more preppy than his best friend Colin. While Colin went in for the Beatle haircut, Steve retained the neater and shorter, but no less revolutionary, JFK hairstyle, the look that took the world by storm in the early sixties. Steve was a little shy, an endearing quality that set him apart from Colin's gregariousness and served to distinguish them. And they were very different. But together, they pretty much cornered the market on the finest catches around, romantic lottery wins for the chosen few.

And here was the winning ticket. All that was required to redeem it was a rubber stamp from my parents.

Well...

The hue and cry that ensued from my straightforward request was explosive, and since the camera store was now closed, the unleashing of the fury was permissible. A more appropriate provocation for the raging intensity of the response I got would have been a similar threat on my side, like trying to strangle my mother to death.

"YOU'LL GO OUT WITH HIM OVER MY DEAD BODY!!!" was my mother's way of saying "no."

What was so terrible about Steve McNally? One might have wondered. Clean-cut, respectful, handsome, interested in me, appeared to be pluses, no?

No.

Steve's fatal flaw was that he wasn't Jewish. The fact that I wanted to go out on a date with him was tantamount to colossal betrayal. As with Brendon, my mother's thinking was dizzyingly metaphysical, namely that this one date would set into motion a chain of events leading to an interfaith marriage and children who were religious pariahs. This coming from an atheist...

My mother was extremely agitated, and seething, which alerted my father. He was instantly mobilized as her robotic protector, ready to defend her against me, and looking at me with severe judgment. "What did you do to make your mother so upset?" I had done the unconscionable. I was a teenager who wanted her parents' permission to go out on one date with a nice boy. My deep affront to my mother was his only reality, his consummate truth. This was how I got blood on my hands.

Calling back my friend to deliver the news that I wasn't able to accept the invitation felt like I was handing the hangman the noose to hang me. My friend was predictably surprised by my response, as in thinking I'd lost my mind. I protected my parents, didn't tell my friend what had really happened. I was ashamed for them, and for me by association. It isolated me.

. Impotent retaliation came in the form of this scathing diary entry:

> My parents are by far the most idiotic prejudiced fools I have ever encountered in my life. I can't go out on dates. I can only go to parties that have Jewish kids there. I can't take it much longer. All I do is cry and cry and cry every time I have to refuse. If I was only older God I would get the hell out of this damn house and never come back to my parents again. I have to do something but as long as I'm still young and dependent I can't.

It took about two minutes and one phone call from my friend to find a willing girl to round out the foursome.

I never got another chance.

Chapter 24

Don't Bogart That Joint

Watching my brother successfully execute the move away from my parents was like the uplifting, vicarious feeling of a prison inmate who knows that one of his peers has managed to outwit the authorities to become a free man.

He escaped to Rochdale, the brand new residence for University of Toronto students, located on the south side of Bloor just west of St. George. With its concrete exterior and hermetically sealed windows, it was an architectural testament to modern design, expressing minimalism through the use of natural materials. While Rochdale, with its French pronunciation—"Roshdale"—was a cataclysmic failure as student housing, it found a way to triumph from its literal ashes and re-emerge, respectfully named after the precious end of a marijuana joint, the roach. And "Roach-dale" lived up to its name, a veritable den so full of drugs and drug dealers, its exhaust vents were like giant, joint-sucking maws emitting marijuana fumes.

My brother's relocation had the salutary side effect of improving my status, as I now moved from my bedroom to his. My former bedroom had always seemed unsettling to me, like scratchy wool on bare skin. I had been Goldilocks in that room, going from one piece of furniture to the next. First I slept in a crib, sharing the room with my brother while we had tenants, then for years on a fold-out couch until I got a proper bed, a dark-stained, wooden, four-poster single from Eaton's.

The room was claustrophobic and scary. An industrial sewing machine took up the space along one wall, parallel to my bed. A coffin-like top and a deep dull green upholstered cover hid the machine when not in use. The overall effect was of a large, expropriating, rectangular object measuring about five feet long by four feet high and three feet deep, in a room that couldn't have been more than ten by eight. On the adjacent wall was an armoire full of clothes that weren't mine. To the right of that was a diminutive, white enameled cabinet storing disparate knickknacks that didn't belong anywhere else.

Between the cabinet and the sewing machine was the small window, right across from the one in the next apartment, which meant that the utilitarian window blind was generally drawn, banishing what little light could come through anyway. The sun, when it was out, shone briefly as it cleared the building, and then disappeared again, because it was blocked by the next building three feet away across the window well. As for air, it too had its hardships. With no ability to flow directly into the window, its strength was severely diminished. I had to lean down into the opening so that my face could catch the slight breeze. Beyond me, the room was stuffy; in the winter, still; in the summer, stifling.

I knew how girls' bedrooms were supposed to look. I saw them on TV and in movies and at friends' houses. All light colors and airy, with plush toys and hairbrushes and lots of room for clothes. Everything in there was in proportion to its occupant, reflecting her interests and laying the foundation for her hopeful future. A feminine desk and chair to match, a petite bookcase with volumes that promoted whimsy and enchantment, like the *Narnia* series, the magical *Carbonel* books, and the clever curiosity of *Nancy Drew*. A big window with beautiful fabric drapes that could be parted and gathered at either end, like a girl with her hair in pigtails.

Fresh air would waft in because the home's blueprint placed windows at particular intervals in order to get a cross breeze. Sunlight would appear for long stretches because of generous side and back setbacks, common in most Toronto residential neighborhoods. There would be pretty pictures on the wall—maybe a Degas ballerina, or an elegant Renoir mademoiselle. The bed would be an inviting sanctuary of soft sheets and frilly pillows and bedspreads where the word "goodnight" would be a promise never broken.

That was what my friend Stacey's room was like. To walk into the space was to enter Stacey's world. A delightful transition

218

from the hall, the room was open and spacious. Her bed sat confidently and squarely in the middle. Having access from either side ensured that bed-making was a task ever done well. In my room, I had to reach across the bed to the opposite corner, try to tuck in the quilt and then the bedspread between the bed and the wall, smooth the fabric as much as possible, and then double back to eliminate the creases I couldn't help but create by having leaned across in the first place. Not to mention what unseemly activity was taking place on the floor along the wall out of my view…dust accumulating, and creepy crawlies having their way.

In addition to all the expected furnishings, Stacey had a number of exceptional pieces, as would befit an only child. I was most impressed with her own, as in personal, mono record player, and a stack of 45s and 33 1/3s. A real, standard issue, Toronto Board of Education blackboard (actually it was green), and real chalk—not the cheap, thin kind you could get at the corner store, which broke maddeningly and looked as though you were buying a deck of cards. No, this was the genuine article. Industrial grade chalk—thick, multicolored, resilient. The same with the eraser, the ruler, the pointer: real. Made playing Teacher beyond pleasurable.

If all good things came to those who waited, then I guess finally moving into my brother's room helped salve the pain of my bedroom history, though I had outgrown the need for good chalk, and playing Teacher was no longer a fantasy that appealed to me.

Time had passed and a tug of war was going on. The preppies tried to cling to their identity, their love of sports, clean-cut looks, and penchant for beer, or rum and coke. The cheerleading spirit of "rah rah rah!" was being eclipsed by a more aloof vibe, that of apathy, evidenced by the reduced numbers attending proms and the growing disinterest in school-wide campaigns to elect the prettiest girl for the position of prom queen.

Hair was getting longer and longer, boys and girls alike. Paisleys and plaids, embroidered peasant tops, denim bell-bottom blue jeans—Levi's first, then Lee's, then Wranglers. Patchouli oil filled the school halls…flowers and beads…trips both actual and figurative. To the head shops on Yonge for dope-smoking paraphernalia. To the Sally Anne for used fur coats and jackets. Instead of throwing around a football, boys were reading Kafka and Proust, Jack Kerouac, Allen Ginsberg.

Instead of shaking pompoms, girls were beginning to learn about feminism from Germaine Greer and Gloria Steinem, wondering about sexuality, gender, and oppression, writing poems, and using psychedelic markers to paint flowers and swirly abstracts onto any surface they could find, signing their names in the tapering and widening fonts that were typical of the "times a- changin'."

Miles Davis and John Coltrane provided the music for the most intellectual among us. Grateful Dead, Crosby, Stills, Nash and Young, Procol Harum, Vanilla Fudge—just a few of the stunning variety of musical offerings celebrating love, peace, and mind-altering drugs.

I was not immune to the fads, and that was why, when it came to choosing a paint color for my room, it was purple. Aside from my homage to the vibrant color scheme of the era, it was the first time I had been given the chance to put my own spin on my own environment. This was MY room.

I had negotiated a kind of privacy with my parents, whereby, if my door was closed, they were to knock first before entering. This took some doing. At first, they knocked and immediately came in the room, paying lip service to this brief, additional gesture. Waiting for instructions from me, after they had knocked, must have felt like an eternity for them. What would they miss in the interim? What mishap could befall me that they might have prevented? What was I up to that they would not find out about in time? What was I keeping from them? But they seemed to be able to learn at least a little patience.

In my room, I did what I could with what I had. The double bed my brother had slept in went into my old bedroom, shrinking that space even more, and the single bed came to my new room. All the furniture was dark wood. The rickety bookcase, built by my brother, was there, as well as his desk and refinished chair, the old night table, and the dresser, which had a round mirror that passed nicely as trendy. These staples were givens. It was now up to unique touches to express the personality of the inhabitant.

A lemon-yellow bedspread, in contrast to the purple walls, worked very well in the room. A bright, lime-green, stuffed animal, not a bear like others had, but a dolphin flourishing its pink, felt mouth, sat just in front of my pillow. On the wooden supports either side of the dresser's mirror was an assortment of personal items. Yarn to adorn hair was very popular for tying pigtails, ponytails, or to be used as a headband. The yarn was very thick and twisted; its color and texture were obvious when worn. I had two long pieces, which I draped over the supports, orange to match an orange tunic, purple to match a purple one. I also had a black ribbon headband and a brown, and another looking like rope, but made out of black velvet. I hung necklaces there as well. One with a cameo pendant, others with strings and beads.

My prized possession, though, was a stereo system, which was a "long time comin'," like in the song on the album *Déjà Vu*. Audio technology had certainly evolved through the fifties, sixties, and seventies. From my humble beginnings as a CHUM Bug, to now, was quite the ascent. The radio was the conduit for music, while TV was about entertainment and news. CHUM AM operating at 1050 kHz, from its premises just north of the Ports of Call on Yonge Street, was *the* radio station to be tuned into. The CHUM Chart may have led to the concept of Top 40, and being a CHUM Bug was my first foray into an exclusive club, although, while I knew I was part of a large group, I didn't know any of the other members.

Every Friday of every week, I would scramble down the stairs and go into the camera store to get the latest chart and see what was Number 1. Usually it was a Beatles' hit, but among the Top 10 were Beatles wannabes like The Dave Clark Five, Gerry and The Pacemakers, Herman's Hermits. There wasn't any money for a mono record player, like Stacey had, which was all the more poignant when, as a CHUM Bug, I entered into a contest and won the latest Monkees' record, a 45, with "I'm A Believer" on one side and "(I'm Not Your) Stepping Stone" on the other. I held the disk in my hand and looked at it in pathetic appreciation of the irony of the moment, *à la* "The Gift of the Magi." However, I did own a cute little transistor radio, which slipped neatly into its tiny lederhosen, its dial and volume control exposed for ease of use.

We also had a main radio, which sat atop the General Electric refrigerator—a plump, round-cornered, enameled block with the name Leonard rendered in the popular font of the '50s. After dinner, when the dishes were cleared away and my parents had retired to the living room to watch TV, the kitchen took on an ambience it didn't have during an ordinary day filled with utilitarian comings and goings. In the evening, the kitchen felt almost romantic; the only light on was an under-cupboard task light, which illuminated the rectangular porcelain sink and cast a glow in the room, bathing the red Arborite kitchen table in a wash that looked like wine.

There was a constant hum from plugged-in electrical objects, which sounded like the happy wife in commercials, who harbored no other sentiment except sheer contentment as she went about her household chores. And above that hum were soothing tunes coming out of the radio, which looked like the refrigerator in miniature, but was made out of Bakelite, its dial set at CKEY, its one speaker delivering the cool, clarinet sound of Acker Bilk's wistful "Stranger on the Shore."

Any music that played in the apartment was chosen for us by the radio jockeys and TV executives. In other homes, like Stacey's, one could decide. A mono player was for the kids. For the adults, there was a permanent piece of furniture, which graced living rooms and was as ubiquitous and necessary as the occasional chairs, long sofas, and wooden coffee tables: the stereo hi-fi cabinet.

It looked like a dining room sideboard, but part of the top lifted to reveal a turntable with a dial for volume control, and bass and treble levels for sounds that would be divided between built-in speakers, one at either end of the piece. Hence, stereo instead of mono. One could easily play 45s by changing the insert, and 33 1/3s could be stacked in anticipation of hours of uninterrupted musical selections, save the time it took for the arm to move away, and for the next album to drop down. The other part housed a built-in radio and storage for albums.

We owned no such item, one which was so common everywhere else, yet another distinguishing difference that I had to shoulder until the day my parents submitted the final mortgage payment on the building. For the first time in many years, my parents were neither in the red, nor just in the black and breaking even. They were up a notch, now able to "capitalize" on the camera store proprietor's rent, and though the unchanged amount was a bargain for him, it still meant a small profit for my parents.

That money translated into "things," my stereo system being one of them. It was my brother who procured it for me. He was savvy when it came to the latest in this and that, and those stereo hi-fi cabinets were now for squares and parents. It was the start of the audiophile age, and with it, the ideology around sound specifications, optimal listening, tweeters and woofers and amps. Now, you had to buy stereo "components." All-in-one systems were for the ill-advised and indiscriminate.

My system consisted of the first component, a changer, the new lingo for record player; the second component, an amp, which housed a tuner, the new lingo for radio (this would be divided into two components in the next few years); and two speakers with enough speaker wire to position them in the room for the best in stereophonic sound. I was actually proud, an emotion with which I was wholly unfamiliar. It had been a few years since I'd received The Monkees' 45 in the mail, and by this point the square, slim, brown paper bag the record slipped into looked aged. Now that I could play it, I didn't care to; my tastes had changed dramatically. That music was for teenyboppers, not for the hip and cool.

A pilgrimage to Yonge Street was in order. There, just north of Eaton's and Simpson's, was Sam the Record Man, the foremost music store in Toronto, and in Canada, for many decades. "Sam" referred to Sam Sniderman. He and Ed Mirvish of Honest Ed's were Jewish entrepreneurs who brashly advertised their wares. Kitschy neon signage that screeched and well-priced stock attracted customers in droves.

For the music lover, Sam the Record Man could always be counted on. Their employees were often musicians or music buffs who educated you regarding the best albums to buy and delighted in your purchases. I went in there and walked out with my very first album, King Crimson's *In the Court of the Crimson King*, with its gargoyle-like face on the cover—mouth agape, tongue poised—and its palette of bright blue and fuchsia.

King Crimson was the next musical incarnation of psychedelic rock, the fusion of atmospheric sounds, jazz, and classical elements. Their songs were very long and developmental, like Moody Blues' "Tuesday Afternoon." I listened over and over to "21st Century Schizoid Man," "The Court of the Crimson King," and the most ethereal, "I Talk to The Wind."

Setting the mood for listening was very important and required two trips, one to the hardware store and the other to the head shop. At the hardware store, I was able to obtain a blue light bulb, which I would screw into the lamp on my night table. The effect would be subdued and tranquil, yet beguiling.

Going to the head shop was like being instantly transported to the Far East and into a composite of Morocco, India, and Thailand. First you had to pass through the beaded curtain, setting off a series of wind chimes, which announced your presence, your nose inhaling drifting aromas of incense and perfume oils, your ears picking up the strum of sitar music.

You greeted the store clerk, who was a personification of the inventory, wearing too many silver rings, and whose manner was endlessly mellow just shy of passing out. A conversation could not be held without the peppering of recurrent terms such as "wow, man," "right on," "groovy," "I dig," and "far out." This form of speech, expressed with the least amount of adrenalin possible, and punctuated at conversation's end with the word that summed up the attitude of the times—"Peace" (with two fingers raised)—meant you were "in" with the in crowd.

So much to look at: pill boxes made of mother-of-pearl and brass, ornate paper-mache containers, embroidered sateen purses with little mirrors sewn in, small jade and ivory figurines from Shiva to Buddha, all types of silver jewelry, ankh, zodiac, and peace sign pendants, dangly beaded earrings, case after black felt-lined case of assorted silver rings, with or without gemstones. Throw

224

pillows in satins and velvets with gold tassels, scarves with gilded threads, Indian cotton tops made of cheesecloth.

For the dope smoker, a cornucopia of accessories was available to make the activity a splendid one. Hookahs and roach clips ranging from simple to fancy, hash pipes forged out of every imaginable material, rolling papers with an endless array of graphics that depicted the times, lighters and matches, and more. There was a flippancy about it that felt good; nothing for sale was illegal except for the substance it exalted, and there wasn't a thing the police could do about it.

Finally, you could choose from an abundance of incense—long and delicately slim packages labeled in Sanskrit, with lovely abstract designs that protected the ten or so fragrant sticks. The scent was everywhere and infused everything, making it hard to decide. I sniffed one package after another, just to find the bouquet that was to my liking. The nicest was a delicious blend of lavender and orange blossom; the lavender was calming, the orange blossom, invigorating. Perfect. I also purchased an incense holder, a small, weighted object with a tiny puncture to secure the stick and ensure safe burning.

The transformation of my bedroom into a listening paradise was now beginning. It was nighttime. The blind was down as usual. I removed the frosted bulb from the night lamp, replaced it with the blue one, and turned off the main ceiling light. A welcome effect I hadn't anticipated was that the lights in the tuner/amp also radiated a blue aura.

I lifted the smoked plastic changer top. Then I drew out the disk from its album cover, careful not to touch the record's surface, using the palms of my hands to maneuver it, just like an audiophile. I placed the record on the turntable and cleaned the vinyl surface with a chamois especially made for the procedure. I had my headphones ready, so as not to disturb my parents by playing music at a rather pronounced decibel level, which teenagers and adults would never agree upon. I put the incense holder on the night table's surface, tore the paper seal off the package, opened the tiny flap so that I could carefully remove one fragile stick and position

225

the stick's end in the hole. I replaced the flap and stored the package in the drawer of the night table. My matches were handy.

I put on my headphones and plugged the cord into the receptacle on the tuner/amp. I pressed "START" on the changer to get the turntable spinning, shifted the lever that raised the arm so that it would clear the album's surface, moved the arm to the cut I wanted to listen to, and shifted the lever again to lower the arm. The diamond needle touched the surface, and the wondrous sounds of "I Talk to the Wind" began to play.

I adjusted the bass and treble levels and then pressed the "LOUDNESS" button, a feature I adored, which augmented the bass and expanded its depth and breadth. I moved over to the night table, picked up the book of matches, tore a match from its grouping, and in one sharp swoop lit it off the igniting strip. I brought the match to the incense tip and held it there until there was a flame, which I blew out so that the tiny, orange ember could continue to burn and fill the room with its mystical scent. I went to my bed and sat upright, a pillow cushioning me against the head-board with my legs outstretched, ensconced in a world of my own, a world that I had made, that I could revel in. A moonbeam somehow found a trajectory that came from the pearly presence in the sky all the way down to earth, through the tiny portal between the blind and the window frame, and settled across my face. I was in sync with the universe.

Suddenly, the door swung open and smashed against the wall. A wide path of light from the hall invaded the room. A figure, lit from behind and in shadow from the front, rushed at me, shrieking madly.

"VOOS STINKT! (WHAT STINKS!)" He was enraged. He jerked this way and that, charging towards one end of the room and then the other, an aggressive beast with nowhere to go to assuage his wrath, his huge presence stifled in this tiny cage.

I was terrified. "What's wrong! What did I do?" Did he think I was smoking dope? "Look, it's nothing. It's just this thing that burns and gives off a nice scent. It's not marijuana!"

"Get rid of it now! How could you do this!" He spoke in Yiddish.

226

"Do what? It's nothing. It's like a perfume."

"It reeks! It's making me sick!"

"What do you mean?" I was incredulous....

"IT SMELLS LIKE THE BURNING BODIES IN THE CAMPS!"

I immediately put out the ember, and he left the room distraught.

I sat down on the bed flabbergasted and looked around at the shattered peace. In an instant, I undid the mood by switching on the main light. Its garish incandescence easily doused the blue.

I contemplated what my father had said. The smell of the burning bodies. Was that what it smelled like? Or was my father horribly confused? Then, I felt so sad. I had brought back this eviscerating memory. I saw the look in his maddened eyes. It looked a lot like blame.

But I hadn't done anything, had I?

I put the incense stick back in its box and sniffed it. It was a lovely fragrance. How bizarre that this could be the same as the smell that spewed out of the crematoria. What does burnt death smell like? What does innocent burnt death smell like?

I never lit another stick, but I never threw out the box.

Chapter 25

When Caesar Crossed the Rubicon in Clogs

It was bound to happen. First Brendon, then Steve, and finally, Kyle. As the saying went, if you were doing the time, may as well have committed the crime. If only one could be that cavalier.

I was immersed in the views and attitudes of the day. It was now clear that not having the preferred beauty traits of cheerleaders had found sweet vindication in the affirmations of the feminists. Any man who objectified a female was a chauvinist, and this identification reconfigured how the sexes comingled. A number of customs fell into disuse, like dancing, dating, and going steady. We hung out in groups, listened to music, philosophized, smoked dope, then found ourselves in the throes of the munchies.

Once again fashion saw opportunity. I was perfectly happy wearing a tight tee shirt that just reached the waistband of my bell-bottom jeans, a burgundy corduroy bomber-style jacket, no makeup, and clogs. The clog craze took hold and was "unisex," the new "thing" in attire. Both sexes wore some version of tee shirts and jeans, and now we were all wearing the same shoes.

I bought a pair that was navy, with a skinny, white band that went around the joints where the navy material met the wooden sole and hid the staples. You could wear clogs with or without socks, and the thick, solid, wooden sole added a couple of inches, which allowed the bottoms of my jeans to coast just above the ground. Funnily, clogs weren't that comfortable, despite the pre-formed grooves for toes and arches. But, pretty soon, skin hardened into calluses, which protected and inured at the same time. Somehow the trend found its way to the medical industry and quickly spread. Nurses and doctors alike wore them and still do to this day.

Another trend was not wearing a bra. Very bad news for the lingerie industry. Born out of a political stance where women burned their bras in a symbolic gesture to free themselves from their oppressors, the ideology was co-opted by the bra companies, who figured out how to make this protestation work for them. It was the age that glorified small, pert breasts, which found perhaps their greatest expression in the ever-erect nipples of Farah Fawcett in the TV show *Charlie's Angels*, where very soft porn met questionable feminism. Fine for anyone who had perfect breasts, but what about the vast majority who didn't?

Enter Warners. No longer in vogue were the large, stiff, fabric cones of Playtex Cross Your Heart bras, with their pointy and prominent shape, very unlike a natural breast. Warners came out with a bra that had enough support for those with some sag, had no manufactured cup shape, just a soft, silky, stretchy triangle of material, the narrowest of straps and back, so that one could still have erect nipples, but not feel completely exposed.

Panties shrank in size from full to bikini and could be bought in many fun colors, like blue and pink and green, instead of the basics—white, which yellowed quickly, flesh-colored, which was bland, and black, which was possibly too risqué for a teenager.

Makeup companies also had to reinvent themselves. Women were no longer interested in pandering to the beauty standards men insisted women adhere to, and so they threw out their powder, foundation, rouge, mascara, eyeliner, false eyelashes, eye shadow, eyelash curler, and tubes upon tubes of sticky, red, pink, and coral lipstick.

Enter Bonne Bell, a company that targeted the teenage girl. Bonne Bell's TEN-O-SIX fragrant astringent was the antidote to many an embarrassing blemish, and Lip Smacker strawberry-flavored lip gloss assuaged the untenable dilemma that, without lipstick, a girl wouldn't draw enough attention, or, with lipstick, a girl was not a feminist. Wearing Lip Smacker gave the impression that one wasn't technically wearing makeup, a look which fit the trend, but still provided the sense of security, however mistaken, that an alluring sheen was better than dull lips. Besides, it tasted and smelled really good.

It would be a while before the hair salons recovered. Teen-agers were growing their hair even longer and not going to the barber or hairdresser to get it cut. A friend with a steady hand, a good eye, and a pair of sharp scissors, was all that was needed to eliminate the split ends and encourage more growth.

I had a circle of friends of both sexes and was happy in the milieu that exemplified the hippie aesthetic and the "make love not war" mantra, which finally overtook the "rah, rah, rah!" of football players and cheerleaders. Though most of the time I hung out with my female friends, the males did make regular appearances, and my eye was on one in particular.

Kyle Rowan was a somber, brooding type, who could benefit immeasurably from a woman's love to make him smile again. He was quiet, unflappable, and went about his business in a state of grace. Teachers were fine with him because of his deferential manner and his uncanny way of reassuring them, even though his assignments were either late or not forthcoming at all.

He was caring and friendly, listened when you talked to him, chuckled softly at your attempts to humor him. He had a lot to be sad about. During last year's Christmas vacation with his family, in South America, his then girlfriend had come to join them. A short, ordinary, hitchhiking ride from a local, who slowed to pick up Kyle, his girlfriend, and his sister, turned tragic. The truck they were in started to fishtail on the road, and in a freak accident, his girlfriend was thrown and died instantly, while Kyle and his sister left the scene without a scratch.

Up until this year, Kyle had been going to an exclusive boys' school in Peterborough; his girlfriend had lived in the town. After this horrific event, he came to our school. I was friends with his sister and had already known her and her parents for three years. Meeting him was like seeing her in duplicate with a sex change.

He had shoulder-length, pure blonde hair, which could only mean his hair would have been practically white as a baby, the envy of so many original blondes who watched helplessly as their hair darkened to brown. His eyes were Greek flag blue and looked hurt. He was a little shorter than most of the other guys I knew, slim, with a trim build, small, strong biceps, tight chest and abdomen. Always casual in his tight white tee, denim jacket, bell-bottoms, and wide, cowboy, leather belt with a bulky, dull, brass buckle. On his left wrist, he wore a watch with a large face housed in a chunky, broad, leather band. He smoked Players Filter regular cigarettes, the square packet fitting nicely into the chest pocket of his jacket, the short, compact sticks a perfect accessory for someone his size, and the brand itself a match to his unpretentious demeanor.

He fit seamlessly into our acquaintance, yet stayed very much on the periphery. In was an age of non-invasiveness in social relations, allowing people to be exactly who they wanted to be, to think and feel whatever they wished, no pressure. The phrase "It's cool, man" accepted all manner of behavior except for aggression, but anger was not "in" anyway. Instead, everyone wanted to be open and loving and peaceful. It was generally assumed that those who seemed preoccupied or distant just had better things to ponder, deeper, profound things. Thus, Kyle was not interfered with, and he came and went as his mood befit him.

At one point, the impromptu shifts of Kyle's comings and goings began to have some method behind them, a little more attention to a specific stimulus. Her name was Jan. She too had this subtle appeal that drew you in and made you careful with her. They gravitated to one another and, as if without discussing it, were found walking together and ostensibly being together. Though I liked Kyle, I had to agree that they were the better match.

We were turning sixteen and getting our driver's licenses, which made an enormous difference to what we could do, where we could venture, and who we would find ourselves with. Having a car was a definite asset, and what kind of car one drove was used as a criterion that did more for the driver than any other personality trait.

None of the females I knew had her own car. Instead they drove the family sedan, often an oversized, unassuming Oldsmobile or Chevrolet in a dark blue or brown, chosen primarily for its practicality rather than flair. If we were fortunate, the car had power steering and power windows. Otherwise, it was a workout to steer the wheel, and required a vigorous cranking of the window handle to get some air. The car's chief asset lay in the fact that we could easily pack in six of us.

232

Some of the males, however, had cars. There were parents who firmly believed that, upon their son's sixteenth birthday, he should have a set of wheels to tour around with. Depending on the arrangement, there might be the stipulation of a part-time job to cover expenses like insurance and gas, or perhaps the son had "earned" the car by being an A student. In some rare instances in our school, very wealthy parents would simply buy their son a car "just because."

That was the case with one of the group, Dan. When he drove to school in his brand new, metallic gold-green, Pontiac Firebird convertible with stick shift and bucket seats, all heads turned. Dan was an amiable, quirky guy, so we never held his good fortune against him. The others without means bought much older cars and dealt with the constant repairs by being somewhat handy.

Kyle's situation was that of having wealthy parents who felt that children needed to learn the hard lessons of fiscal responsibility. He drove something lightly used and quite utilitarian and, by a stroke of brilliant advertising, one of the hippest cars around, simply because it would never have thought of itself that way: the Volkswagen Beetle.

The ad that took the car's ineffable modesty and used it to its fullest money-making advantage was the one that began with a funeral procession and a voice-over of the deceased reading aloud his last will and testament. In an elegant litany of just retribution, the deceased itemized what little he bequeathed to those closest to him, who had flagrantly spent his money. One by one the limousines drove by. The last in the procession was his nephew Harold driving a Volkswagen, drying his tears with a tissue. The deceased had remembered his nephew always said "A penny saved is a penny earned," and "Gee, Uncle Max, it sure pays to own a Volkswagen." This so impressed the deceased, that Harold was left his uncle's entire fortune of one hundred billion dollars.

Kyle's Volkswagen was off-white with a tan interior, understated in style, like Kyle. Inside, it felt like a cute toy, with its small windows, thin doors, few knobs on the dash as if to indicate that we really only need the essentials—heat in the cold, an AM radio, and a lighter. The bare stick shift with its diminutive diagram on the knob took care of every speed the car could go and immersed you in the essence of the actual ride; the immediacy between the driver and the car left nothing to the imagination. The buzzing engine sound that came through the vents in the rear belonged unmistakably to a Volkswagen. The fact that the "front" was in the back and the "trunk" was in the front, and that a vertical, chrome handle, which opened the trunk, looked at first glance like a hood ornament or the car's "nose," was absolutely charming, as were the innocent, round, bug-like eyes of the headlights, the inspiration for the nickname: "Bug."

Our collective mobility, now that there were cars, was not the only perk of getting older. We could also go away without our parents for long weekends, or during Christmas and March Break, and being that independent was prized highly among us.

Easter was coming up, and there was much presupposition in the question "So what are you doing for Easter weekend?" as if no other option existed but to have plans that necessitated getting out of town, particularly leaving the big, bad, concrete city for the bucolic bliss of parts rural. Kyle, Jan, and one of Kyle's childhood friends were going to do just that, but as the date neared, Jan ended up not being able to go. Kyle opened the invitation to a few of us.

I accepted.

Once again, the dialogue…

"Mom, Dad?"

"Yes, dear."

"You know Kyle Rowan, Linda's brother."

"Yes, you've mentioned him."

"He's a friend of mine, a really nice guy. You know his family. They're good people."

"Of course, you've spoken highly of them and you've been friends with Linda for a quite a while now."

"Yes…. This coming weekend, Kyle invited me to come along with his friend to Peterborough. We have a place to stay and we've been invited for dinner at Kyle's other friends' house and then for Easter dinner. I think it'll be a lot of fun. You don't have to worry. Kyle is a very good driver and he knows Peterborough well. Can I go?"

234

"Yes, I think that would be all right. Remember to be safe."

"I will."

…was *not* how it went.

As soon as my mother was aware of what I was asking, she erupted. Whatever fixation she had around sex, which came out in the disastrous confrontation stemming from my wanting to invite Brendon to my party, came out again.

"YOU WANT TO GO TO BED WITH HIM!" she accused, as if she had uncovered a lascivious plot.

"NO! He has a girlfriend. He's not interested in me." *Would that he were*, I kept thinking, which somehow implicated me and confirmed my mother's wacky suspicions. Once again, I felt the way I had during the argument about Brendon. I defended Kyle's rejection of me by putting myself down in an uneasy sacrifice.

Nevertheless, I persevered.

"You're not going!" my mother yelled at me.

"Oh yes I am."

"I said no, you understand me!"

"There is no reason for me not to go. He's a good person, he's my friend, he's a safe driver. You're making no sense," I told her.

She was furious and left the room raging. Glad that was over. I thought I was done. But it was a tag team.

In swooped a tornado.

"WHAT DID YOU SAY TO YOUR MOTHER?"

"I didn't say anything to her!"

"Then why is she so upset! WHAT DID YOU DO TO HER!"

"I didn't do anything!"

"You're aggravating her! You'll make her sick! Give her a heart attack! You are not going away with a boy, do you hear!"

"Yes I am!"

He grabbed the first thing he could and raised it over his head. My arms reached up to protect my face. He held it so that the thickest part of the wooden sole was towards me. Down it came: the gavel. I felt the bone break on the knuckle of the middle finger of my left hand. It was the break of redemption, the price for my freedom.

He knew he had gone too far. I knew he had gone too far. He knew that I knew. He left the room, his shoulders hunched, and never mentioned it to me again, except for once.

Now, there was nothing they could do to keep me at home. Whatever physical pain I felt was alleviated by a weird feeling of justification, a sensation far more appealing than guilt.

The next morning, I watched from the living room window until I saw an off-white Volkswagen Beetle pull up in front of the building. I grabbed my bag, ran down the stairs, disappeared into the passenger side, and we took off.

Once we were on the highway, I told Kyle I thought I might have broken my finger when "I fell" the day before. He said that we could stop at the hospital on the way and get it checked out. No interrogation. I wasn't familiar with such ease of communication, such respect, such acceptance. I was actually being taken at my word.

Getting to the local Peterborough hospital was simple, quick, and convenient. It was a far cry from the long, onerous journey by TTC to any downtown Toronto hospital. Whether it was Mount Sinai or Toronto General, they sprawled and took up many city blocks. They seemed like fortresses barring your entrance, and then, when you did get inside, you were paralyzed with confusion as to which way to go. In Peterborough, we parked the car practically at the door of the hospital, got me admitted, seen, x-rayed, seen again, and discharged, in under an hour.

The x-ray did in fact show a fracture on the knuckle of the middle finger of my left hand, and the confirmation intensified my entitlement to this weekend away. My finger had to be immobilized in a large splint, which doubled the size of my finger in every which way and crowded the others. The entire splint was wrapped in a flesh-colored bandage extending to the palm of my hand.

That evening, we were invited to visit with a family Kyle knew. They lived in a huge Victorian home on a number of acres with a pond and deep woods. The family was American. The father had been a CEO for a large corporation and, upon retirement, had been given a diamond-studded golden parachute. There were eight

236

children in the family, and Kyle was friends with the two eldest boys.

I felt like I was with an unblended *Brady Bunch*. All the family members were upbeat and affable and good-looking. It really could have been TV, except for one glitch. After the perfunctory, introductory moments with the parents, the eldest boys invited us upstairs to their bedroom—an innocuous move, teenagers needing a little privacy. Once there, an elaborate business venture was under-way. Siblings in the know and old enough came in one by one to contribute their allowance and to place an order with the two eldest brothers. In the meantime, we sampled the merchandise.

Carefully rolled, fitted with a tiny cylinder—a piece torn from a book of matches serving as a filter tip—the joint passed among us. Soon, all the visuals were brought into sharper focus and our utterances became humorous, leading to more humorous utter-ances.

We got up, went downstairs, got our coats, hats, boots. There was still a lot more snow here than in Toronto, and we began walking in the woods behind the house. Before we got to the thick, dark cluster of evergreen trees, we walked through a clearing. Instantly, I was in a Christmas card or in the carol "Good King Wenceslas." The clear, indigo sky, the twinkling stars, the moon's rays making the snow's surface sparkle, the crunch underfoot. It was remarkably still outside. The joint made its rounds again.

We got back late to the place we were staying at. The implications of having a broken bone began to present themselves to me. Basically, I had one good hand. All crucial grooming systems would have to be revised. Since I couldn't get my hand wet, I was really at a loss when it came to washing my hair. Kyle helped me. I knelt by the tub and lowered my head so that my hair fell over my face. Kyle did the rest, gently wetting my hair, shampooing it, rinsing it, drying it with a towel, and carefully brushing it through. We went to sleep in the same bed. First, he made sure that the blanket covered me; then he stroked my cheek, and bade me goodnight. I slept well.

The next day was a bustle of activity, from breakfast, to the evening, when we went to see a play at the local theater. Kyle had friends everywhere, his kind, sweet nature a joy to be around. Too soon came Sunday and an invitation to Easter Sunday dinner—the biggest event next to Christmas—with Kyle's friend's parents. Why we decided to smoke a joint first had more to do with being young and adventurous than with having much common sense.

Dinner was actually quite grueling and taught me the lesson that being high in unsympathetic environments was a waste of a good stone, because of the tension it caused inside—trying not to react to what was "stoned" funny, and worrying about being found out.

We endured the excruciating pleasantries, the painfully benign chitchat, answering questions about what we wanted to do with our schooling, paying compliments on the delicious ham and the fixings, barely containing our propensity to burst out laughing, all the while agonizing over our glazy, bloodshot eyes, which would be a telltale sign if anyone knew about marijuana. Luckily, no one noticed anything amiss. Finally, it was over, and now we could freely howl about what it was like being stoned and trapped at the dinner table.

On the drive back home to Toronto, we were subdued. For me there was a tranquility brought about by having had a wonderful weekend, which I would always remember, mixed with a tremendous sadness because of what it took to get away and what I would be going back to. The lowest point was being dropped off.

I came up the stairs, met my parents with a flat hello, and went into my room. There was some small talk of having had a good time, but conversation was at a minimum. I felt justified in my being upset with them, but also sorry for my father that he had to resort to striking me in order to make a point that didn't even stand up to scrutiny. This led to a feeling that I had "taken one for the team." In sustaining my injury, I refuted two invariable principles my mother held to: first, that it was possible to come back if you went away, and second, that you could sleep with a male and not have sex.

Then, a wholly unrelated "good" came of having a broken finger.

A necessary evil of being young, and pretty by virtue of being young, was having to suffer the incessant catcalls coming from men who hadn't read the feminist manifesto. Often, the men were recent immigrants on construction sites and battle-weary from the dearth of female company, so it was about showing off to their co-workers, breaking the monotony of their day by hailing "Hey, Baby. Where you go?" in imperfect English. Other times, walking past you, they would whistle or make salacious clucking sounds.

It might have been a cultural thing, a common way of addressing women in other places, or a biological thing, an elaborate display of their appreciation for you because the female gets to choose. But, for the average Toronto teenaged girl, it was extremely annoying and very creepy. There was nothing you could do, because any form of engagement with their banter, even your rage, felt to them like they had successfully interacted with you.

St. Clair had seen a number of changes in small businesses. Café/bars with pool tables cropped up, precursors of the trend towards "ristorantes," followed by "bistros." These places were favorite hang-outs for men from young to old. Those with similar backgrounds congregated and spoke in their first language. Patrons could be found anytime from morning 'til close, probably owing to shift work and sporadic employment, drinking and talking and carrying on. No "nice" women of their culture, whose presence might have mitigated the men's inappropriateness, would be caught dead there. And so unbridled male attitude and bravado were rampant.

I found myself approaching one of these dubious establishments after school had let out. My arrival on the scene seemed to cause a stir within, and a number of men flocked to the floor-to-ceiling windows at the front to "honor" my passing by. They were particularly effusive in their praise, boisterous and rowdy, banging on the glass and yelling, which sounded muffled to me on the street, but must have been very noisy inside. I slowed my gait, and their delight erupted into whistles and huge smiles, pursed lips and kisses.

I stopped in front of the window and took my left hand out of my pocket. I raised the middle finger—an enormous, flesh-

239

colored digit, which resembled an erect penis more than it did a finger—and shook it at them for emphasis. From the inside it must have looked like a horrible hand deformity, judging by the shock on the faces of the men and their sudden silence.

It was a lovely retaliatory moment.

Chapter 26

Wiedergutmachung, Part I

Much of my parents' rage had to do with the German government's compensatory policy, which began in 1953 and was known as *Wiedergutmachung*. A feature of the German language was its "word collage," and this one was made up of three parts to express its intention: *"Wieder"* meaning "again," *"gut"* meaning "good," and *"machung"* meaning "making." *Wiedergutmachung* (making good again) was the reparation settlement by which Holocaust survivors were recompensed for their loss and suffering, though it could never be made good again.

It is September 1945, and my parents have just been married. They are talking a lot about what to do now. They are among those who have survived the Holocaust, yes, but otherwise have absolutely nothing else—no papers, no home, no family, no country. Word travels fast, and ideas circulate, and options present themselves for the group they are now part of the DPs, displaced persons. Where will they go? Germany is one of the choices. My parents cannot stomach the thought of going to the country that is responsible for the tragedies that have befallen them. In fact, everywhere in Europe haunts them, as they consider how easily nation after nation gave up its Jews to the Nazis. Even the Pope blessed Hitler. But there is somewhere else. Palestine...Israel.

It makes perfect sense. A place where they can be with others just like them, and where they are protected, patriated. To be the same as other nationalities, like Danes in Denmark and Spaniards in Spain. My mother has an aunt in Israel—her father's sister— who left before the war and who has made a good living there for herself and her husband. Finally, a home, family, and country. That's where my parents will go.

241

Would that it could be so simple. Life, after the war has ended, doesn't really feel any different, except for the obvious absence of SS guards and the threat of bombs. But humans don't forget that easily. The end of the war doesn't lessen anti-Semitism and even violence against Jews. DPs are housed in refugee camps, which in fact are former concentration camps, a bizarre contrast: the nightmarish echo of the mandate that systematically shrank life to the point of extinction, and the foreign aid that sustains the survivors now. Now the threat exists outside the DP camp walls instead of inside, because of the lawlessness that characterizes post-war Europe.

These camps dot the countryside, from Germany, through Austria, to Italy. My parents, along with many others participating in B'richah, the Hebrew word for flight, make their circuitous way to an imagined haven. One of the highlights is Bad Gastein, a picturesque alpine town in Austria. Traveling is not something my parents are familiar with. Those who travel are wealthy and can afford to flit here and there to take in the sights. If not for the war, travel would be prohibitive for most people in my parents' situation. As working-class folk, they would have been born, married, and buried in the same town, barring life-altering decisions to embark on a faraway voyage to North America—an impossible concept for each of my parents, as their attachment to family would have trumped any ambition for a different life in a distant land.

There is a photo of the two of them in Bad Gastein, standing awkwardly, almost happy, the scene of a mountainscape behind them, as if their image has been superimposed and they are actually not there at all. It is December of 1945. They lean against a railing at a lookout point. Snowcapped mountains loom beyond, and valleys swoop and reappear in a geological interplay. It is too brief a moment in time.

Two other photographs really tell the tale. In the first, four figures stand in front of an enormous pile of rubble, with another pile of rubble further back, debris lying randomly on the trodden ground they stand upon. In the second, there are three figures at a tall wooden fence, as if they've been backed up against it. All around them is winter grass playing dead until spring; a bare tree and the hint of a rooftop are behind the barricade. The routine is to pack and move stealthily to the next camp, pack and move stealthily to the next....

Eventually, they make it to Italy. My mother's heart lights up momentarily as she sees that not only has the landscape changed, but the features of the people as well, from the tall, fair Austrians to the shorter, olive-skinned Italians. About the Roman Catholic Italians my mother says, in an excited expression of what is in fact the saddest naïveté: "Look, they are so many Jews here!"

My parents are in a constant state of not believing what is happening, of never expecting to be doing what they're doing, in a present that has been impossible to predict, ripped from a rhythm they counted on as secure in pre-war Czestochowa, Poland, and thrown into being nomads with nothing, belonging to a group that inspires hatred, pity, denial.

In a fourth photo, three figures are leaning on another railing at a lookout point. It is clear that the mountains have descended into hills, the valleys are within reach, the trees smaller, the foliage lush. The figures have shed their winter coats in favor of blazer jackets for the two men, one of whom is my father, and a short-sleeved, print dress for my mother. They peer expectantly at the camera, hoping that the snap of the shutter will confirm their existence. They are heading towards sea level.

The vastness of the environment has been completely reduced, and the numbers of people have increased dramatically, bloating the southern tip of Italy. Refugees congregate at certain ports, shepherded by those who seem to know, but no one really does know which port will be the best shot at safe passage.

The British have been negligent in their mandate to create a Jewish state, and pressure is put upon them by the American government to get going. It is a perfect case of the pot calling the kettle black, while Jews are held in the balance. The other game these superpowers play is hot potato, Jews being the potato.

Brindisi is sultry and bustling. The sales pitches of various vendors pierce the ambient noise, like the boys at a baseball game selling Cracker Jacks. The learning curve is too steep for my parents, *who are trying to understand what they're in for and are figuring out whom to trust when information is contradictory.*

Boats are allegedly leaving for Palestine; it's just a matter of which vendor to buy passage from. The vendors are like any entrepreneur who gauges a business opportunity. Boats and crews are required, and the price of passage is assessed on the basis of supply and demand. Profit margins can be increased if the seaworthiness of the boats isn't looked into too much, if boat crews are minimal, amenities are scarce, necessities on board are curtailed, and the boats are filled to capacity.

The vendors have sized up their peers, and competition is rife. How my parents choose a vendor is based on the feeling they get. Can it be because he's Jewish that they decide to go with him? Passage is sold in American dollars. Vendors don't take chances. Somehow, American dollars have been painstakingly saved by my parents. There's no customer service here. Those embarking will never be back to complain about what they find once they get on board. The voyagers buy passage based on a transaction unconfirmed; the vendors get paid, incur zero risk and reap all of the benefits.

It's departure time. My parents are hustled onto the boat along with a horde of others. Every space is filled with an arm, a leg, a head. Someone's knees are right behind yours, their forehead is at the nape of your neck, you hear and feel breathing. Is it yours or theirs?

My parents steel themselves on the voyage, believing that a better life awaits them in Palestine. The many boats that leave Italian ports and return emptied of their passengers look like proof. It's just a matter of hours. They know all about waiting through anguish.

What they don't know about is boats and what happens when the number of passengers exceeds the limit.

The voyage on the Mediterranean is relatively easy. A fairly calm sea, and though land at times is not visible, it is not like being on the Atlantic in the middle of nowhere. Which turns out to be hugely significant when the boat starts to take on water.

Chaos, panic, trapped, can't swim, boat is sinking...

244

A Mayday call is issued: vessel in distress, threat to life is imminent.

The British Navy responds and races to the area to commence rescue efforts. All passengers are successfully transferred from the failing boat to the British one. My parents feel eternally grateful to the British for resurrecting the almost abandoned notion that human life, especially Jewish life, is worth saving. They are unconcerned that this may be more about nautical codes of ethics, and are wholly unaware of the irony that the British actually contribute to my parents' plight and that of many like them.

Of the ships leaving ports for Palestine, the overwhelming majority never arrive because the British are there to prevent it. My parents are two out of tens of thousands hoping to immigrate under the illegal process called **Aliyeh "Bet,"** *Immigration "B," as opposed to* **Aliyeh "Aleph,"** *Immigration "A," which is legal. What is promised in Brindisi turns out not to be the case. The Royal Navy and their blockade can't be penetrated that easily. Immigration to Palestine is slowed to a trickle, and the goal is to turn off the tap entirely. My parents are grateful not to have drowned, but instead of arriving in Palestine, the British ship makes landfall in Cyprus, where the passengers are interned without trial in prison camps and accused of illegal immigration.*

The camps are surrounded by high, barbed wire fences. Watchtowers built at regular intervals, with convenient machine gun supports, facilitate the ever-shifting guard, ready to impose their authority. Soldiers man the gates. Not exactly a homecoming party. There are tented summer camps, and more weather-impervious winter camps, as the numbers of illegal immigrants continue to rise. Life within becomes absurdly mundane, while history limps along towards the creation of a Jewish state.

Subscribers to "the glass is half empty" may be suspicious of the number of pregnancies among the detainees, since a criterion for immigration prioritizes pregnant women. If "the glass is half full," these pregnancies are testimonials to the resilience of a persecuted culture that makes a triumphant comeback. Or maybe it's as basic as finding some comfort in the pleasures of the flesh. In any event, my mother is one of these pregnant women. With this

245

gesture, she withdraws one of the two conditions upon which my father agrees to marry her. She is surprised that she has regained feelings, that she is not dead in that regard, and that she wants to have and care for a baby. Conception likely takes place in December of 1947.

The State of Israel is officially proclaimed on May 14th, 1948, an event that is ridiculously incompatible with the continued strife, acts of terrorism, and bloodshed, before, during, and to date. This is the "better life" my parents are about to become part of.

What May 14th does signify, however, is the augmenting of immigration quotas, and as my parents wait in the queue, my mother's belly grows and grows. Women and children are still going first. On September 7th, my mother is given the go-ahead as a very pregnant woman, but is now faced with the awful predicament of having to leave my father behind. They plead with the officials not to be separated. The officer in charge seems moved and can't argue with the size of my mother's stomach. He allows my father to go with her.

Once again they are on a boat to Palestine.

On this voyage the boat also takes on water, the amniotic fluid from the ruptured sac signifying the onset of birth. My mother lies on the ship's floor and is administered to by the captain, who delivers to her a baby boy, on September 8th, 1948. He is named after the boat, in the masculine form. Then there is panic. My mother has failed to pass the placenta and if she doesn't get immediate medical care she will hemorrhage and die. The boat lands in Haifa, and my mother is hurried to the nearest hospital. My father is sick with worry until he hears that she has pulled through.

Haifa is no picnic either. As he faces conscription into the Israeli army, my father's trauma owing to the war comes in handy. At thirty-four, he has lost his hair, and what little is left has turned white. He decides to grow a beard to add more credibility to his older man disguise. When it comes to creating papers that will vouch for him, and information to which he will be held accountable all his days forward, he lies about his age and evades enlistment. He easily passes as too old for the army, which is a huge relief, since the last thing he can possibly consider is putting his life on the line for another senseless cause.

They go to Holon, on the outskirts of Tel Aviv, where my mother's aunt Rebecca resides. Rebecca's life is moneyed. She and her husband don't just have a yard, they have "grounds," including an orange grove and almond trees. One can live on those alone. The property is circumscribed by a wrought iron fence, and a gracious path leads to an elegant facade. The place, both inside and out, looks like the movie set of **Sunset Boulevard,** *minus the outdoor pool. Despite all their money, though, they have no children. Upon meeting her niece, and her nephew by marriage, Rebecca becomes completely smitten with the baby boy, her grand nephew.*

With time, my mother picks up the subtle, undeniable message that Rebecca is treating her as subservient. My brother, on the other hand, is brought into the "big house" and lavished with attention. Rebecca's husband owns a toy factory. No more marvelous a profession can be found to delight the heart of a young boy. There are toys galore, and especially a bicycle. Rebecca's husband is a nice, kind man. Never an occasion goes by that he doesn't call my brother over. Then, when no one is looking, he reaches into his pocket to draw out some almonds he carries like a secret stash, which he shares with my brother, who is made to feel very special. My brother is active and clever and expands into their space, running through the fragrant orange grove, being made to believe it belongs to him.

Rebecca's condescending treatment of my mother does not abate; in fact it becomes more and more obvious. Rebecca is adamant about being owed a debt of gratitude for helping my parents out when they arrived in a new country. Her idea of my mother returning the favor is, for all intents and purposes, to act as her "mishoorus," Yiddish for "maid." That way, my parents can live there, my mother can "give back," and Rebecca can have unlimited access to my brother.

My mother is filled with mixed emotions—hurt, insult, loss, betrayal, outrage. Her first act of defiance is to rent a small apartment for the three of them. My father finds work as a tailor in a factory that cranks out ready-made suits, emblematic of the effects of industrialization. Custom-made work, where tailor fits fabric to measurement specifications of patron, now gives way to assembly-line piecework, though the very wealthy continue to be fitted. The wage my father receives helps set them free from Rebecca and allows them to be financially independent. Sustaining this unencumbered state becomes an inviolable credo from now on. Make sure you don't owe anybody anything, not like poor Mephistopheles.

Still, my parents and brother have to visit. After all, Rebecca and her husband are "family."

Rebecca takes advantage of every opportunity to indulge my brother, and there's no mistaking how excited he gets whenever he hears they are going over to Auntie Rebecca's. My mother is appalled, not jealous, but feels stymied about what to do. Why shouldn't my brother have a wonderful time, why shouldn't he play and laugh and reap the rewards of continuous gift-giving? Rebecca, in turn, treats my mother with something that now approaches contempt. My mother experiences an untenable internal contradiction: her natural instinct to put her son's needs before hers, set against the injustice of being constantly put down and having her role as the mother of this child strenuously mocked in a kind of familial expropriation.

As time goes on, it becomes painfully clear to my parents that the advertisement depicting Israel as the "Land of Milk and Honey" is pure hyperbole, for a number of reasons. Chief among these is the fact that there is no getting used to the violence between Israelis and Palestinians as the daily norm, like juice with breakfast. That is anguish enough. But there is more.

What they see is that, sadly, Jews are not immune to racism, even when it comes to one other. There is conflict and prejudice among the three main cultural groups: the Ashkenazim, the Sephardim, and the Temanim. In a hierarchy akin to India's caste system, at the top are the Ashkenazim, noticeably whiter and of European descent; next, the Sephardim, somewhat darker and originating from the Iberian Peninsula; and last, the Temanim, darker still and sharing a longstanding history with Arabs. Each group regards the other with disdain. The Ashkenazim look down *on the Sephardim, who look down on the Temanim. Added to all that is Rebecca pressuring my parents to embrace both Zionism and Judaism, which makes them feel as though their heads are in a vise.*

While my brother is dizzy with the smell of orange zest, soothed by the kiss of the warm weather on every exposed part of his skin, and free to roam in a huge playground, which extends beyond Rebecca's fence to the lovely beaches and luminescent waters of the Tel Aviv coastline, my parents are feeling trapped and controlled.

My mother has family in New York, and my father some in Australia. It all seems so hard to imagine going through: moving again, starting over.... Letters are written, responses weighed. The first choice would be New York. Inquiring into the logistics of, and prospects for, immigration takes time.

My mother decides to share this information with Rebecca, perhaps to "caution" her. She makes oblique reference to Rebecca's persistent encroachment, implying that, instead of eliciting their deference, it is having the opposite effect. But it seems Rebecca takes her job as matriarch very seriously, or that she particularly identifies with the orphanage master in Oliver Twist, *aghast that Oliver should deign to ask for more gruel.*

She looks at my mother with level scorn and repugnance. To be challenged in this way after all she has done for her! Rebecca can only be pushed so far. My mother doesn't realize with whom she is dealing, Rebecca thinks to herself. She delivers a blow. The message is clear: If my mother, father, and brother leave, Rebecca will disinherit her. Rebecca knows that her wealth can make the difference between hardship and ease, which are at her discretion to bestow. Rebecca, also in this declaration, makes no small point that my mother's impudence will have a disastrous impact, not only on the wellbeing of her husband but, more poignantly, of her innocent son. Does she really want to disadvantage him in this way? Is that the kind of mother she is?

My mother reels from the effects of Rebecca's edict and cruel allegations and feels beaten down. But my mother continues to look into leaving Israel. She is in constant contact with her uncle in the Bronx, who makes inquiries into sponsorship. The back and forth

249

keeps hope in the air for my parents, but ultimately, the circumstances are against them. New York will not happen. But there is another possibility: Toronto.

My mother's first cousin left Poland as a young man before the war and now lives in Toronto with his wife and two children. He is willing to sponsor them. The paperwork begins. Once it is all worked out, my parents' stay in Israel will have spanned five years.

My mother now has to impart the latest news to Rebecca. She prepares herself for the conversation, which she hopes will evoke some small understanding from Rebecca that this is the best option for them. More importantly, she wishes to demonstrate to Rebecca that deciding to leave Israel proves that she is not after Rebecca's money. My mother expects that her integrity will impress Rebecca and soften Rebecca's manner towards her.

Rebecca erupts in fury and admonishes my mother for her egregious ingratitude.

"If you want to go, then go! Remember, not a penny will you get!" My mother is shocked.

Then Rebecca's tune changes. She pleads and condemns, all in the same breath.

"Go! I can't convince you to stay, but leave the boy here with me!" she demands and sobs.

My mother is horrified.

Rebecca goes on. "He will be better off with us than with you. Everything he will ever need he will have. I love him so much, as if he were my own son. You can be assured of that. Taking him on this journey to nowhere with nothing is the most selfish thing you can do. He is so happy here. Why can't you see it! How could you do this to him!"

Passenger ships are now in full operation with professional crews, captains, regulation-issue amenities on board. The route is from Haifa to Marseille. Three people have booked passage: two adults and one child.

Chapter 27

Wiedergutmachung, Part II

The second leg of the journey is on a train from Marseille to Paris. It's in Paris that papers have to be picked up to bring to Canada. My mother has cousins in Paris who left before the war. The three of them stay with these cousins for two weeks before the big Atlantic voyage. Then it's time to go to the train station again for the ride from Paris to Le Havre, where they will board a ship bound for Halifax.

This ship is huge in comparison to the two they've two previously experienced. Along the way, my mother begins to sense how far away she is traveling—day, after day, after day, of nothing but water—which conveys to my mother that with each successive knot between her, Israel, and Rebecca, there is no going back. She is filled with sorrow and relief and fear of what is to come.

Once in Halifax, my brother is perplexed by the fact that there is such commotion in the middle of the night. But the shock of the intense cold against his skin, the likes of which he has never known, is what really gets him. Where are they taking him? On the train ride to somewhere called Toronto, he stares out the window, unable to conceptualize what he is seeing: white debris that fills the air and intensifies, covering trees, many of which are leafless for some reason, and, more white falling on the ground, the ground disappearing. "Snow," someone says. All these new words. He doesn't want to learn them, and feels strangely low. He stops absorbing the information and gives in to sleep.

Too many things continue to be thrown at him. He meets the people who have brought them over, more cousins—adults, and two girls around his age. Then another rented apartment, a job for my father, and schooling for my brother. The buildings are totally different from the ones he knows. More like fortresses, really. The broad streets of Tel Aviv don't exist here. No palm trees, no sand, no

251

beach, no warm breezes all the time. No wearing shorts and a tee shirt all day, every day. It's freezing here. Everyone speaks in a foreign language, which at first is novel, but when it lasts and lasts it's isolating and disheartening. He is five years old; the year is 1953.

My parents adjust as best they can. They are living in a part of town close to Kensington Market, and among a lot of Jews, so at least they can communicate in Yiddish. Nevertheless, my mother is adamant about learning the language and so enrolls in night school to study English. In her first year, she is one of three women in a class of seventeen. In the second, she is one of five women in a class of twenty-two. In the third, she is one of nine women in a class of twenty-five. Sometime between the taking of the first and second year class photographs, my mother has cut off her thick, chestnut-brown braids, which she had worn wound around the crown of her head. She opts for a bob hairdo instead and sheds the knitted dress in favor of a pencil skirt with blouse.

My parents are reunited with a group of Holocaust survivors, originally from the same home town. They have been in Toronto for roughly the same amount of time that my parents and brother spent in Israel. This is when my parents first hear the word Wiedergutmachung. Each survivor is receiving a monthly lifetime pension from the German government. In many households, there are two pensions, one for the husband and one for the wife. This money is making the difference between struggling and getting on their feet. It is money that is not easy to accept; the recipients are not capitulating, the losses will never be mitigated. But it does ease what would otherwise spell financial difficulty: new country, little education, new language, fractured souls. How does one get this money? My parents ask and are informed of the process. They apply.

In the meantime, their apartment on Oxford Street is too small, and the landlord is troublesome and invasive. My parents find a better alternative on the third floor of a triplex on McCaul Street, where they can begin to have the autonomy they yearn for. My mother is now pregnant with what will be her second child—me.

A pension would help immeasurably. Life is hard. Finally, the envelope arrives. It is from the German consulate, with its official logo and seal, austere and definitive. There is excitement and a hope, long buried, that push through with the force of reckoning. My mother carefully tears open the paper along the top edge and draws out the tri-folded document, which will determine their financial future....

Then it is October 15, 1954. For over a week prior, rain has been falling steadily and uncharacteristically in Toronto, while a tropical storm called Hazel has already devastated Haiti, leaving 1,000 people dead, having defied predictions that the storm's path was directed at Jamaica.

It is hurricane season in the Atlantic, a remote concept for Torontonians. Hazel continues to travel unexpectedly up through the Unites States, packing winds of 140 mph, instead of losing power over Florida. It is considered a Category 4 storm as it makes landfall in the Carolinas and claims 19 people, but Canada knows no such weather systems, and the Carolinas are far enough away.

Still moving north, now a Category 3 storm, Hazel takes a gander at Pennsylvania, Delaware, Maryland, Virginia, West Virginia, and New York, claiming another 95 lives. The meteorologists are confident that Hazel is going to dissipate, but instead, the storm partners with a cold front and is potentiated. The course of the storm suggests that it will pass east of Toronto, and so no evacuations are ordered, and few warnings are issued. Toronto Hydro crews on standby are almost sent home because of a lull in the storm, when the unthinkable happens.

Within hours, record amounts of rain are not absorbed by the water table, which is already saturated, and so intense flash flooding ensues, taking with it Toronto's infrastructure. Over 50 bridges fall like houses of cards; roads and highways are taken out in the wake of the fierce currents. Five volunteer firefighters responding to a stranded motorist are swept away in their fire truck. Highway 400 at the Holland Marsh is submerged under 10 feet of water when 20 feet back up. The marsh is now a huge lake, and the one landmark visible is the tip of the steeple of Springdale

Christian Reformed Church. It takes until November 13th to drain the marsh. All told, 300 million tons of water fall during the storm.

The Humber River bursts its banks and swallows 14 homes with their occupants still inside, plus another 18 homes, and 1,201 feet of Raymore Drive. Etobicoke Creek also gulps down homes and people. In Woodbridge, the river swells from its typical width of 66 feet, to 351 feet at its narrowest. The death toll is the worst to date for any natural disaster in Canada. There are 81 people who lose their lives; 4,000 are rendered homeless. The damage is estimated at $138 million, the equivalent of $1.2 billion now.

Because of the catastrophic destruction and heavy losses of life in the Caribbean, United States, and Canada, the name Hazel will never again be used for any Atlantic hurricane.

For those who believe that a drop in barometric pressure stimulates labor, this may make sense of the fact that on this atmosphere-crazed day I am born. For my parents, it must seem that the dogged legs of misfortune, like bounty hunters, have pursued them clear across the Atlantic.

Chapter 28

Wiedergutmachung, Part III

Wiedergutmachung was a strong theme within the group my parents were part of. And like those who joined yacht clubs, tennis clubs, golf clubs, etc., the group shared the same interests. For Jews, the common interest was death. Akin to volunteer firefighters of yore, certain people were representatives in a neighborhood and came to the assistance of those in need. Jewish burial societies served a similar purpose. Based on a tradition called "chevra kadisha," the idea was that Jews buried their own dead, and the processes of cleaning and shrouding and praying for the body were key ways of showing respect.

The modern burial society my parents belonged to offered many perks, among them a prepaid funeral, and plot designation. God forbid you should leave that to your children to sort out. The organization was run strictly *à la Robert's Rules*, with members elected to a board of directors, along with an executive board. A membership booklet was published and distributed yearly, listing alphabetically all members, their mailing addresses and telephone numbers. The members were Holocaust survivors, and much of their "business" had to do with the Holocaust, in one way or another.

The society had been allocated a section of land in a Jewish cemetery in North York. This parcel was then divided into plots for the members. Among the group's projects was a permanent banner bearing the name of the society and demarcating the area. But the proudest initiative was a huge bronze plaque annotating names upon names in commemoration of the members' relatives who had perished during the war, under horrible circumstances, and robbed of the dignity of a proper Jewish burial.

Every year in September, around the High Holidays, an event was put on by the membership. The purpose was manifold. It was a solemn time, a time to remember the dead. It was also a time to be social, chat with other members, and catch up on the latest in one another's lives, mostly centered around "nachas," the "proud parent" commodity so coveted by everyone. This son was graduating from medical school, and that daughter was marrying into a good family, etc. No bad news was overtly discussed, though it was known, in all likelihood, which offspring had fallen through the cracks by not amounting to anything career-wise, by divorce, or by not getting married and producing grandchildren (maybe they were homosexuals), never mind those who were drug addicts and/or criminals.

The event was also a fundraiser and a big "we love America and Israel" fest. The members were fiercely pro-American, in a world that still openly voiced much hatred against Jews. Having a superpower in your corner was a prime example of not biting the hand that feeds you.

Politically, the Americans and the Israelis delighted in scratching each other's backs. The Americans were happy to have a Western, democratic presence in the Middle East, and by extension the Soviet Union, and the Israelis, all too aware of being a tiny country surrounded by Arab states, were grateful to be associated with a team that, for once, had a shot at winning.

The members circulated and mingled, congratulated each other for living well, and freely pronounced their fervent wish—"Le'Shana Ha'ba'ah Bi'Yrushalim"—which meant "Next year in Je-rusalem," suggesting that their lives wouldn't be complete until they had settled in the Jewish homeland.

Certain well-to-do members made pledges of donations for Israel, and this show of philanthropy impressed the others. "How generous!" and "What a *mensch!*" (literally meaning "man," but figuratively meaning "a fine human being") were among the many accolades, voiced aloud or sotto voce amid rounds of applause.

My parents walked around in a bubble made for two. Words coming from the outside sounded distorted, and visions were blurry. Everything looked normal on the surface. All Holocaust survivors, all from the same town, they spoke the same languages, all the men wore suits, the women had their hair dyed and coiffed in

256

the same, short style, they were all raising families. But on the inside, the differences burned.

On the subject of pro-America, my parents were resolute. My father's experience of "liberation," where the Americans were involved, was like watching the ineptitude of the Keystone Cops. If only it were that funny. The Russians were the real heroes, in my parents' estimation. When the Russians had freed my mother, it was clear to her that they knew all about suffering. They handed her a baton and said, "Here. Do to them what they did to you!" And though she didn't have it in her once the roles had been reversed, she never forgot the fervor of revenge stirring within her liberators, which only injustice can engender. The Russians had sustained record-breaking fatalities and overwhelming numbers of injured in their battle with Germany. What were the Americans doing? Making ammunition, which meant big business, and waiting until June, 1944 to make a move. Too little too late. Or, like my mother loved to quote, "With friends like these, who needs enemies."

On the subject of Israel, they felt nothing but bitterness.

None of their peers had been in Israel like they had, when it counted, from the state's very beginning in 1948, of all the times to be there. This display of "Next year in Jerusalem" was the epitome of hypocrisy. No one would trade in their split-level, four-bedroom, three-bathroom, modern home on a sizable lot, for life on a kibbutz or in cramped housing. No one would exchange their safe, quiet existence in banal North York, for living in dread of terrorist attacks, the frequency of which kept you on unrelenting alert. It was easy to say "Next year in Jerusalem," but no one was going to do it. A few of their peers' offspring got the wrong message and bought the pro-Israel propaganda, to their parents' alarm, like Dr. Frankenstein's shock when he realized he'd created a monster.

Pro-Russian and anti-Zionist meant that my parents couldn't relate to their peers. They didn't live in the same neighborhoods. Their children didn't go to school with their peers' children. They didn't have a car like their peers, or money to spend on bar mitzvahs. My father wasn't a businessman or a builder like his peers. And it was all owing to *Wiedergutmachung*.

257

The greatest philanthropists, in terms of percentage of income donated to Israel, turned out to be my parents, rather than the wealthiest members of the society. Whatever these members gave would be a fraction of what my parents had literally sacrificed for Israel and literally donated, though no one was lauding them. Sometimes members would forget this fact, caught up in their enthusiasm to rally financial support for Israel. "So how much did you give?" someone would challenge them, elated by the fundraising drive. My parents would counter, and the mood plummeted from spirited to bleak. "We gave plenty, more than anyone here." For a moment, the member would look confused by the cryptic comment, and then a flash of recognition would pass over his face. "Oh yes," he'd say awkwardly, before he wandered off.

For some time now, my parents had known about the extent of their capacity to be philanthropic, which they were unable to curb. The impact on my parents of this knowledge had never diminished and in fact was exacerbated on these fundraising occasions, particularly because there were so many opportunities to compare themselves to the other survivors. It was obvious how much my parents had struggled.

From the first shock of the reply, to the explanation they had come to learn, the upshot was this: *Wiedergutmachung*, which ought to have been their chief benefactor, had eluded them somehow.

The Germans were methodical and had been meticulous about dotting their *is* and crossing their *ts*. So when my mother opened up the envelope containing the official response to the application for *Wiedergutmachung* and sat with my father to read their fortune, they were stunned by the word that sealed their fate: "INELIGIBLE."

How could that be? They were victims of the Holocaust just like everyone else who was getting a pension. What was the problem? They hired a lawyer to find out, spending money they didn't have. What they learned shook them to the core, in the most devastating version of the adage "Hindsight is 20/20." Under the terms of *Wiedergutmachung*, victims of the Holocaust would be given a lifelong pension. Anyone who had survived the Holocaust qualified for reparations. Anyone...except the ones who went to Israel.

If one went to Germany, or Canada, or the United States, etc., then the payment went directly to each survivor. But the Israeli government lobbied strenuously that Israel ought to be compensated for absorbing a vast number of refugees after the war. This influx had taken its toll on the young country. After difficult de-liberations, a lump sum of money was allocated to Israel as a whole, to be used towards providing infrastructure, instead of being given to the individual immigrants. These talks were held without the input of the survivors. No live coverage on TV spread the news. My parents had had no idea.

For the Jew who left Europe before the war, knowing that the German government had accepted responsibility for the tragedy of the Holocaust and had paid Israel this money, there was a sense of vindication and a surge of pro-Israeli sentiment.

For the Jew who emigrated to North America after the war and was a Holocaust survivor getting a life-time pension, the fact that this money would contribute to the development of a Jewish state approached a kind of restitution.

But for two people who ended up in Canada anyway, after an excruciatingly ill-fated, five-year detour to Israel, it was almost too much to take. From the mortal risk of being DPs after the war, to the near-sinking of the ship, which was never going to reach Palestine anyway, to the arduous two and a half year prison stay awaiting immigration in the internment camps in Cyprus, to the war-torn and violent reality of an emerging Jewish state, amid Arab outrage resulting from the debacle caused by the political powers involved, my parents epitomized being pro-Israeli, before the term had even been coined, and where had it got them?

Who could they turn to for solace?

Not to their peers who were getting pensions. It was hard for my parents to be connected to them when the issue at hand had so greatly benefitted the one and severely constrained the other, in very real, monetary terms. My parents couldn't shake their anger, and their friends had no choice but to feel defensive.

Not to their peers who had come over on the boat before the war, starting anew, establishing themselves as small businessmen, like my mother's cousin had done.

259

And especially *not* to their peers who had been born on North American soil and had grown up in cities like New York and Toronto, who were schooled and well-heeled, who had subscriptions to the Symphony, belonged to tennis clubs, dined in fine restaurants, and who were happy to give to the Israeli cause, to plant trees, and sing Hebrew songs and dance the "hora."

This peer group was the most different from my parents. Though they were all about the same age, my parents were more like the parents and grandparents than they were anything like the peers. My parents discounted them, certain that there was no way they could possibly understand my parents' torment. And this group didn't really know how to relate to my parents. As the first generation, they were relieved that being born in Canada or the U.S. meant that they didn't have the dead giveaway of a heavy Jewish accent and Jewish-sounding surnames, because anti-Semitism operated covertly, as well as overtly, in North America. Their refinement and polish and money protected them from prejudice and earned them a secure place in Anglo society. Maybe it was instinctive to recede from immigrants like my parents and to show solidarity and support in other ways, such as founding organizations and building community, embracing both Judaism and Zionism, writing checks to various Jewish charities, reading books and watching movies about the atrocities of the Holocaust, rapt and riveted, but safe.

There was no one for my parents to talk to about the money that could have been theirs. It would have been evisceratingly hurtful to my parents to be judged as not caring about the future of the Jewish homeland and reducing the Holocaust to a matter of money. My parents, in turn, would have felt raging contempt, because those passing judgment would be saying this from the comfort of the very homes that those pensions had afforded them. The conversation could never take place.

And, for the icing on the cake, Rebecca was as good as her word. When she died, she left my mother nothing. My brother was the recipient of some inheritance money redeemable upon his twenty-first birthday, which by then, and with inflation, had retained only a tenth of its original purchasing power.

Chapter 29

Why It's Useful to Watch *Perry Mason*

Because of the investigation that was undertaken by my parents' lawyer to determine if there was any way around the *Wiedergutmachung* policies, the Germans had a lot of information about my parents. They knew that my mother had worked in a slave labor camp. And while this did not figure in the bid for reparations, it did provide for an all-expenses-paid trip to Frankfurt, Germany for herself, and for someone to accompany her, which turned out to be me.

The departure date was set for the end of May, which in Canada meant that winter was hanging on with its two-fisted cold spells, while in Europe the spring flowers had already been on view in all their splendor. I was a little scared about going to "Germany," the country that came up with the accepted, mainstream notion that Jews were basically vermin to be stamped out by jackboots, wherever and whenever necessary. Would they be able to tell that I was Jewish? Even though the country tried hard to dissociate itself from its infamous reputation as the Third Reich and had found respect for the products of car manufacturers like Mercedes Benz, BMW, Audi, and Volkswagen, and of kitchen appliance companies like Braun and Miele, I still felt very ill at ease.

But I was also mollified by the very qualities that scared me: German obedience, quality workmanship, attention to detail, and striving for a job perfectly executed. I had developed over the years, and had graduated from fear of the dark to more refined phobias like fear of flying, though inherent in both was a strict belief in catastrophe. My parents had pretty much cornered the market on flukes happening to them, so why would a plane crash be so out of the ordinary?

Somehow, Lufthansa inspired confidence. A fleet made up mostly of Boeing jets, each plane with its yellow and blue colors, vi-

vid in the searing blue skies above the clouds. Standing at attention in crisp uniforms, ready for work, were the pilots—the secular contingent of the Luftwaffe. Stewardesses like runway models, in short-sleeved, figure-outlining, above-the-knee dresses, with smart jackets, and hats evocative of riding caps, either all in yellow or all in blue, hair in soft flips and side parts or up in French twists. The logo of the encircled crane in flight was displayed on the tail of the aircraft, sported on hat brims, and embossed on small brass buttons for pocket flaps. Much less terrifying than the Third Reich's eagle, with its wings permanently spread and ready to prey, perched above a swastika.

Interestingly enough, my mother wasn't frightened at all about flying, and luckily for me, the plane ride over was uneventful. When we landed, we got into a cab—a Mercedes Benz, the first one I'd ever been in, certainly a rare occurrence where I came from (didn't know anyone that rich), but here they were as common as air.

My mother's Yiddishisms were Germanic-enough-sounding to tide her over where her German failed her, but I worried constantly that our Jewishness was obvious, if not linguistically, then by our looks: my mother squat and matronly with dark hair and blue eyes, myself of average height with hazel eyes, and more olive-skinned than fair. In my mind, we stood out as shamefully as those forced to wear yellow Stars of David during the war. All the time I was there, I walked around anticipating the inevitable re- cognition, the "I know you're Jewish" look and some attendant wave of distaste, though I must say I didn't really encounter it. Everyone was actually quite nice, polite in a respectful way, as if to assume that one would prefer distance to closeness and to assure that the space between people would be protected.

We were booked at a quaint, old hotel, where we could also dine, and for a couple of days we got over our jet lag and prepared for the reason why we had ventured to Frankfurt in the first place.

Our presence was required at precisely 10:00 a.m. A Mer- cedes Benz taxi picked us up and drove us downtown, where the buildings loomed and the streets narrowed. We disembarked.

Upon entering the huge lobby, we were greeted by a tall, skinny man, who spoke German. I could catch the odd word or two because I understood Yiddish and could stretch my ear to associate, by comparing pronunciations, the gist of what he said.

He led us to the elevator and then down a wide hall to a set of double doors. He ushered us in, asked us to sit to the right of the main aisle close to the front of the room, and there we waited.

Various people came in and took their seats. As more and more congregated, and the German language filled the room, I felt more and more isolated. I turned to my mother, but she looked like she was in a daze. There was activity at the front, a few personnel shuffling papers and getting ready. As the minutes ticked by, my nervousness increased. The configuration of the space, with its bench-like seats, center aisle, and stage-like front, could have been the setting for a play, a church sermon, or a concert. But we were there for none of those.

Instead, my mother had been summoned as the key witness for the prosecution in the trial of a Nazi war criminal.

Suddenly, a door opened to the right of the front of the room, and in swooped the judge. "All rise, court is in session, Judge Something or Other presiding," was said in German which, for me, meant that there was a slight delay in comprehension as I processed what was happening visually and so aped the others. Then we sat back down, and the proceedings commenced.

Opening remarks were heard on both sides. While meaning was elusive, the snap, gutturals, and long-windedness of the tones of the German language were not lost on me; it sounded like I was being yelled at. I knew that the man on trial was charged with something quite weighty, murder definitely, and I also knew that the actual terms of the allegation were being challenged by the defense, to the extent of a not guilty plea.

And then it hit me. Was my mother's testimony the hope upon which the prosecution's case depended? Was it going to be up to her to put him away for life?

She was called to the stand.

For starters, my mother was offered an interpreter, an idea that confused her. Why did she need one? Did they think she couldn't communicate in German? She hesitated and began to wonder whether she really could manage in German—hemming and hawing in shades of gray not appropriate in this context of black and white—and now the lawyers looked confused. She ended up taking the offer.

The preliminary ritual of swearing on the Bible didn't go over that well, as my mother couldn't understand why one hand had more ability to take an oath than another. But finally, she complied with what was asked, while maintaining her opinion that the difference between hands was trivial at best.

The questioning began in earnest.

In the course of the next ten minutes, it was established that she had worked in a slave labor camp as a welder, making ammunition for the Nazis. She testified that there was a foreman in charge who was given to acts of cruelty when he deemed it necessary. Workers were beaten with a stick of some kind, and these beatings could be fatal. Or, if he didn't wish to expend the energy, he simply shot them. He made himself quite visible walking around, supervising, always with his rifle. She saw him much of the time and would never forget him.

Somewhere during these exchanges, my mother got way ahead of herself. At first, things were going well; the question was asked in German, the translation was given in English, my mother answered in English, and the translation was given in German. The problem was that she could catch a lot of what was asked in German. It seemed unnatural and ridiculous to her to wait for the translation, and she grew impatient, so she began to answer in the strangest hybrid of German, Yiddish, and English, which then effectively put the interpreter out of work. After the first few times when she was reminded to listen to the translation before responding, they just gave up on her and let her answer the questions directly.

Now came the crucial part of the trial: the establishment of her credibility. Two very simple but profound questions would ensure that.

"Please tell the court how old you are?"

Easy answer, one would think. But a few things contributed to why the answer was actually quite complicated. Asking women their age sent many into a state of panic. The instantaneous reaction under these circumstances was to obfuscate, squirm, and do whatever was necessary to evade this seemingly innocent question, as if they were wise to the trap. Most would be willing to go to extremes, their truth unspoken, rather than give up the goods.

Those in polite society knew better than to ask at all. A woman's age, anyone's political affiliation, and yearly income were all verboten topics. If a woman were inclined to discuss her age, then she did so with a fair degree of humor, hanging on to the perception of youth with gusto. Either she would leave them wondering, or would invoke what came to be the oft-quoted rejoinder, for which *The Jack Benny Program* was most remembered: the perpetual state of being thirty-nine years old. To this, my mother added her own spin. Maybe because of women's pervasive attitude of denial, or "Don't ask, don't tell," her age didn't matter to her, and she didn't spend her time counting. Also, in European culture, one spoke of one's age in terms of the year, rather than the day. So, come January, one would speak of being forty-five, for example, as being "in one's forty-sixth year." But on the stand, age was calculated by birth date.

For all these reasons, my mother sat there trying to figure out the answer. When she finally gave it, she wasn't really sure, sounded like she was in fact guessing, with a cavalier air about her, which expressed that she thought it a rather inconsequential point in light of all the other aspects of her testimony.

The lawyer tried to help her tell "the truth." He coached her a little by saying he knew when her actual birthday was and that she was not a year older than what she testified, a distinction he hoped would warm her to the notion of being one year younger. To which she responded, "A year more, a year less, what does it matter," which was in fact her honest answer, but not in keeping with what it meant to be under oath. There was no point in continuing this line of questioning, so he moved on to the most implicitly significant, yet explicitly straightforward question, the one that would confirm her testimony.

"Do you think you could you identify the man who beat those workers?"

"Yes," my mother said assuredly.

"Then, please, point him out in the courtroom."

My mind drifted.

From the popular TV show's theme song's opening bars, you could tell the content would be eerie. The strings' vibrating sounds, followed by an orchestral pounce, then the sleazy, gritty beat thumped out in triplets by the piano, like in the song "A Summer Place," but seedier, an elephant roar from the trumpets in the melody, and a dissonant final chord. This unforgettable musical jingle foretold that the show was going to be dealing with the slimy underbelly of the human condition, the criminal element, those who murdered, those who were murdered, and everyone else who had to get involved, namely Perry Mason, Lawyer for the Defense.

The plot line was formulaic. A murder victim, a suspect charged, and Perry Mason to the rescue. But, in the show, you could also learn about the rules of the courtroom. It was all explained in action: swearing in, objections, what was allowed and not allowed in testimony, how to address the court and the judge, perjury, contempt of court, eye witness testimony, etc. If only my mother had watched.

Neither my mother nor my father could stomach seeing any shows with the slightest degree of violence; all guns were anathema, as were spy dramas, westerns. Even Boris, the tiny, round, bumbling spy, and Natasha, the svelte Amazon—both clearly the brunt of American political satire aimed to mock the Russians—and silly characters in *Rocky and Bullwinkle*—an afternoon, children's cartoon show—were too much for my parents. The *Perry Mason* theme song's forty second intro alone would have sent a paroxysm of pain through both my parents, rendering them incapable of continuing to stay tuned.

A preliminary meeting with the lawyer wouldn't have helped either. My mother would simply have been told to answer the questions as best she could and to tell the truth, which was exactly what she was doing anyway.

At this stage in the *Perry Mason* episode, the witness would declare "That's him!" pointing out the person beside the defense lawyer, in the spot where the defendant always sat.

"The court will recognize that the witness has identified the defendant," would be the customary response substantiating the eye witness's testimony.

When my mother was asked to identify the foreman, she began to seek him out in the packed courtroom, looking intently at every single person there, her eyes moving systematically up and down the aisles and back and forth along the rows. She had constituted an image in her mind, a kind of time-lapse photograph, to account for the many intervening years. Where was that gray-haired, balding man? This was the moment. Those horrible, interminable days she spent in acquiescence so as not to call attention to herself. The many victims she knew had succumbed to his violence. Decade upon decade distancing herself from the experience, but never the memory, only to return to a now-sanctified environment, where the one on trial was finally the one who was guilty. Nemesis was within reach.

After an exhaustive search, she concluded, "He's not here."

My heart sank for her. She had tried so hard, scrutinizing the assembled, comparing them to the artist's rendering in her mind. She had no idea how her answer had affected the outcome. I could only imagine the exasperation of the district attorney, what the look on his face must have been, since his back was towards me. I did hear him, however. His voice sounded worn out. This was unbelievably unfortunate for the prosecution. He tried to make the best of it. "He's right over there." The lawyer indicated the defendant sitting exactly where he would be in every courtroom all over the world and in every TV courtroom drama.

Her eyes alighted on the man who had terrified her throughout the indelible years of working long, grueling hours, with death looking over her shoulder. To her surprise, he had not only retained all his hair, which was plentiful, but it was also jet black, not a single gray hair in sight.

There was one thing she could think of to say. "He looks good," she conceded. The statement was delivered so plainly, was even complimentary, with a "Go figure…" undertone.

The prosecution rested; I suspected this would register in the district attorney's mind as "having had a very bad day at work."

269

It was now time for cross-examination. The burden of proof was not much of a burden, and toppling the prosecution's case akin to kicking a sand castle.

The defense attorney began gently. "So you didn't recognize him?" he asked, as if it were no big deal.

"No," she said. "I was expecting him to look much older." The defense attorney smiled to himself.

He moved on to the particulars of her testimony, mainly the beatings and alleged murders.

"You testified that he beat some of the workers."

"Yes."

"Did you see him do that?"

"Everyone knew he did."

"But did you actually see him beat someone."

"I don't understand."

"Were you there when he took a stick, as you told the court, and hit someone with it?"

"We all knew he did it, because we talked about it after. The workers were bruised and injured."

"But did you actually *see* him do it, even though everyone talked about it?"

"We didn't watch."

"So you didn't see him beat one of the workers."

My mother was puzzled.

"Is it possible then that another person could have beaten those workers, and everyone thought it was the foreman?"

This speculation, another common courtroom strategy of which my mother was ignorant, was totally beyond her scope of understanding reality. She looked at him like he was insane.

He continued. "And the ones that died...how do you know it was this man who had something to do with it?" He pointed to the defendant.

"Believe me, I know," she said, as if her word ought to be enough.

He continued, unaffected by her naïve sincerity.

"And those that were shot...did you see this man," he pointed again, "shoot them?"

270

"They were there one day and gone the next. We all knew why," she expressed a little sarcastically, as if it was obvious that there was no other plausible explanation.

"So you didn't actually *see* him do it?"

My mother looked irritated.

"Let me put it another way…. Did he shoot anyone in front of you?"

"No, but…"

"Thank you. No further questions."

My mother was perplexed. She didn't understand why she had been interrupted in midstream.

"The witness may step down," the judge said.

My mother returned to her seat beside me. I saw that the vacant look had once again rooted in her eyes. It seemed she had been on a boomerang journey that had offered the possibility of redemption, more valuable than any restitution. Neither was to be. Ultimately, she was led back to the same, desolate, haunted place where there was no justice, no rectification, no accountability—the all-too-familiar feelings that began when her world forever changed.

I didn't know what to tell her. I had watched a lot of *Perry Mason*.

Chapter 30

Shame

Some recompense for my mother's tribulations as a slave laborer did come many years later. The Claims Conference created a special category and outlined provisions in what was called the Article 2 Fund. A friend of my parents had told them to apply, and this time they were eligible for a small sum of money, which came in handy now that they were seniors. I noticed a triple-folded document lying on the kitchen table in my parents' spacious three-bedroom apartment, the place I convinced them to move to after I woke up with a cockroach on my pajamas. I read it and froze.

Shame was a powerful thing.

My mother had made no secret of the tragic end suffered by her brother, her sisters and their families, and her parents. My father too told us about his beginnings, and about the fate of his widowed mother, which led to the dispersal of her three sons and the dismantling of his immediate family.

My mother also spoke of a man she would have married had the war not broken out. They were seeing each other seriously and were on the brink of engagement. He did not survive. Among the members of the burial society, there were many stories of those who had lost their boyfriends or girlfriends, fiancés or fiancées, wives, husbands, or children, and after the war had remarried and had new families.

My mother was twenty-two when the cacophony of jackboots, and startling, iconic graphics of the Nazi brand on banners filled the air of her hometown on September 1st, 1939. My father was twenty-five. After the war was over, they looked at themselves in shock at their survival, reanimated their bodies, and tried to live again. What else was there to do? Who would judge them?

Two conditions my mother laid down during their pivotal night out, which led to marriage—that she didn't cook, and didn't want children—were both withdrawn. But there was another promise, which was never broken. Why he ever agreed to it I couldn't figure out. Maybe it was easier to hang on to some petty convention, when the world had lost its soul.

Keeping that promise was like baking sponge cakes and cleaning house, or worrying about my going out at night or dating non-Jewish boys: manageable matters with outcomes that could be controlled.

But what was the cost of keeping the secret?

Now that I knew, I looked at both of them as if they had finally removed their face masks.

"Why didn't you tell me?" I implored.

It was my mother who spoke, of course. Her usual self-righteousness and condescension was toned down, but still there wasn't a sense of the impact this omission might have had on me. Perhaps that was too risky for her. Thinking of another's perspective might mean feeling more than she could bear. But that left me without support, as if I had rogue emotions.

My father said nothing, ever loyal to her, though his look belied something. But it wasn't collusion with me. It was more like respect for her viewpoint, than agreement

So I was on my own, left to feel the weight of the news in Technicolor, from the facts to the reverberations therein. I was enormously saddened, angered, and I pitied them both.

He is standing in line waiting to be greeted and to register his family's name. No one speaks. Pleasantries are a fiction, as fantastical and remote as life on another planet. You can hear deep whispers as the one who approaches the ledge exchanges information with the one in charge. Those next in line are fighting a conflicting urge to listen in while wishing desperately not to hear anything. There's no rush to receive what may be the worst news of all, that no one in your family has survived. Standing in line offers the greatest odds of someone still being alive.

274

When he gets to the front of the line, he recognizes the woman in charge. She's from his hometown. His heart lifts for a second. When she sees him, she remembers him as well. It's a bittersweet moment, being reacquainted on the other side of the abyss. Everything has changed, except here they both are.

They reestablish how they know each other. "I remember your father, his fine reputation," he says to her. "I remember your mother, so young to be widowed," she says back. They are careful not to ask who's alive or dead, but to reference the others as if this makes the others' existence somehow fixed in time. They can only continue in this vein for so long, before the obvious reason for why he is here pushes through belligerently.

"My mother?" he asks her.

"No."

"My brothers?"

"Not the older one. No trace of the younger one."

"My wife and baby?"

"No."

A wife and baby, a girl. I was flooded with thoughts about these two dead women who were loved by my father. My father's first wife. My stepsister. And never to speak of them.

I knew there was no reasonable answer to account for why my father never betrayed his own grief, when my mother went on about the loss of her family. And when it was his turn, there was only his mother to publicly commemorate. He had been separated from both his brothers at such an early age and then lost track of them to the point of feeling estranged. The younger one, who went to the orphanage as a child and then escaped to Russia as an adult, thus avoiding Europe, did make it through the war alive, and when he contacted my father there was a feeling of mistrust, real or imagined. My uncle naturally assumed that my father must have struck it rich in North America, which implied to my father that he was being prepped to be asked for a loan. My uncle had also been in the midst of a tale of two wives, another red flag for my father. It seemed that the first wife survived the war, my uncle had married the second wife in the meantime, and hadn't come clean to either.

275

This was unscrupulous, as far as my father was concerned. So even though, technically, my father hadn't lost everyone, his feelings for his brother didn't survive. He had only his mother to grieve, while my mother grieved an entire family, and thus a lot of attention went to her.

I couldn't get the thought of my father's other life out of my mind. The only pre-war fact my brother and I were actually told, other than what we knew of his childhood, was that he had spent some time in the Polish army as a cavalryman. Trivial in comparison to what was now revealed. He'd had a wife, which meant he'd met someone, spent time getting to know her, his feelings had grown, he'd fallen in love, and married her. They decided to have a child together, and they did—a baby girl. How happy they must have been. Then the war. His wife was killed by the Nazis. There was probably no chance for the baby—just a nuisance, like a kitten that needed to be drowned. It was a rather important chapter. And to keep this from my brother and me felt so wrong. But my father had done that for my mother.

Somehow, the two of them had conspired to prevent us from knowing about my father's earlier family. There was some bizarre taboo regarding my parents' union not being my father's first. Was he used goods? If my mother had to resort to someone who had already been married, did that mean she wasn't much of a commodity herself? This, which I presumed was the basis of their shame, sounded to me like the epitome of nonsense, not unlike many other examples of their strange thought processes.

The deeper implications of his not being allowed to speak of his loss, while my mother availed herself of the opportunity, was what kept bothering me. If it had been me, I would have felt like I was going to implode. Was anything remotely like that going on for him?

I tried to ask, now that it was out in the open.
"What was she like, your wife?"
"She was a nice woman."
"And your baby...how old was she?"
"Almost a year old..." He wasn't really sure.

276

His answers seemed vague and distant, as if his promise to my mother still held. This led him back to the present and talking instead about his love for my mother, as if no other reality existed.

I asked my mother.

"Did you know Dad's wife?"

"Yes, I knew her as someone in the town." In other words, the town was small; a marriage would have been common knowledge.

Once again, I found myself on the outskirts of this discussion. I was the one with the deep sentiment, not they, which isolated me from them and kept nagging at me.

His devotion was really something. He stood by her no matter what, and it wasn't easy when she would insist on her outlandish opinions, of which she had an arsenal. During moments when her wrath was directed at him, he sometimes let slip a word or two—a tiny break in the ranks—but it wasn't ever in the form of what would grow into mutiny. Rather, he would just laugh at the absurdity of her complaint, look at me as if to say, "There she goes again," shake his head, and do her bidding.

He was her support when they walked arm and arm down the street. She was the one who took care of the home and family, the one to whom he entrusted his earnings, the only person in the world to whom he could relate.

He revered her.

Chapter 31

The Beginning of...

My mother's strange notions—her mistrust, misgivings, prejudices, blindnesses, worries—about almost everything didn't arouse any suspicions at first. Just more of her usual, obstinate postures, which infuriated me, but at the same time made me feel helpless.

Then things occurred that were harder to deny. Episodes of faintness, disorientation, forgetfulness. That was what happened to arteries—they thickened, restricting oxygen to the brain, which changed "perceptions." My mother was diagnosed with dementia. Unlike Alzheimer's with its steady decline, dementia moved through plateaus, with sudden drops followed by a stationary period until the next drop.

One such drop took place at my father's birthday celebration. She opened a card for him and blithely read aloud these words: "Dear Turkey, lots of love and hate and lucks." Nothing seemed amiss to her. The words were spoken without any attention to their inanity. My father burst into tears and pronounced, "The days of happiness are over."

Still, he tried. He was her mind, her body, and her spirit. Wherever and whenever she slipped up, he interceded. Every forgetful comment was followed by a reminder, as if it would stick, but it never did. Like grains of sand precariously close to the shore, solidifying in the sun only to be dissolved by the lapping waves, again and again and again.

As my mother's need for care increased, it became necessary for my father to get help, an untenable predicament for private people. So, over the course of two years, caregivers were hired to do what my mother couldn't do any longer and what my father couldn't manage without her.

With every aspect of his being, he clung to the way they had lived, explaining to the women who tended to my mother how to do what. But they had their own ideas, cooking in unfamiliar ways, cleaning, doing laundry, etc., differently from my mother. It was a constant affront to him. These women weren't used to getting orders from men regarding how to run households, so they generally placated him and went ahead and did what they felt was right. Clearly, my mother was no ally to him in all of this. He was alone in his frustration and indignation, as well as the growing desolation of witnessing my mother's persona disappear.

The strain wore him down several times. At one point, both my mother and father were hospitalized, and I was traveling daily from one facility to the other.

Eventually, it really got to him, the constant effort of swimming against the current of the inevitable.

He called me. He'd had a sleepless night and much trouble breathing. It frightened him. We went to the hospital, and he was admitted. That night set in motion the events of the next three weeks.

At about 11:30 p.m., my father coughed up blood. I called the nurses, who alerted the doctors, who ministered to him. I was asked to leave, as if it was assumed I wouldn't want to be present. One look at my face, and the doctor in charge decided to abandon that presumption. I kept my eyes on my father, and he kept his eyes on me. In that reciprocal stare, I felt he was counting on me to ensure that what was being done to him was what was required, as he wasn't exactly keen on "personnel," medical or otherwise, tampering with his body. In my gaze back I relayed that I wouldn't betray his trust. The mundane truth was that the doctors and nurses were tending to someone experiencing a mild heart attack.

They needed to intubate him and take him to the ICU, where he could be closely monitored. The next twenty-four to forty-eight hours would be crucial. I stayed with him throughout, sat by his side in the ICU until well into the wee hours, at which point he started feeling drowsy. I assured him I would be there when he awoke.

The ICU had its own waiting room and a few private rooms reserved for consultation with doctors and families. In these rooms were chairs that could be unfolded to become cots. This was where I slept, if you could call it sleep. A few hours later, I was back with him.

Since he was intubated, he couldn't speak, but he was conscious. I tried to explain, as best I could, what had happened to him. In addition to his having had a mild heart attack, his kidneys had become compromised. The following days would show whether kidney function would return, or not.

Something seemed deeply troubling to him. He was gesturing and trying to cast his eyes to his left. For several frustrating minutes, I didn't know what he wanted. I felt as if I was failing him. At times like these, those close to you should know instinctively what you are trying to communicate. Then I understood. His watch. An orange-gold Tissot he had acquired after the war. His agitation and reasoning were heartbreaking. He wanted me to take his watch, in case someone might steal it from him while he was sleeping, or worse, when he was unable to protest because of the tube in his throat. I gently removed the watch and placed it on my own wrist, which was where it remained. I assured him it was safe now. He relaxed.

I had to inform my parents' caregiver of the events that had ensued. I spoke to my mother as well, who heard what I said, but couldn't register it. My father so wanted my mother to visit him. I arranged for the caregiver to take my mother and herself by cab to the hospital. I would meet them at the entrance, with a hospital wheelchair, so that my mother could be easily transported; the long walk to the ICU would be too difficult for her.

I wheeled my mother in. When my father saw her, he looked expectant, as if her seeing him thus would mean something to her along the lines of "Look at me. I'm in here; this is what has happened to me," the kind of dark humor both had enjoyed in each other. She stood beside him and rested her hand upon his arm. He couldn't speak to her, so he gazed at her lovingly. She smiled at him. I watched her. I couldn't shake the notion that she was on her best behavior, like a child being told what was proper when visiting someone in the hospital. She looked so sweet.

She sidled down the length of the bed, over to where I was standing, and purposely turned her back to my father so that he wouldn't hear her.

Then she whispered to me, *"Who is that old man?"*

My heart sank for him.

I answered, "Siz de tateh," literally "It's the father," colloquially, "It's Dad."

"Oh," she said, with an understanding that still didn't make the accurate connection. I wasn't sure if she thought I was telling her it was my father—information which somehow still bore no relation to her—or someone else's father, which would better explain her inability to recognize who he was to her. This, after fifty-two years of marriage...

In the next few days, discussions with the doctor were worrisome. The prevailing euphemism used by the medical profession—"We can make him very comfortable"—far from calming me, disturbed me instead. My father's kidneys had stopped functioning, his heart was weak, and so, too, the capacity for fluid to be dissipated by his lungs. The doctor asked me if there was any one else besides me to inform—a sibling perhaps?

"Yes. My brother."

"Where is he?" "He lives in London, as in England."

"I think he should get on a plane as soon as possible."

Living in Rochdale at Bloor and St. George had not been far enough away. With more education and relationships that lasted, my brother made the move to England, distinguishing himself as a respected academic, and there he settled, making occasional trips to Toronto, being visited by my parents, or by me on nail-biting journeys overseas. But geographical distance was the rule.

I phoned and told him that the doctors thought the situation dire, and that they had suggested an immediate visit. I also told him that I was holding on to some kind of hope. My brother came through. He seemed to arrive instantly, as if he had been around the corner when he heard the news, or had grabbed a coat, run down the stairs of his flat, and boarded a plane waiting for him outside his door.

I had impressed upon the doctors that I was not going to give up on my father and that getting the fluid out of his lungs, putting him on dialysis, taking his tube out so that he could eat and communicate on his own were ways to give him the best shot at some kind of life. And that would be the plan. It appeared to work.

He was released from the ICU two days later and was given a room on the ward. All this time, he was conscious, his mind sharp and alert. My brother and I spent every day and night there with him, in the routine of dialysis, furosemide, and daily suctioning of the accumulated lung fluid, a three-pronged ordeal, which was still better than the alternative. It became a kind of normal.

My mother was slated for another visit, and arrangements were being made. My father tried to talk to her on the phone. I could hear only his side and imagined that on the other end there was confusion, the last thing my father needed to deal with. His voice was raspy and brittle, more air than anything, really. He had to repeat himself a number of times, so I surmised she hadn't really caught his drift. When he decided there was little point in continuing, and that he was getting tired from the exertion, he pushed his vocal chords to their limit and yelled, although the sound he actually made was hoarse and feeble. "I love you!" and then, "I love you!" again. When he handed me the phone, he looked dejected.

In the meantime, my brother and I made the best we could of the situation, providing happy-go-lucky conversation and attending to my father's needs. One evening, the two of us came up with an idea for an outing. We discussed it with the nurses and were able to rig up all of the necessary drips and IVs to make a wheelchair self-sufficient. We transferred my father comfortably, covered him with blankets, and took him on an excursion within the hospital. For my father, it was sheer joy.

He was never one to be cooped up or stay still, not restless or anxious, but someone so attuned to his body that he knew he had to be moving, walking mostly. He had read no self-help books, nor was he versed in the health benefits of exercise; he simply knew himself physically. He loved to walk and was the one always eager to get bread or milk, or pick up odds and ends at the supermarket. On days of inclement weather, and throughout the winter, he could be found pacing back and forth, using whatever space was available as a makeshift track.

Hallway after hallway, we traveled throughout the hospital, which was a huge complex. With tunnels and corridors opening into lobbies and departments, there was no shortage of avenues to take, and with no destination in mind, it was about the pleasure of the ride, which we took at a fair clip to keep it stimulating. My father beamed, the sensation of air moving against the skin of his face.

Back in the room, the air stood still. But back to the room was where we had to return. The day's endlessness was broken up by nurses checking blood pressure, taking temperature, and monitoring tubes. He had started to eat on his own, a double-edged sword—good from the point of view of independence, but not so good for the lungs. A special nurse would come in for that procedure of sticking a hose down his throat to vacuum out excess fluid. Did I detect a mild flirtation? My father, practically immobilized, with three major body systems—respiratory, heart, and kidneys—not working anywhere near enough to sustain life, yet he had a sparkle and a smile when he saw her.

But it was a momentary respite from an inescapable reality. Four salient exchanges told the tale.

In the first, he came straight to the point, regarding my mother's next visit. "Do you think she'll recognize me?" Whatever I said was belied by my expression, which he caught, and which I saw move through him. Like dye on cloth, he darkened.

The second started off quite innocently. "Will I be able to go home?"

I championed his intent and responded, "We'll do everything we can to get you there."

My enthusiasm didn't fool him for a second. For him, the subtext was "maybe not," and the message there was grave. Still, I knew I sounded heroic, but what I said was true. I had already thought through what his life could be like, coming to the hospital for dialysis treatments several times a week for approximately four-hour stints. It seemed almost unfathomable, though people did live that way, and awe-striking, that two little organs could cause so much trouble for the body.

Then the third one.

Television was a vast teacher, showing us how to act, dress, live, and be. Did mores follow ads and plot lines, or vice versa? There was no point in unraveling that conundrum. So many TV scenes of love, sex, and death—how could anyone, even if they'd never experienced it, not have some idea of what to do in these circumstances? Were they clichés, what turned out to be final statements—blessings at the side of the bed, last instructions, unloading of the soul? My father was not a man to observe others and imitate them. His instincts came from within, unencumbered by the acceptable way to be. That had been both a burden and a boon for me.

I think he must have known the end was possible, and so he broached the topic he had never mentioned since the day it had happened: the incident with the clog.

The words were few and in Yiddish. It seemed he had carried the weight of what he imagined my feelings to have been towards him, believing I held a grudge against him, which he felt I was justified in doing. He had accepted what he assumed was my stance and had operated under its blemish.

"Can you forgive me for that?"

I looked at him with deep regard, and also sadness for us both.

"I forgave you a long time ago."

I had made peace with what had happened. Like him, I had an acute sense of right and wrong, deep inside, hard to reach, but intensely felt. I knew why he had struck me, how desperately afraid he was when my mother was terribly distressed. If anything happened to her, he would never recover. I knew that my unbending bid for permission to go away for the weekend was a bold confrontation to her. I knew that what drove her was a terror unrelated to me. All three of us were stirred by forces that collided in this one, awful moment. But I knew that hitting me with an object changed the nature of the act from a disciplinary measure into to a serious breach, and I knew then that he knew it too.

He seemed surprised at my answer. All these years, he had thought differently and behaved accordingly, thinking I held this transgression against him. All these years, I had never expected him to say what he did today. I felt for him. I hoped he believed me.

This same day, my mother was supposed to visit, but the caregiver phoned to say that my mother wasn't feeling well enough to come. It was disappointing, in ways that were about to become monumental.

My brother and I left the hospital late that night. It was our usual routine to leave when he was sleepy and be back upon his awakening, thereby maximizing the number of hours we spent with him.

The next morning, when we arrived to greet him, he told us he hadn't slept much that night. He was so thirsty, he said, could he not have something to drink? Giving him fluids put pressure on his heart and lungs. But I gave him a little something, as well as ice, which he was allowed. It was a day like any other. The intermittent visits from nurses, and hospital staff bringing food trays. The doctor popped in to have a look and asked me if my father was usually this sleepy. I told him that my father hadn't slept well. That seemed to be a reasonable answer, though it became a pivotal signal, which went unnoticed or noticed, but not interfered with. Either way, it would have ended the same.

By mid-afternoon, my father could barely keep his eyes open, so my brother and I decided to go home and return in the evening after he had rested.

"You sleep. We'll see you later." I kissed his cheek.

Several hours passed at home, and then the phone rang.

I couldn't understand what I was being told.

When we arrived at the hospital, he was sleeping, but not the kind you awake from. He had already slipped into unconsciousness. Carbon dioxide gases, and not enough oxygen, had that effect. He was in the process of dying. An oxygen mask was on him, more for appearances than anything.

I just sat there all through the night and watched him go. In the morning, the doctor came in again. During the vigil, I hadn't allowed him to remove the mask. In my resistance to conceptualizing what was happening, I deduced that, if oxygen were what was missing, then surely oxygen would help. It was the logic of a child. The doctor had indulged me this unscientific reasoning. Now, when he looked at me, we both knew it was a sweet standoff. I would never remove the mask, and therefore I knew he would have to.

Not long after that, my father's hand grew cold, and after a penultimate gasp of breath, and a last, shallow one, he stopped.

I stayed with him. While the doctor did the paperwork, and the funeral home was notified, I didn't take my eyes off him. When the process of taking him out of the hospital was underway, I followed. As the funeral home attendants transferred him into their vehicle, I stood by. I didn't know that I was fulfilling a Jewish burial rite—that the deceased never be left unaccompanied. I just knew that I wanted to be with him.

Chapter 32

...the End

How was I going to explain my father's death to my mother?

I spoke with gravity and emphasis, in Yiddish: "De tateh hoht gishtorben" ("Dad has died"). She seemed moved, but again I couldn't tell whose father she thought had passed away. I stressed, "Da Mann" ("Your husband"). She looked at me as if she didn't even know that she was married, or what "married" meant. It was just as well, except for the fact that I had one less significant person to mourn with.

The funeral went on around her. She was there when we stood behind the curtain to have a private final moment with him, to look at his face, the rest of him shrouded in natural cotton, and to see him lying in the casket. She was there to greet people at the shiva—relatives and friends who had come to pay their respects, many of them my parents' "landsmanner" (fellow countrymen) from the burial society.

The fourth exchange my father and I had before he died, came as no surprise. It had been instilled in me on many prior occasions, mostly as a wry comment, but this time it was serious. In Yiddish, he reminded me, almost as an admonishment, "I don't want a rabbi to speak for me." It was an adamant position, which never altered. No rabbis! He had heard enough eulogies to catch the irony in their words. The polished phrases with blanks to be filled with the name of the deceased, the recently acquired information made to sound familiar, and an opportunity to preach Judaism, was how he understood the rabbi's job. He wanted none of it. No stranger with a religious agenda was going to ride on my father's coattails. I assured him that his request would be respected and that I wholeheartedly agreed. The last time he'd been in a synagogue was decades ago, in Israel, at Rebecca's insistence. Both my father

289

and mother had gone unwillingly, to say the least. Staying in Israel would be impossible. They never looked back at their decision to leave except with profound regret that they had ever gone in the first place.

It was my brother who spoke for my father. And he delivered the eulogy eloquently, elegantly, and concisely. No rabbi officiated. This may have been one of the only occasions when such a thing had taken place among the members of the burial society. Our family was either viewed sympathetically as being close-knit, or as wanting to break with tradition, which led to criticism that we were irreverent. We were executing my father's wishes; that was the only thing that mattered to the two of us.

After the shiva, life went on without my father. Interestingly enough, from time to time, my mother would ask where he was. "Vie is de tateh?" ("Where is Dad?") She seemed to be able to connect to the idea only when she herself brought up the topic. At first, I told her he had died, and then I began to reconsider the logic of that. Why have her go through the shock of receiving this news, and then having to relive it each time she asked, which she would continue to do? Even if it were about someone else's father. A couple of times, she offered her own explanation in the body of questions like "Is he still at work?" or "Did he go to the supermarket?" I found it increasingly easy just to say yes and have my father stay in her world, where she knew his whereabouts.

She would outlive him by five years.

There were further lifestyle adjustments, with my father being gone, and to compensate for my mother's continuing cognitive dysfunction. A full-time caregiver looked after her. She couldn't be left alone, lest she try to get up from her wheelchair. If she succeeded, she'd either end up wandering, or worse, falling. She was incapable of doing anything for herself like cooking, cleaning, bathing, or going to the washroom. The sides of her bed had to be equipped with railings so that she didn't, upon instinct well-honed, try to make the trek from bed to toilet. These restraints caused frustration in her, and she would make griping noises, which alerted the caregiver, and that was the chain of command. But everything was temporary, as her increasing debility required constant tweaking of her care.

Whenever I came to visit her, we had our greeting routine.

"Do you know who I am?" I would ask her.

"Perila," she'd say, her answer tinged with a sense that it went without saying, all the while smiling at me, so excited to see me.

As for questions she didn't know the answers to, she had learned to maneuver around the missing information, a tactic I marveled at. Her standard response, which worked very well, was "Chell de bahld zuhggen" ("I'll tell you in a minute"). Of course, the conversation would then move on, her lack of understanding remaining undetected, it seemed.

Others, whom she ought to have remembered, asked "Do you know who I am?" and steadily she lost her way of retrieving that data. It was curiously unsettling to them, the feeling of not being recognized, the initial rejection, slight hurt, then rationalizing based on the mitigating circumstances, even though, for a split second when someone didn't know you, you could feel as though you didn't exist.

She was beyond that now.

I would sit there with her, and time stopped pushing. There was contentment in the moment, such as Buddhists and Taoists espouse. I'd hold her hand and look at her, her big blue eyes, her voluminous, thick, straight hair, now pure white, her thumbs, her chest, her neck. There was really nothing to talk about, which felt boundlessly calming.

The strangest implication of all was the change in my mother's demeanor. She softened. Her agitation subsided, her worries receded. She seemed, dare I say it, happy. No more constrained muscles in her face, no narrowing of the eyes in suspicion, no inherent "I told you so" or "You'd better watch out," the admonishing tones I'd heard my entire life. Just the gleeful outpouring of her love, love beneath all the sick pain of her loss, a loss so profound, it had led to the terror of loss recurring, which in turn required her to wield a powerful force, for so long, to shield her from that threat.

"Do you know who I am?" I would ask.

"Perila!" she'd say, her whole body expanded, proud that she'd answered correctly and overjoyed with my presence. I felt honored and special and loved.

It was then that I felt my sense of peril lifting, as if there were another channel to turn to on the dial of the way the world operated, other than impending doom.

She continued to decline, talking less, moving less, though her basic instinct for food and drink never changed. She may not have known that she had finished her tea, but she continued to bring the cup to her lips and to raise it higher and higher, knowing somewhere deep inside what was required to get the last drop. Only with the cup's removal would the behavior stop.

A number of years before, I had prudently anticipated the inevitability of her needing increasing help. Her name was put on a waiting list for the Baycrest nursing home, which catered to a Jewish clientele and was among the best facilities for geriatric care in Toronto. The wait could take at least three years. But if you refused once your name came up, you dropped to the bottom of the list.

Perhaps it was good timing, then. When the call came, and I thought about how much literal, backbreaking difficulty the caregiver was experiencing—moving my mother from bed to wheelchair, from wheelchair to toilet or, most strenuous, to the bath—it seemed the right move to make. The round-the-clock nursing staff, access to the hospital, meds, meals, baths, hygiene, would all be provided. I also arranged for the caregiver to come during the day to attend to my mother, to take her to the atrium to hear music, or outside for some fresh air, to feed her, filling in the gaps in regular care.

Her sane protests, voiced in the past, regarding the effrontery of moving to "an old age home" were erased by dementia. Instead, she adjusted seamlessly to the loss of her environment and was as easygoing as could be, another instance of the huge paradigm shift from the personality I had known. I liked her this way, not that I would ever have wished upon her the loss of her mind which, when she was compos mentis, she considered to be her most precious attribute. And she was fiercely intelligent.

I saw that she was in there somewhere—the ethos of her without the trauma. Her sense of "things" came through. Her strength, her passion, her mark.

"Do you know who I am?"

"*Perila!*" she hollered, with delight at seeing me. My heart swelled with love for her. More hours would pass as we sat together, hand in hand, in peace.

Soon I would be the only person she could recognize.

She had stopped laboring for thoughts she couldn't master and words she couldn't formulate. But she still communicated surprisingly well.

Her world had been distilled into a binary system, which reduced every single concept and the vastness of a nuanced vocabulary to two syllables with opposite meanings, repeated three times each. For all things good, she chirped liltingly "*La, La, La,*" and for all things bad, she railed "*Na! Na! Na!*" There was never a hesitation when she proclaimed the one or the other. Efficient, effective, precise. It was truly brilliant.

CPSIA information can be obtained at www.ICGtesting.com
Printed in the USA
BVOW081110090413

317695BV00001B/3/P